TRAVELS IN INDIA CEYLON AND BORNEO

TRAVELS IN INDIA CEYLON AND BORNEO

BASIL HALL

SELECTED AND EDITED WITH A BIOGRAPHICAL INTRODUCTION BY

H.G. RAWLINSON

GYAN

Published by

Gyan Publishing House
5, Ansari Road
Daryaganj, New Delhi-110002
Phone: 011-47034999, 9811692060
E-mail: books@gyanbooks.com

Distribution Network
gyanbooks.com
India, USA, Canada, UK, Australia, France

ISBN : 978-81-212-4145-8 (PB)
First Published, London, 1931

2nd Impression 2020

Printed at: Gyan Press, Delhi.

Travels in India Ceylon and Borneo
Author: Basil Hall

By Raeburn

CAPTAIN BASIL HALL

[*front.*

THE BROADWAY TRAVELLERS

EDITED BY SIR E. DENISON ROSS
AND EILEEN POWER

CAPTAIN BASIL HALL

R.N., F.R.S.

TRAVELS IN INDIA CEYLON AND BORNEO

Selected and edited with a Biographical Introduction by

PROFESSOR H. G. RAWLINSON
Indian Educational Service

Published by

GEORGE ROUTLEDGE & SONS, LTD.
BROADWAY HOUSE, CARTER LANE, LONDON

PREFACE

Captain Basil Hall's *Fragments of Voyages and Travels* originally appeared in nine volumes. They are of a most miscellaneous character, dealing with almost every conceivable topic bearing upon life at sea, arranged with little idea of order. As it was impossible to reprint the whole of the work in this series, it was decided to select what appeared to be most entertaining portion,—the author's experiences in India, Ceylon and Borneo. The present work, therefore, comprises chapters I, VI, and VII of Volume II of the Second Series, and Volume II of the Third Series of the *Fragments*.

CONTENTS

LIST OF ILLUSTRATIONS

CAPTAIN BASIL HALL, R.N., F.R.S.

TRAVELS IN INDIA, CEYLON, AND BORNEO

INTRODUCTION

CAPTAIN BASIL HALL, R.N., the subject of this memoir, was the second son of Sir James Hall, Fourth Baronet of Dunglass, Haddingtonshire, [1761-1832]. The house in which he was born was built on the site of an ancient castle on the Berwick Burn, a stream which witnessed many border skirmishes between English and Scots in the old days. It is a spot pregnant with historic memories. It was the last place in Scotland at which a Scottish king slept, for here James IV passed his last night before crossing the Border to become James I of England. It was the "Ravenswood" of Sir Walter Scott's famous novel, and is described by Robert Burns as one of the most beautiful places he ever saw. Sir James was a remarkable man. Educated at Christ's College, Cambridge, he afterwards went over to Brienne to stay with a relation, William Hamilton of Bangour. He attended classes at the Military School, and here he met Napoleon Buonaparte, also a pupil there, and was "the first Englishman Napoleon ever saw." He held advanced opinions, and in 1791 crossed over to Paris to study the French Revolution, where he came into contact with Robespierre, the Abbé Sieyès, Condorcet, and the famous chemist Lavoisier, with whom he found much in common. Cockburn, in his *Memorials*, speaks of Sir James as being "the most scientific of our country gentlemen," held in great admiration by all deep philosophers, and describes his house in George Street as, "distinguished by its hospitality both to science and fashion."

Early in life he turned his attention to geology; he was the first scientist to test geological hypotheses by practical experiments in the laboratory. From geology he passed on to the study of Gothic architecture, where he anticipated Ruskin by endeavouring to shew that all Gothic architectural forms were derived from simple wattle-buildings, the arch from flexible poles tied together, crockets from sprouting buds on willow-staves and so forth. Basil Hall, when travelling in the Mysore jungles, found an apt illustration of his father's theories in the graceful avenues of overarching bamboos. "It seemed," he said, "as if I were travelling amid the clustered column of some enormous and enchanted Gothic cathedral, compared to which, the Minster of York, or the cathedral at Winchester, would have seemed mere baby-houses."[1] He sat for some years in the House of Commons. Sir James Hall had, by his marriage with Helen, daughter of the Earl of Selkirk, three sons and three daughters. The boys inherited their father's talents. John, the eldest was F.R.S. James, the second, the friend of Sir David Wilkie and Sir Walter Scott, was a well-known painter of portraits and Scottish scenery. Basil, born December 31, 1788, was the most gifted of the trio. He came into the world, he tells us, on a night of violent storm. The tempest, he thinks, got into his blood; "long before I shipped a pair of trousers, I felt that a salt-water destiny was to be mine." He derived little benefit from his education at Edinburgh High School, where the tawse, the Scotch counterpart for the birch, was chiefly relied upon for the inculcation of knowledge. He read, however, a good deal in his own way, though he

[1] See pp. 223-4, *infra*.

spent the term in counting the days until the time would arrive when he would once more find himself "at sunrise in a fishing boat, half a league from the coast, surrounded by congenial spirits, fellows who had no idea of grammar." The joyous excitement of this prospect placed the dull drudgery of syntax in sad contrast. When not spending the night in fishing-boats—often, as he confesses, violently sea-sick!—the boy was roaming about the rock-bound cliffs at Dunglass, dreaming as he gazed on Fast Castle, [the Wolf's Crag of the Waverley Novels] and all the panorama of sea and sky and multi-coloured sails of that romantic coast. Not infrequently his dreams were rudely disturbed by scenes of real tragedy : wrecks upon that cruel shore, not yet lighted by the genius of the elder Stevenson, were then terribly frequent.[1] About this time he read Shakespeare, chiefly, he owns, because the *Tempest* and other plays have nautical passages in them such as the one about the shipboy reposing on the high and giddy mast, which were congenial to a "sailor-elect." Young Hall, like others after him, wondered where Shakespeare picked up his seamanship, which he considers wonderfully correct. One day his father introduced the lad as "a future brother seaman," to the great Duncan of Camperdown, and the old veteran won the boy's heart for ever by showing him the flag he captured from De Winter on October 11, 1797.

On June 12, 1802, Master Basil realised the ambition of his young life, when he found himself, arrayed in new uniform and dirk, in the cockpit of H.M. frigate *Leander*, fifty guns, flagship of Sir Andrew Mitchell, Commander-in-Chief of the North American station. There were fourteen midshipmen in all. "We were very merry in this dark hole, where there are only two candles," he writes to his father. The *Leander* sailed for Halifax in July. "A pretty

[1] R. L. Stevenson, *A Family of Engineers*, Chap. III.

ship of her class, and permanently endeared to the memory of all who sailed on board, especially to those who first went to sea in her," notes Hall who, years after, remembered "every corner about her—every beam—every cabin—every gun."

Life in the Navy in those days was as exciting and eventful as in the Great War a century later, and while cruising in a fog off Bermuda, the *Leander* found herself almost abreast of the *Ville de Milan*, which was making off with the *Cleopatra*, just captured after a smart fight. The *Ville de Milan*, taken utterly by surprise, surrendered without firing a shot ! Shortly after this Sir George Berkeley, who succeeded to the command, transferred his flag to the *Leopard* taking Hall with him. In 1803 the *Leopard* returned home, and Hall passed his lieutenant's examination, an amusing farce of which he gives an entertaining account. He was now promoted to the *Endymion*, commander the Hon. Thomas Bladen Capel, "one of the finest, if not the very finest, frigates afloat," and shortly afterwards, proceeded to Corunna with reinforcements for Sir John Moore. At Corunna, to his great delight, Lieutenant Hall obtained permission to land. He was with the troops during the whole of the day's engagement, which he describes very vividly, saw Sir John Moore and Sir David Baird carried off the field, and witnessed the embarkation. Afterwards, he and his brother officers spent their time in administering to the wants of the exhausted soldiers on board, with truly naval hospitality. His future chief, Sir Samuel Hood, was in charge of these operations.

In 1812, Basil Hall was transferred to the East India Station. With his keen interest in everything new, and his unique powers of observation, Hall plunged with avidity into the study of his novel and romantic surroundings. "No buccaneer indeed," he says, "ever sought 'El Dorados in the sky' with more fervour than I longed to visit those brilliant scenes." He had as a passenger Sir Evan Nepean, the new Governor of Bombay. The voyage, on the old *Volage*, acting as part of the escort to a convoy of East Indiamen, was a slow one. Leaving in March, they reached Bombay in August. Hall describes the passage and its incidents, the Madeira islands, the Trades, the Cape, Johanna, porpoise-catching and the like, in his usual lively style. On his arrival at Bombay, he was sent on to Trincomalee, where he was transferred, as Fifth Lieutenant, to the *Illustrious*, flagship of Admiral Sir Samuel Hood, a veteran sailor belonging to a famous naval family.

Sir Samuel Hood had had an extraordinary career, typical of the "fighting Hoods", who did so much to make our navy's reputation during the French wars of the 18th century. These included Sir Samuel and his brother, Alexander, who served in Captain Cook's voyage in 1772, and was killed in action 1798; the famous Viscount Samuel Hood, who made his name under Rodney in the West Indies; and his almost equally famous brother, Admiral Alexander Hood, Lord Bridport. A descendant, Rear-Admiral Hood, went down in the *Invincible* at Jutland, *more majorum*, while leading the 3rd Battle Cruiser Squadron into action. *Stirbt ein held.* Sir Samuel had been present at Ushant in 1778; at the actions off Martinique, Cape Henry, St. Kitts, Dominica, and Mona Passage, 1781-2; he had served under Nelson at Santa Cruz and the Nile: captured St. Lucia and Tobago, 1803; lost an arm off Rochefort in 1805; fought at Copenhagen in 1807, and taken part in the operations to embark Sir John Moore's troops at Corunna in 1809. In 1812, he was sent to command the East India Station. In Sir Samuel Hood, Basil Hall found a chief after his own heart. Gifted with an inexhaustible love of adventure, an unbounded curiosity, and a fund of humour, the gallant admiral was intent on seeing and trying everything he came across in the course of his travels. "There was ever observable," writes Hall, "a boyish hilarity about this great officer, which made it equally delightful to serve officially under him, and to enjoy his friendly companionship; in either case, we always felt certain of making the most of our opportunities." Whether they were engaged in digging out a white ant's nest, or exploring Ceylon rivers for precious stones, hunting crocodiles on foot, or ascending a Borneo creek to visit a local Sultan, Sir Samuel was always to the fore, nor was Lady Hood ever behindhand in sharing her husband's adventures. The "Sam Hood school" became proverbial in the Navy. This gallant officer eventually paid the penalty for his love of travel. He died in Madras in 1814, of a violent jungle fever contracted in Seringapatam, probably while sleeping in Tipu Sultan's palace, which was notoriously unhealthy. Even to-day, Seringapatam has a bad reputation for malaria. The complaint was aggravated by exposure to the sun: the Admiral, finding his palanquin bearers not ready, actually walked a stage of the road on foot.[1] On his deathbed he said to Lieutenant Walcott, his faithful follower in many actions, "It will be hard, Walcott to die in this cursed place: but should I go off, let nothing deter you from going home and accounting to the Admiralty for my command of the East India Station." It is characteristic of the "Hood tradition", that Walcott went straight home to fulfil this last behest, though he lost six years' promotion by doing so! Hall's maiden effort in literature was an obituary notice of his beloved chief, which appeared in the *Bombay Courier*.[2]

The *Illustrious* then went from Trincomalee to Bombay, where Hall spent his time in characteristic

[1] *Fragments*, iii, 1, 3.

[2] *Ibid.* ii, iii, 177*ff*., and iii, ii. Chap. ix, *passim*.

fashion exploring the famous Elephanta Caves. After this they proceeded to Madras.

In the middle of 1813, Hall was sent by Sir Samuel to take over charge of the *Theban* frigate. He was then in Madras, and received permission, if he preferred, to make the journey overland.[1] Hall, thrilled at the prospect of seeing India, accepted the offer with alacrity. He could hardly believe, he tells us, that within a week, he would be sleeping in the palace of Tipu Sahib, or scrambling up the blood-stained breaches of Seringapatam. Travelling by palanquin, a mode of conveyance now happily obsolete, of which he gives us a detailed and highly diverting account, he reached Mysore in the nick of time to witness the great Hindu festival known as the Dussera, which the restored line of Hindu rajahs was celebrating with barbaric splendour. Hall had a unique glimpse into the life of a native state in "the good old days of John Company." The Maharaja received him on a throne of gold, silver, and ivory, the canopy being set with gigantic pearls, and surmounted with a gigantic peacock, apparently composed of diamonds and precious stones of untold value. His Highness was so weighed down with jewels that he could hardly stand, and his enormous golden head-piece gave his head "a slight list to starboard!" though, as one of the party remarked, a man might well go with a crick in his neck for life in return for such ballast! At intervals, attendants popped betel-nut into his mouth, and loaded him with perfumed garlands. One of the great features of the festival was a wild-beast fight, in which a tiger, a buffalo, donkeys with leather bottles full of peas tied to their tails, and a number of savage hounds participated. The indescribable din was augmented by twelve military bands which played simultaneously different tunes, and the unfortunate tiger was only

[1] *Ibid.* iii, ii, p. 148*ff*.

prevented in its terror from leaping among the audience, by the presence of mind of a small boy, who rapped it smartly on the nose. "Just the sort of thing," whispered an aged Mahommedan soldier, regretfully, "that my old master, Haider Ali, would have done when he was young!"[1] The scene was diversified by Oriental boxing and wrestling, the combatants wearing a formidable *cestus*, capable of laying open the opponent's scalp at a blow, stilt dancers who balanced ploughs on their shoulders, and a strange amusement, which consisted in throwing cocoanuts high in the air, so that, falling upon the hard heads of the throwers, they would burst, scattering their milk far and wide. It is not altogether surprising to learn that this monarch was subsequently deposed by Lord Bentinck.

Similar diversions were afforded for Captain Hall's entertainment at the hill-state of Coorg, which he next visited. Here a tiger and a bear were harnessed together. The tiger promptly leapt through the palace window, to the great derangement of the furniture, while the bear, who refused to follow suit, hung down on the other side of the ledge. Presently the Rajah sent for a gun, a proceeding which caused something of a flutter in the court, as his late Highness had been in the habit of practising shooting at unpopular members of his Cabinet on similar occasions. We can without much effort imagine the delight with which Hall, with his keen sense of humour and quick power of observation, enjoyed these extraordinary *tamashas*. From Mysore he went down the ghats to Mangalore, where he caught a ship for Bombay.

In 1814, Hall accompanied Sir Samuel on a prolonged cruise in the *Minden*, touching at Acheen in Sumatra, once the seat of a flourishing English factory going back to Elizabethan days, when the spice trade

[1] After the death of Tipu in 1799, the Hindu dynasty was restored by the British Government.

was an all-important element in the Company's business, Pulo Penang or Prince of Wales' Island, and then going down the straits of Malacca in order to pay a state visit to the Sultan of Pontiana in Borneo, who dwelt in a ramshackle palace at the head of a creek overgrown with creepers and infested with crocodiles.

The *Minden* was a fine 74, one of the many beautiful vessels built on the Bombay slips by the celebrated Parsee master-builder, Jamsetjee Bomanjee, the head of the great ship-building firm of Lowjee Wadia. Next year Hall got command of the *Victor* sloop, also built in Bombay, and took her home.

His visit to England was short. Almost immediately he was ordered to join the *Lyra* sloop, acting as escort to the *Alceste*, which was taking out Lord Amherst as our Ambassador Extraordinary to the Court of Pekin. The *Lyra* incidentally carried out some valuable survey work in the Gulf of Pechili, the west coast of Korea, and among the Loochoo, of which little or nothing was then known. Of these attractive islands Hall gives an interesting narrative in his *Account of a Voyage of Discovery to the West Coast of Corea and the Great Loo Choo Islands*, including a valuable comparative vocabulary of Japanese and Loochoo words which Hall compiled. Canton was reached on November 2nd, and the Chinese forts had to be silenced by gunfire. The Embassy, after some futile negotiations, re-embarked on January 21st. On their return journey, the *Alceste* was wrecked in Gaspar Straits, and Lord Amherst had to make for Batavia in an open boat. Meanwhile, the *Lyra* had gone on to Calcutta with despatches.

On the homeward voyage, St. Helena was reached on August 11th, 1817, and Hall took the opportunity to pay his respects to the Emperor Napoleon, who, as we have seen, had been a classmate of his father's at Brienne over forty years before. The interview was arranged, through the good offices of Dr. O'Meara, the Emperor's surgeon, and General Bertrand, after many tantalising delays, the latter acting as interpreter. Hall describes his sensations, on hearing the footstep of one who a short time ago had ruled the world, as comparable to those raised in his breast by approaching for the first time the Niagara Falls.[1] The Emperor received him courteously, and recalled many little details of his father's career at Brienne. On Hall expressing surprise at his recollection of these bygone incidents, Napoleon replied: "It is not in the least extraordinary, because he was the first Englishman I ever saw, and I have recollected your father on that account ever since." The conversation drifted on to the Edinburgh Royal Society, of which Sir James was President, Hall's adventures among the Loochoo Islands, and kindred topics. "Was Sir James one of the Edinburgh Reviewers?" was one of Napoleon's queries: and he was much amused at Basil Hall's reply that he was not, but that his books had often come under their clutches! The interview lasted twenty-five minutes. Hall was struck with the fallen hero's tranquillity of bearing. "Were it not for an occasional lighting-up of the eyes, and a sort of determined, commanding glance—which pierced, as it were, into one's most hidden thoughts, I should have been disposed to describe his look as being placid or gentle, and at all times lively, never stern."[2]

Hall reached England in October, 1817, and soon after was posted to the rank of Captain. During his absence, he had the rare honour of being elected a Fellow of the Royal Society. After a holiday of two years, spent mostly in Continental travel, he was

[1] *Travels in America*, iii. 181.

[2] *Account of a Voyage of Discovery to the West Coast of Corea*, 3rd edn., 1840. Chap. vii. *The First Englishman Napoleon ever saw*, by Lady Hall, in the *Nineteenth Century*, Oct. 1927.

posted to the *Conway*, a 26 gun frigate on the South American Station. His experiences are narrated in *Extracts from a Journal written on the coasts of Chile, Peru and Mexico, in the years 1820-1821-1822*, which had a great vogue in its day. In 1825, having married Margaret, daughter of Sir John Hunter, Consul-General of Spain, he retired. In 1829, after spending a holiday in North America, with his wife, he wrote a book entitled *Travels in North America in the years 1827 and 1828*, which was very widely read and discussed, and translated into French. This work caused a sort of "moral earthquake" in the United States, especially when it was followed and confirmed in 1832, by Frances Trollope's *Domestic Manners of the Americans*. American bookshelves banned it. Many persons even believed that both books really proceeded from the same pen : "Either Captain Basil Hall was Mrs. Trollope in breeches, or Mrs. Trollope was Captain Basil Hall in petticoats."[1] *Domestic Manners*, declared the sapient writer of the preface to the American edition, with its coarse delineations and indelicate allusions, and its "bug and spitting stories", was obviously the work of "some conceited, ignorant Jack Tar, breaking his forecastle jests, with a quid of tobacco in his mouth, and his canvas hat knowingly adjusted on one side of his head." It may be thought that there is a certain feline touch in Frances Trollope, but it can scarcely be said of Basil Hall's *Travels in North America*. The book is written in Hall's usual good-natured, breezy, conscientious, observant manner. His object is obviously, to

> nothing extenuate,
> Nor ought set down in malice.

[1] See *Domestic Manners of the Americans*, Chap. 31 *passim*. But Hall found a stout defender in Mark Twain, who declared the book contained "not one exaggerated statement," [appendix to *Life on the Mississippi*.]

He thinks that, as America was always boasting of her right of freedom of speech, she was logically bound to extend the same privilege to visitors to her shores When asked to state the chief difference between America and England, he replies candidly, "The want of Loyalty."[1] But nothing but unqualified approbation would satisfy his critics. They cited, as examples of Hall's "shocking moral coarseness", his story how, owing to lack of bells in America, he once had to wander half-dressed and half-shaved, all over a hotel, at the imminent risk of stumbling into a lady's chamber, in search of water to fill his jug, or his seemingly harmless remark that in the whole of America, he never once came across a flirtation! Hall was very hurt at the reception given to his book. He refused to read American criticisms of it: he had lively recollections of the kindness which he had received in New York as a midshipman on the North American Station, and was at a loss to understand the commotion he had excited. "In all my travels," he says, "both among heathens and among Christians, I have never encountered any people by whom I found it nearly so difficult to make myself understood as by the Americans."

In 1831, Hall had the privilege of laying before the First Lord of the Admiralty the recommendation that Sir Walter Scott, as a last chance of recovering his health, should go for a cruise in the Mediterranean. Largely owing to Hall's exertions, the *Barham* frigate was placed at Sir Walter's disposal. Sir Walter was a friend of the family—James Hall had painted his portrait—and, before sailing, the great writer added a long note in his own hand to the manuscript of the *Antiquary*, of which Basil Hall was the possessor. In 1831, Hall published his most popular work, his famous *Fragments of Voyages and Travels*, 3 series, each

[1] *Travels in America*, Vol. III., Chap. xvii. Hall's defence of the old unreformed House of Commons makes amusing reading.

in 3 volumes, 12mo, 1831-3. These nine little volumes once so well-known, are now comparatively rare and almost forgotten. The fortunate book-lover who picks them up on a bookstall or a library shelf will soon be rewarded for his pains. They are, indeed, a lasting joy to the reader. Written "chiefly for young persons", they are also intended, the writer tells us, "to engage the attention of those who, from having entered the Service in less stirring times, may find it more difficult to gain experience for themselves." Few books ever penned give a more graphic and entertaining picture of the Royal Navy a century ago. Those of us who have been brought up on Smollett and Marryat have heard too much and have dwelt, perhaps too exclusively, on its rough and brutal side. Hall shews us the reverse of the picture. True, he believes that, in view of the character of the material enlisted, and the necessity of an iron discipline where the life of the crew often depended upon the instantaneous carrying out of an order, corporal punishment was essential, though only applied in extreme cases and after patient and exhaustive investigation. That such a view was deliberately held by a humane and enlightened man like Hall is a very significant fact indeed.[1] Hall himself gives us many instances where the wonderful discipline of a man-of-war saved numbers of lives, when death seemed almost certain. A "slack ship", he says, was a danger to herself and her consorts, and a constant source of discomfort to all aboard her. Naval life, where a large number of persons are forced to live in close proximity, without contact with the outer world, sometimes for many months together, in cramped quarters and under trying conditions, is unique in its way. Of the wonderful *esprit de corps* of the Navy, where a man got

[1] *Cf.* what he says on the subject in *Travels in America*, Vol. III. Chap. v.

to love his ship as a Public School boy loves his school, he speaks in feeling terms. "This character indeed," says Hall, "gives the Navy of England its peculiar character, and mainly contributes to its success. We do truly make the ship our home: we have no other thoughts of professional duty or happiness but what are connected with the vessel in which we swim: we take a pride in her very looks, as we might in those of a daughter and bring up her crew to honourable deeds, as we should wish to instruct our sons."

And of the lighter and more humorous side of the life, the pranks of the middies,—the story, for instance of dressing up the pigs in mourning when the Captain ordered Shakings, the cockpit mongrel, to be thrown overboard, or of the filing of the teeth of Jacko, the ship's monkey, or of Jean, the pet sow, who followed the crew like a dog, and was accorded a naval funeral —what inimitable descriptions we glean from Hall's pages! His volumes are full of nautical information for landsmen, charmingly served up. We learn all about bells and knots, toeing the line and casting the lead, how a great gun is served and aimed, how a man of war is put into commission or paid off. The whole panorama of life in our wooden walls in the Trafalgar period is displayed before our eyes. Hall was an indefatigable traveller and a keen and humorous observer. Wherever he went, he tried to learn all he could. In India, he works hard at Hindustani. In Eastern waters he takes up Malay and Japanese. His description of Hindu mythology, as illustrated by the Elephanta Caves, could hardly be bettered to-day: and for one who was not a professed Orientalist, it is simply wonderful. In the Loo Choo Islands, he made valuable notes of the flora, fauna, and geology, and compiled the first vocabulary of the language. His descriptions of India and Ceylon, the Elephanta Caves, the jungles, the Rajahs' courts, and all the panorama of

Eastern life, have the same vivid, illuminating human touch, which makes them hard to put down. He is the ideal travel-writer. He never wearies his readers: he makes them not merely read him, but love him.

Fragments of Voyages and Travels is Hall's best and most abiding work. After it, he did little of note. In 1836 he published his historical romance, partly founded on fact, *Schless Hainfield*, or *A Winter in Lower Styria*, and in the following year, *Spain and the Seat of War in Spain*. *Patchwork* [1841] a collection of sketches and tales, which shews signs of failing powers, was the last product of a prolific pen and fertile brain, for shortly afterwards, Captain Basil Hall was seized with brain fever from which he was only released by death, at Haslar Hospital, Portsmouth, September 11th., 1844.[1]

[1] For the above biography, the writer is deeply indebted to Captain Basil Hall, R.N., [retired], the author's grandson, who has supplied numerous facts from unpublished family papers and records.

CHAPTER I

BOMBAY[1]

I HAVE seen some persons, who, after losing their friends, their health, or their fortunes in India, have looked back to that bright country without pleasure; but I am not sure that I ever met anyone who arrived in it without great satisfaction, or who could hail the first glimpse of a world so totally new without feelings of curiosity more than commonly excited. For my own part, I was thrown into a high fever of wonder and enjoyment; and assuredly, as long as I have a trace of memory left, must retain the recollection of that happy period carved brightly and distinctly on my mind.

Early on the morning of the 11th of August, 1812, we first made the coast of Asia; and, on steering towards the shore, discovered, close under the land, a single sail, as white as snow, of a cut quite new to our seamanship, and swelled out with the last faint airs of the land-breeze, which, in the night, had carried us briskly along shore. As we came nearer, we observed that the boat, with her head directed to the northward, was piled half-mast high with fruits and vegetables, cocoa-nuts, yams, plantains, intended evidently for the market of Bombay. The water lay as smooth as that of a lake; so we sheered close alongside, and hailed, to ask the distance we still were from our port. None of the

[1] [Basil Hall had come out in the *Volage* frigate, as Second Lieutenant, to join Sir Samuel Hood, Commander-in-Chief of the East India Station. The *Volage* formed part of the escort to a convoy of East Indiamen bound for China. They were also bringing out Sir E. Nepean, the new Governor of Bombay [1812-1819]. They left Spithead on March 25th.]

officers of the *Volage* could speak a word of Hindustanee; and I well remember our feeling of humiliation when a poor scullion, one of the cook's assistants, belonging to the governor's suite, was dragged on deck, with all his grease and other imperfections on his head, to act as interpreter. Sad work he made of it; for, though the fellow had been in the East on some ten or twelve former voyages, the languages of the countries he visited had not formed so important a part of his studies as the quality of the arrack and toddy which they produced. The word Bombaya, however, struck the ear of the native boatmen, who pointed in the direction to which they themselves were steering, and called out "Mombay! Mombay!" This word, I am told by an oriental scholar, is a corruption of Moomba-devy,[1] or the Goddess of Moomba, from an idol to which a temple is still dedicated on the island. Others, less fanciful in their etymology, say that the Portuguese gave it the name of Bom-Bahia, on account of the excellence of its port. That nation held possession of Bombay from the year 1530 to 1661, when it was ceded by the crown of Portugal in full sovereignty to Charles II.

It was not long before we came in sight of several headlands, which are so well described by that great hydrographer, my excellent friend Captain James Horsburgh, that we knew our place almost as well as if we had been sailing between the Motherbank and Spithead. When the next day broke, and the sun

[1] [Hall is as accurate as usual. Bombay receives its name from the Koli goddess Mumba Bai or Mumba Devi, who still has a shrine in Phydonie Bazaar. The present name doubtless arose from false analogy with the Portuguese *Bom bahia*, Good Bay. Bombay is, of course, far older than the Portuguese, to whom it was ceded by Sultan Bahadur Shah of Gujarat in 1534. In 1661, the Portuguese surrendered it to Charles II, as part of the dowry of Catherine of Braganza, and seven years later, Charles made it over to the East India Company for the sum of £10 per annum!]

rose upon us over the flat-topped Gauts or mountains of the Mahratta country, I remember feeling almost at a loss whether I had been sleeping and dreaming during the night, or whether the gay reality, with its boundless vista of promises, was still before my eyes. The imagination and the reason were both more or less heated by the simple facts of having actually seen the shores of India, having heard the language of the East from the mouths of its natives, and beheld the forms and figures, and that dusky aspect which induced its northern and fair-complexioned conquerors of old to style their new possession Hindoo-stan, or land of "black men." All these circumstances, though trivial, it is true, in themselves, were well calculated to give reality to pictures which, for many a long year before, I had busied my fancy with painting in colours drawn partly from the Arabian Nights and Persian Tales, and partly, if not chiefly, from those brilliant clusters of Oriental images which crowd and adorn the pages of Scripture.

Besides, the mere picturesque feelings excited by such reflections, I had accidentally acquired others somewhat more substantial perhaps, and practically useful, from being thrown a good deal into the society of officers who had served in various parts of India, and called my attention to the histories and to the political arrangements of our possessions in the East. What with fiction and what with truth, therefore, my head was pretty full of combustible materials, ready to be acted upon at once by anything and everything that should meet the eye on landing.

Captain Cook asserts somewhere, when speaking of the delights of voyaging and travelling, that to such rovers as he and his companions, nothing came amiss; and I can safely venture to boast, that, as far as this goes, I may claim a corner of my great brother-officer's mantle. At all events, in sailing over the Indian seas, or travelling in those countries by land, I not only never met anything that came amiss, but hardly ever met anything which did not so much exceed in interest what I had looked for, that the grand perplexity became, how to record what was felt, or in any adequate terms to describe even the simplest facts, which struck the eye at every turn in that "wide realm of wild reality."

Of all places in the noble range of countries so happily called the Eastern world, from the pitch of the Cape to the islands of Japan, from Bengal to Batavia, nearly every hole and corner of which I have visited in the course of my peregrinations, there are few which can compare with Bombay. If, indeed, I were consulted by anyone who wished as expeditiously and economically as possible to see all that was essentially characteristic of the Oriental world, I would say, without hesitation: "Take a run to Bombay; remain there a week or two; and, having also visited the scenes in the immediate neighbourhood, Elephanta,[1] Carli,[2] and Poonah, you will have examined good specimens of most things that are curious or interesting in the East."

For this remarkable distinction, quite peculiar, as far as I know, to that one spot on the earth's surface, this presidency is indebted to a variety of interesting circumstances. Bombay, as perhaps many people may never have heard before, is an island, and by no means a large one, being only between six and seven miles long by one or two broad. It is not, however, by geographi-

[1] *Elephanta. Vide supra.* p.55, note.

[2] [The famous *vihâra*, or cave-temple, of Karla, hewn out of the living rock, stands not far from the Poona-Bombay road, about thirty miles from the former place. It is of Buddhist origin, and probably dates from about the 1st century, B.C. Poona, the old Maratha capital of the Deccan, was taken by us after the Battle of Kirkee in 1817. It is now the summer residence of the Bombay Government: it stands on the Ghauts, about 1,850 feet above the sea and about 120 miles from Bombay.]

cal dimensions that the wealth of towns, any more than the power and wealth of nations, is determined. The harbour unites every possible desideratum of a great sea-port: it is easy of access and egress; affords excellent anchoring ground; is capacious beyond the utmost probable demands of commerce; and, owing to the great rise and fall of the tides, is admirably adapted for docks of every description. The climate is healthy; and the ground, being diversified by numerous small ridges and hills, furnishes an endless choice of situations for forts, towns, bazaars, and villages, not to say bungalows or villas, and all sorts of country-houses, and some very splendid retreats from the bustle of business. The roads which intersect this charming island were beautifully macadamised, as I well remember, long before that grand improvement was heard of in England; and as the soil of the island is made up of that rich kind of mould resulting from decomposed basalt or lava, the whole surface affords a good sample of the perennial verdure of tropical scenery, which dazzles and surprises the new-comer, while its interest seldom, if ever, fails to rise still higher upon a more prolonged and intimate acquaintance.

Such are among the eminent physical advantages enjoyed by Bombay; but even these, had they been many times greater, would have been light in the balance compared to those of a moral, or rather of a political nature, which conspired in 1812 to render it one of the most important spots in that quarter of the globe. At the time I speak of, it was almost the only possession exclusively British within several hundred miles in any direction. The enormous territory of the Mahrattas lay close to Bombay on the east; and I mention this one district because the name is more or less familiar to English ears, chiefly, perhaps, from its having been the scene of the Duke of Wellington's earliest campaign in command of an army. The brilliant course of that service was wound up by the well-known battle of Assaye, not the least hard fought of his hundred fields. Assaye is about twice as far from Bombay as Waterloo from London. To anyone familiar with modern Indian history, the name of Basseen[1], where one of the most celebrated treaties that ever statesmen agreed upon was signed, will be well remembered. Then who is there that has not heard of the caves of Elephanta, those singular temples of the old Hindoos, excavated on the side of a hill on an island in the very harbour, and within one hour's row from the fort?

These, and many other circumstances, some military, some historical, give a very peculiar degree of liveliness to the interest we feel in that spot; and I certainly have as yet seen very few places on the globe which fasten themselves with more tenacity on the memory. I allude chiefly to matters of taste, association, and other refinements, with which the natives of the countries surrounding Bombay have no concern. To them it possesses, or did then possess, exclusively, an interest of a different and far more important character. At that time it was almost the only spot in that range of country where persons and property were perfectly secure, and in which all men might safely display and enjoy their wealth to the utmost limits of their taste for ostentatious parade, or hoard it as parsimoniously as they pleased, without the slightest chance of arbitrary

[1] [Bassein, now a picturesque ruin, was a great Portuguese fortress, taken by the Marathas in 1739, which lies on a creek of the same name some twenty-five miles north of Bombay. Here Colonel Close concluded a treaty with the Peshwa, virtually reducing him to a state of dependency, in 1802. In the following year, Sir Arthur Wellesley decisively defeated the great Maratha prince, Daulatrao Sindia of Gwalior, at Assaye, in the N.W. corner of the Nizam's dominions. In 1817, the Peshwa repented of his actions and tried to throw off the British yoke, but was beaten at Kirkee, after which the Deccan fell into our hands.]

interference. In addition to this, every form of religious worship was not merely tolerated, but allowed to exercise itself with the most ample and equal freedom. Every native of Asia, or of any other country in the world, so long as he infringed none of the established laws of the Presidency, was allowed equal privileges; and as the advantages of security and freedom, in the most genuine senses of these words, were enjoyed under none of the native governments adjacent, but, on the contrary, were almost entirely unknown in them all, Bombay became the natural place of resort for the wealthy from all parts of India, lying on that side of the Peninsula, and indeed from many other regions much more remote.[1]

The population of Bombay is about two hundred thousand; and I think it may be said with truth that we can see nothing in China, or Java, or the Philippine Islands, or along the Malay Peninsula, or even in the interior parts of India, any single caste, or dress, or custom, or form of superstition, or anything else belonging peculiarly to Eastern manners, which we may not witness at Bombay in as genuine and apparently unsophisticated a condition as on the spot to which it properly belongs. In twenty minutes' walk through the bazaar of Bombay, my ear has been struck by the sounds of every language that I have heard in any other part of the world, uttered not in corners and by chance, as it were, but in a tone and manner which implied that the speakers felt quite at home. In the same short

[1] [Religious toleration, unknown in Portuguese India, was introduced by the great and good Gerald Aungier, Governor of Bombay, 1669-77, and the real founder of the city. He allowed all races to worship and build temples as they desired, and induced a number of Parsees and Banyas from Gujarat by this means to settle in the island. From this innovation, attracting as it did the mercantile classes of Western India, dates the rise of Bombay as a great commercial city. The population in 1672 was 10,000: in Hall's time it was 200,000: in 1921 it was 1,175,914.]

space of time I have counted several dozens of temples, pagodas,[1] joss-houses,[2] and churches; and have beheld the Parsees,[3] the lineal religious descendants of Zoroaster, worshipping fire; the Hindoos, with equal earnestess, bowing their heads to Baal in the shape of a well-oiled black stone, covered with chaplets of flowers and patches of rice; while in the next street the Mahometan ceremonies of the grand Moharem[4] were in full display; and in the midst of all a Portuguese procession bearing an immense cross, and other Roman Catholic emblems, as large as life.

I have no language competent to give expression to the feelings produced by the first contemplation of so strange a spectacle. I was startled, amused, deeply interested, and sometimes not a little shocked. The novelty of the scene was scarcely diminished by a further inspection; which may appear a contradiction in terms, but is not so in reality. The multitude of ideas caused by the first view of such an astonishing crowd of new and curious objects, obscures and confuses

[1] [This strange word, perhaps from Persian *but kadah*, "idol house," means, in Anglo-Indian parlance, a Hindu temple. See p. 183, note 2.]

[2] [A Chinese temple. Joss is "pidgin" for Portuguese *deos*, god.]

[3] [The Parsees are the descendants of the ancient Persians, who fled to the coast of Gujarat before the oncoming wave of Mahommedan invasion about 720 A.D. General Aungier's toleration edict attracted them to Bombay in 1672, where they settled down as traders and ship builders. Before this, their principal occupation had been agriculture and weaving.]

[4] [Muharram, the Sacred Month, the first in the Lunar Year, during which the Mahommedan Shiahs celebrate the martyrdom of Husain, the grandson of the Prophet, at the battle of Kerbela, 680 A.D. *Tabuts* or model mausolea, made of tinsel and paper, are carried in procession and thrown into the nearest water. The word Muharram is, however, usually applied to the festival itself, which in places like Bombay is carried out amidst scenes of great excitement, often culminating in dangerous riots.]

the observation, in a certain sense, and prevents us from distinguishing one part from another. In like manner, I remember being almost stupefied with astonishment, when Sir John Herschel first shewed me one of the great nebulæ or clusters of stars in his telescope at Slough. When, however, the philosopher unfolded the results of his own observations, and ventured to separate and distinguish the different orders of nebulæ and double stars, or pointed the instrument to the planet which his illustrious father discovered, and made me understand, or tried to make me understand, the revolutions of its satellites, I felt the confusion by which at first I was distracted gradually subsiding, while the fresh interest of the spectacle, strictly speaking, was greatly increased. And so I found it in India, especially at that most curious of places, Bombay, where the more I saw of the natives the more there seemed still to discover that was new. It would be absurd to pretend that all this pedantic kind of reasoning process took place at the moment, for, in truth, I was too much enchanted to speculate much on the causes of the enjoyment. I shall never forget, however, the pleasure with which I heard a native, with a bowl in his hand, apply to a dealer in corn for some of the grain called sesamé.[1] The word, in strictness, is not the Indian name for this seed, though it is used generally in the peninsula of Hindustan, and forms one of the ingredients of curry-powder. Til is the native word for the plant from which the oil of sesamé is expressed. I need not say how immediately the sound recalled the "Open, sesamé!" of the *Arabian Nights;* and the whole of the surrounding scene being in strict character with that of the tale, I felt as if I had been touched with some magic wand, and transported into the highest heaven of Eastern invention.

[1] [This is the seed of the *Sesamum Indicum* or Gingelly, called *Til* in Marathi.]

As I gazed at all things round me in wonder and delight, I could fix my eye on nothing I had ever seen before. The dresses, in endless variety of flowing robes and twisted turbans, flitted like a vision before me. The Hindoos, of innumerable castes, were there, each distinguished from the other by marks drawn with brilliant colours on his brow. There stood Persian merchants with shawls and other goods from Cashmere, mingled with numerous Arab horse-dealers careering about; Malays from the straits of Malacca, chatting familiarly with those good-natured, merry fellows, the long-tailed Chinese, whose most ungraceful Tartar dress and tuft contrast curiously in such a crowd with the tastefully arranged drapery and gorgeous turbans of the Mahometans and Hindoos.

Some of these groups were fully as much distinguished by their sandals and slippers as by their head-gear; others arrested the attention by the sound of their voices, and many by the peculiarity of their features and complexion. It really signified little which way the eye was turned, for it could rest on nothing, animate or inanimate, which was not strange and full of interest. Most of the trees which shaded us, and especially the tall variety of the palm tribe, commonly called the Brab,[1] I had never seen before. It is called by botanists Borassus flabelliformis, or Tara Palm; Tara or Tair being the native word for the toddy which is yielded by these trees. It grows, in respect to its stem, like the cocoanut, with a glorious set of projecting arms at the top. But these branches, unlike those of the cocoanut, do not send out lateral leaves along their whole length like the ostrich feather, which the cocoanut leaf resembles very much in form. They are smooth and naked to the end, on which is opened out, rather fantastically, a huge circular leaf, marked with divisions

[1] [From Portuguese *brava*, wild; a name given to the Palmyra palm, Hindustani *tal* or *tar*.]

like those of a fan, radiating from a centre, each ray or division being sharp-pointed.

But the chief object of attraction, and I may well say of admiration, in this gay scene, was the appearance of the women, who are not only not concealed, but go about freely, and, generally speaking, occupy themselves out of doors in works not requiring any considerable strength, but a good deal of dexterity. Of course, this does not include the highest classes, who are kept quite secluded. The females appear to be the great water-carriers; and the pots or chatties, as they are called, which are invariably borne on the head, are of the most elegant forms imaginable. Indeed, when standing by the side of a Hindoo tank, or reservoir, as I have often done for hours together, I have been reminded of those beautiful Etruscan vases, the discovery of which has given so new a character to modern forms. This practice of carrying all loads on the head is necessarily accompanied by an erect carriage of body, and accordingly the most graceful of dancers, even the matchless Bigottini herself, might have

"Snatched a grace beyond the reach of art"

from observing the most ordinary Hindoo girl on her return from the tank, with her hand sometimes just touching the vessel poised on her head, and sometimes not, so true is the balance, and so certain the bearer's step. The dress of these women consists chiefly of one strip of cloth, many yards in length. This narrow web is wound round the body and limbs with so much propriety, that while the most scrupulous delicacy could find nothing to censure on the score of deficiency in covering, it is arranged with such innate and judicious taste that even the eye of a sculptor could hardly wish many of its folds removed. The figure of the Hindoos, both male and female, is small and delicate; and, although their features are not always handsome, there is something about their expression which strikes every stranger as singularly pleasing, perhaps from its being indicative of that patience, docility, and contentment, which are certainly their chief characteristics. We see at least, in every part of our Eastern empire, that with a little care, coupled with a full understanding of their habits and wishes, and backed by a thorough disinterestedness and genuine public spirit on the part of their rulers, the above-mentioned qualities of the Hindoos may be turned to the highest account in all the arts of war, and many of the arts of peace.

Perhaps not the least curious sight in the bazaar of Bombay are the ornaments worn by the women and children, by which, with the most lavish profusion, and the most ill-directed taste, they succeed in disfiguring themselves as much as possible. And this might lead us almost to suspect that their taste in the other parts of their dress, like the gracefulness of their carriage, is the result, not of choice and study, but of happy accident. The custom of carrying their water-vessels on the head requires an erectness of gait during the performance of that duty, which may become the easiest and most natural at other times. And probably some circumstance incident to the climate may, in like manner, direct the fashion in adjusting their drapery.

Most of the women wear nose-rings of great dimensions. I have seen many which hung below the chin; and certainly to us this seems a strange ornament. I forget whether or not the Hindoo women cover their fingers with rings as our ladies do, but their principal fashion seems to consist in loading the wrists and ankles with armlets and bangles, as they are called, of gold and silver. The virgin gold generally used for this purpose, is almost always rich and grateful to the eye. But, I imagine, no art can make a silver ornament look anything but vulgar. Just as we sometimes see persons in Europe crowd ring upon ring on their fingers till all beauty is lost in the heap, and all taste sacrificed for the mere sake of ostentatious display; so, in India, I have observed women whose legs were covered with huge circles of gold and silver from the instep nearly to the knee, and their arms similarly hooped round almost to the elbow. The jingle made by these ornaments striking against one another gives ample warning of a woman's approach; a circumstance which has probably led to the notion that this custom of attaching, as it were, a set of bells to the heels of the ladies, may have been an institution of jealousy devised by the husbands of those warm latitudes to aid their researches after their gadding spouses. I cannot say how this theory squares with history; but I have never heard any hypothesis equally good to account for the still more ridiculous, not to say cruel, custom of covering the legs and arms of their poor little children with these rings. I have seen a girl three years old so loaded with them that she could not walk or hold out her arms; and I once counted no fewer than twenty heavy gold chains on a child's neck, besides such numbers of rings on its arms and legs that the little thing looked more like an armadillo of the picture-books than a human being. Such is the passion of some Hindoo parents for this practice, that I have been assured they often convert their whole wordlly substance into this most useless form of the precious metals, and thus transform their progeny into a sort of money-chest. Small happiness is it for these innocent wretches, however, who, as the head police-magistrate informed me, are not infrequently murdered for the sake of the property they carry about with them.

I have before remarked, that when a traveller is first thrown into such a scene as I have here alluded to, although his enjoyment certainly is very great, there often comes across him a feeling of hopelessness, when he admits to himself his total inability to record one hundredth, one millionth part, I may say of the splendid original. Everything is totally new to him; even the commonest implements of husbandry, the pots and pans, the baskets and barrels, the carts and carriages, all are strange to his eyes, and far beyond the reach of his pen; while things which stand higher in the scale come still less within its range. Then what is he to do with the sounds he hears, or the motion he perceives? And strange it is to admit, but true, that the interest is at times actually increased by circumstances which are in themselves very annoying. I well remember submitting even to the intense heat and glare with great patience, and almost relish, in consideration of their being strictly in character with a scene I had so long ardently desired to witness. The formidable smell of assafœtida,[1] which reigns in every Indian market, I nearly learned to bear without a qualm, for the same reason. Other annoyances I cared very little about; and had it not been for the well-cursed mosquitoes, I should not hesitate to declare, that, as far as travelling human nature is capable of happiness, I was perfectly happy when cruising about the bazaars of Bombay.

Full well am I aware that much of all this will appear to many excellent persons who have been in the East, or who may visit it after me, as sufficiently fanciful and exaggerated; and there are many who will pass through the very scenes which excited in me so much rapture, and will have no more anxious wish than to get safely out of it before they are splashed with mud from the feet of the wild-looking, blue-skinned buffaloes, or have their toes trodden upon by bullocks with great humps between their shoulders. It is impossible to expect general sympathy for such things; and accordingly my English friends at Bombay used often to laugh heartily when I returned from these Arabian

[1] [This is silphium or *hing*, a repulsively smelling substance beloved of Hindus as a condiment.]

Night sort of excursions, with my head brim full of turbaned Turks, Hindoo pagodas, and all kinds of Oriental associations about the Indus and the Ganges, or Brahma and Vishnoo, or with speculations on the customs, languages, and manners, of the extraordinary collection of people I had been rambling amongst.

But there is one set of images and delightful illustrations, meeting the eye at every turn in India, which I have never seen any person so insensible as not to attend to with unaffected interest. I allude to those numerous every-day customs of the East so often mentioned incidentally in the Scriptures, and with which our minds have become familiar from earliest infancy. We so naturally associate these customs with the sacred writings, that we are easily drawn to link the two indissolubly together. Before visiting Eastern countries, we almost fancy that because the events related in the Bible, and the characters who acted in them, have passed away and become matter of history, so also must the customs have disappeared which served as familiar illustrations between man and man, or between our Saviour and the human beings whom it was the object of his mission to impress with his doctrine. We are apt to be startled, therefore, when we find ourselves actually surrounded by scenes almost identical with those described in the Bible. Be all this as it may, I could never see a Hindoo female sitting by the steps of a well in India, with her arm thrown wearily over the unfilled water-pot, without thinking of the beautiful story of the woman of Samaria, the association being perhaps helped by the recollection of a well-known Italian picture, in which the figures and the scenery are represented quite in the Eastern style, such as I was now beholding it for the first time.

"Two women shall be grinding at the mill, the one shall be taken, the other left," conveys scarcely any meaning to European readers. But in India, where we see constantly two female millers, sitting cross-legged on the ground, turning by one handle the upper of two small stones, we are at once struck with the force of the illustration used to explain the uncertainty which should prevail at the destruction of the City. It is difficult, on looking at two persons so engaged, to conceive a situation in which it would be less easy to remove the one without interfering with the other; and this point was admirably enforced by reference to a custom with which every listener in those countries must have been quite familiar. The industry of commentators on the Bible has, I observe, long ago discovered the true explanation of this, and many other passages apparently obscure, but pregnant with meaning when duly investigated. Nevertheless, I aver that a whole quarto of commentaries on the above verse could not have impressed my mind with a tenth part of the conviction which flashed upon me when I first saw two women actually "grinding at the mill;" all unconscious, poor folks, of the cause of my admiration, and as yet ignorant, alas! of the sublime lessons, to enforce and explain which their humble task was referred to.

On the morning after my arrival at Bombay, I got up with the first blush of the dawn, and hastily drawing on my clothes, proceeded alone greedily in search of adventures. I had not gone far before I saw a native sleeping on a mat spread in the little verandah extending along the front of his house, which was made of basket-work plastered over with mud. He was wrapped up in a long web of white linen, or cotton cloth, called, I think, his cummerbund, or waist-cloth. As soon as the first rays of the sun peeped into his rude sleeping chamber, he "arose, took up his bed, and went into his house." I saw immediately an explanation of this expression which, with slight variations, occurs frequently in the Bible, in connection with several of the most striking and impressive of Christ's miracles, particularly with that of the man sick of the palsy. My honest friend the Hindoo got on his feet, cast the long folds of his wrapper over his shoulder, stooped down, and having rolled up his mat, which was all the bed he required, he walked into the house with it, and then proceeded to the nearest tank to perform his morning ablutions.

I remember mentioning this, amongst many other illustrations of the incidents recorded in Scripture, to a worthy old Scotch lady, upon whom I expected it to produce the same pleasing and satisfactory effect which it had wrought on me. I made, however a great mistake, for so far from raising myself in her estimation, on the score of correct observation, I sunk, I fear irrecoverably, in her good graces, by presuming, as she alleged, to interfere with the wonder of the miracle, the essence of which, according to her, I discovered to consist, not in the recovery of "the man, who was made whole," but in his being able to shoulder a four-post bed, and carry it off without inconvenience!

CHAPTER II

SIR SAMUEL HOOD AND THE ALLIGATOR HUNT

As soon as the *Volage* was refitted, and her crew refreshed, after our voyage from England of four months and a half, we sailed from Bombay to the southward along the western coast of India; and having rounded Ceylon, at the extreme south-western corner of which, Point de Galle, where we merely touched to land the governor's despatches, we hauled up to the northward, and, after twelve days' passage, sailed into the beautiful harbour of Trincomalee.[1] There, to my great joy, we found the commander-in-chief, Sir Samuel Hood; who, to my still greater joy, communicated that a vacancy had been kept open for me in his flag-ship, the *Illustrious.* In a few minutes my traps were packed up, my commission made out, and I had the honour and the happiness of hailing myself a professional follower of one of the first officers in His Majesty's service. It is true, I was only fifth lieutenant of the ship, and not even fifth on the Admiral's list for promotion; for I came after a number of old officers who had served under Sir Samuel for many long years of patient, or rather impatient expectation. But my first and grand purpose was attained, viz. that of getting fairly into the line of promotion; and for a time I did not fret much, or consider myself the most ill-used man in the service, merely because my chance of advancement was very small, and remote.

In capstans, and other machines, there is a mechanical device with which every person is acquainted, termed a pawl or catch, by which the work gained by the effort last made shall be secured, and the machine prevented

[1] [See p. 88, note 2.]

from turning back again. Something of this kind takes place in life, particularly in naval life; and happy is the officer who hears the pawl of his fortunes play "click! click!" as he rapidly spins up to the highest stations in his profession. Proportionately deep is the despair of the poor wretch who, after struggling and tugging with all his might at the weary windlass of his hopes, can never bring it quite far enough round to hear the joyous sound of the pawl dropping into its berth! I well remember most of these important moments of my own life; and I could readily describe the different sensations to which their successive occurrence gave rise, from the startling hour [thirty years ago] when my father first told me that my own request was now to be granted, for on the very next day I was to go to sea—up to that instant when the still more important and awful announcement met my ear, "Those whom God hath joined together let no man put asunder!"

Nothing perhaps more distinctly characterises men than the different manner in which they behave on these occasions. One person acquiring fresh spirits from the consciousness of so much of his fortunes being secured, plants his foot more firmly on the deck, and grasping the handspike anew, springs aloft to command by a still more vigorous effort of his strength, the next revolution of the windlass; while another man, similarly circumstanced, remains content with the first step gained. It is wrong, however, to say that he remains content, for there is no contentment in the sluggishness with which he waits till someone helps him to accomplish that purpose which he has not energy enough to attempt single-handed. In two words: the classes of people we are speaking of may be divided into those who know how to avail themselves of the opportunities within their reach, and those who will not, or, at all events, who do not, screw up their courage to the sticking-place alluded to. There is a charming sea-song by Dibdin[1] [that prince of nautical minstrels!] one part of which often came to my aid in seasons of professional despondency:

> "So I seized the capstan-bar
> Like a true-hearted tar,
> And in spite of sighs and tears sung out, Yo heave ho."

"It is easy to be cheerful when one is successful," says a high authority; and there are "few people who are not good-natured when they have nothing to cross them," says another equally profound recorder of commonplaces; but the secret of good fortune seems to lie far less in making the most of favourable incidents, or in submitting manfully to disastrous ones, than in studying how to fill up to advantage the long intervals between these great epochs in our lives. Perhaps, therefore, there is no point of duty which affords more scope for the talents of a superior than the useful and cheerful employment of the heads and hands of his officers and people during those trying periods of inaction which occur in every service. Sir Samuel Hood possessed this faculty in a wonderful degree, as he not only kept us all busy when there was nothing to be done, but contrived to make us happy and contented, though some of our prospects were poor enough in all conscience. My own, for example; for I was placed at the tip of the tail of his long string of private followers; and when the Admiralty List came out, on which I had built so many beautiful castles in the air, my poor name was not upon it at all. I had not expected to be first or second, or even third; fourth I had reckoned upon as possible; fifth as probable; sixth as certain; so that my horror and disappointment were

[1] [Charles Dibdin (1745-1814), author and composer of the famous sea-songs and ballads which so powerfully influenced national spirit during the Napoleonic war at sea.]

excessive when this kindest of commanders-in-chief broke to me the fatal news, in the following characteristic manner.

A telegraphic signal had been made from the flag-staff at the Admiral's house to the ship, in these words:

"Send Mr. Hall on shore, with a crowbar, two pick-axes, and two spades."

All the way to the landing-place I puzzled myself with thinking what on earth could be the object of these tools; little dreaming, good easy lieutenant! that I was so soon to dig the grave of my own hopes. The Admiral received me at the door with his coat off; and holding out his remaining hand [his right arm was shot away in action], he squeezed mine with even more than his wonted kindness.

"I have been waiting for you with some impatience," he said, "to be present at the hunt after a white ant's nest, a sort of thing I know you like. These rogues, the *Termites bellicosi*, as I find the naturalists call them, have made their way into the house; and having carried their galleries up the walls and along the roof, have come down in great force upon a trunk of clothes which they would have destroyed entirely before night had I not caught sight of them. Now let us to work; for I propose to rip up the floor of the verandah, in order to follow their passages and galleries till I reach their nest, if it be a mile off; won't this be a glorious piece of service?" exclaimed the Admiral, as he warmed himself by anticipating the chase. He could hardly have been more delighted, I am persuaded, had he been giving orders for a fleet under his command to bear down upon the enemy's line. Of course I failed not to feign or feel the enthusiasm of my commander-in-chief—a little of both, perhaps; for the utmost possible, or even conceivable, familiarity of an Admiral, will scarcely ever crack the ice of a lieutenant's reserve in his commander-in-chief's presence. We may cherish and obey him, as much, or more, than any wife ever did, or promised to do, her spouse; but I never yet saw a naval man, in uniform or in plain clothes, on shore or afloat, sober or merry, that could, even in appearance, bring himself to take a liberty with one who, in times past—no matter how long—had once been his commanding officer. This truth is doubly, trebly true at moments of actual service; and though Sir Samuel was all smiles and favour, standing without his coat in the verandah with a crowbar in his grasp, his bare breast and single arm exposed naked to the sea-breeze, then just beginning to puff at intervals over the low, red-hot isthmus or neck of land between the inner harbour and the eastern beach, I could not venture to do more than bow, and say I was much obliged to him for having so considerately thought of me at such a moment.

"Oh!" cried he, apparently recollecting himself, "but I have something else to shew you, or rather to tell you, for I must not shew it to you; though I fear it will not please you quite so much as the prospect of a white ant hunt. Here, Gigna," called the Admiral to his steward, who stood by with a tea-kettle of hot water ready to pour over the ants, "put away that affair, which we shall not require this half hour yet; and hold this crowbar while I step into the office with Mr. Hall."

"It is of no use to mince the matter," said the veteran, shutting the door, and turning to me with somewhat of the air which he might be supposed to have put on had he been instructed from home to tell me that one or both my parents were dead; "it is no use to conceal the fact from you; but here is the Admiralty List, just come to my hands, and your name, in spite of all you tell me of promises, verbal and written, is NOT ON IT!"

Had the Admiral fired one of the flagship's thirty-two pounders, double-shotted, down my throat, he could not have demolished more completely my bodily framework than this fatal announcement shattered to pieces the gilded crockery-ware of my fondest hopes. All the gay visions of command, and power, and independence, in which I had indulged my fancy during the voyage, vanished like the shadows of a dream I fain would recall, but could not. I stood at first quite stupefied, and can remember nothing that passed for some minutes. As I recovered my scattered senses, however, I recollect gazing at the anchorage from the open window of the Admiralty House, near which we stood. The flag-ship then lay just off Osnaburgh Point, with her ensign, or, as it used to be called in old books, her Ancient, the "meteor flag of England," dropped, in the calm, so perpendicularly from the gaff end, that it looked like a rope more than a flag; while its reflection, as well as that of the ship herself, with every mast, yard, and line of the rigging, seemed, as it were, engraved on the surface of the tranquil pool, as distinctly as if another vessel had actually been inverted and placed beneath. I have seldom witnessed so complete a calm. The sea-breeze, with which the shore had been refreshed for twenty minutes, had not as yet found its way into the recesses of the inner harbour, which, take it all in all, is one of the snuggest and most beautiful coves ln the world. And such is the commodious nature of this admirable port, that even the *Illustrious*, though a large 74-gun ship, rode at anchor in perfect security, within a very few yards of the beach, which at that spot is quite steep-to, and is wooded down to the very edge of the water. I gazed for some minutes, almost unconsciously, at this quiet scene, so different from that which was boiling and bubbling in my own distracted breast, and swelling up with indignation against some of my truest friends at home, whom I had such good reason to believe had either betrayed or neglected me, maugre all sorts of promises.

In the midst of my reverie—which the kind-hearted Admiral did not interrupt—I observed the wind just touch the drooping flag; but the air was so light and transient, that it merely produced on it a gentle motion from side to side, like that of a pendulum, imitated in the mirror beneath, which lay as yet totally unbroken by the sea-breeze. Presently the whole mighty flag, after a faint struggle or two, gradually unfolded itself, and, buoyed up by the new-born gale, spread far beyond the gallant line-of-battle ship's stern, and waved gracefully over the harbour. It is well known to nice observers of the human mind, that the strangest fancies often come into the thoughts at a moment when we might least expect them; and though, assuredly, I was not then in a very poetical or imaginative humour, I contrived to shape out of the inspiring scene I was looking upon, a figure to soothe my disappointed spirit. As I saw the ensign uncurl itself to the wind, I said internally, "If I have but life, and health, and opportunity, I trust—for all the bitterness of this disappointment—I shall yet contrive to unfold, in like manner, the flag of my own fortunes to the world."

Just as this magnanimous thought crossed my mind's eye, the Admiral placed his hand so gently on my shoulder that the pressure would not have hurt a fly, and said, in a cheerful tone, "Never mind this mishap, Master Hall; everything will come right in time; and if you only resolve to take it in the proper and manly temper, it may even prove all the better that this has happened. Nothing is without a remedy in this world; and I'll do what I can to make good this maxim in your case. In the meantime, however, come along and help me to rout out these rascally white ants. Off coat, however, if you please; for we shall have a tough job of it."

It cost us an hour's hard work; for we had to rip up the planks along the whole of the verandah, then to shape a course across two cellars, or godongs,[1] as they are called in the East, and finally, the traverses of these singular animals obliged us to cut a trench to the huge hillock or nest, which rose to the height of five or six feet from the ground, in numberless shoots, like pinnacles round the roof of a Gothic church. We might have attacked them at head-quarters in the first instance, had we wished it; but the Admiral chose to go more technically to work, and to sap up to his enemy by regular approaches. In this way we had the means of seeing the principles upon which these ants proceed in securing themselves at every step of their progress by galleries or covered ways, which, though extremely feeble, are sufficiently strong to keep off the attacks of every other kind of ant. It is curious enough, that although the white ant be the most destructive of its species, it is said to be, individually, by far the weakest, and cannot move a step without the artificial protection of the galleries it constructs as it goes along; just as the besiegers of a fortification secure themselves in their trenches and zig-zags.

We now brought our spades into play; and having cut the hill across, laid open the secrets of these most curious of all the ant tribe. At last, we reached the great queen ant, the mother of millions of her race, a most enormous personage to be sure, nearly four inches long, and as thick as a man's finger, with a head not bigger than that of a bee, but a body such as I have described, filled with eggs, which continually rolled out like a fluid from a reservoir. Never shall I forget the shout of rapture which the gallant Admiral sent over half the harbour, as he succeeded in gaining the object of his labour.[2]

[1] [A Malay word meaning 'a warehouse'; usually Anglicized as 'godown'.]

[2] See an exceedingly interesting account of the *Termes bellicosus*, or white ant, in Shaw's *Zoology*, vol. vi., taken chiefly from the *Philosophical Transactions* for the year 1781.

There are some men who go about everything they undertake with all their hearts and souls, and this great officer was one of those. He did nothing by halves and quarters like so many other men. The greatest deeds of arms, or the most trivial objects of passing amusement, engrossed his whole concentrated attention for the time. He was equally in earnest when holding out examples of private generosity, or lending the heartiest and kindest encouragement even to the least distinguished of his followers, as when performing acts of the highest public spirit, or making the greatest sacrifices to what he considered his duty. Everything, in short, that he did, or thought, or uttered, bore the stamp of the same peculiar impress of genuine zeal. So eminently exciting, and even fascinating, was this truly officer-like conduct, that even those who had served under him the longest often wondered at the extent of their own exertions when roused by his example, and were led almost to believe that his very look had something stimulating in it which actually gave fresh vigour to their arms as well as to their thoughts. With all this, he was the gentlest of the gentle, and accomplished all he undertook without apparent effort, or the least consciousness that what he was doing was remarkable.

I remember an instance of his skill in the small way. One morning, near the spot where he had headed the storming-party against the white ants, a working party of the crew of the *Illustrious* had commenced constructing a wharf before the dock-yard. The stones of which this platform or landing-place was to be built were, by Sir Samuel Hood's orders, selected of very large dimensions, so much so, that the sailors came at last to deal with a mass of rock so heavy, that their combined strength proved unequal to moving it beyond a few inches towards its final position at the top of one corner. The Admiral sat on his horse looking at the workmen for some time, occasionally laughing and occasionally calling out directions, which the baffled engineers could by no means apply. At length His Excellency the commander-in-chief became fidgety, and having dismounted, he tried to direct them in detail; but never a bit would the stone budge. Finally, losing all patience, he leaped from the top of the bank, and roared out, in a voice of reproach and provocation, "Give me the crowbar!" Thus armed, he pushed the officers and men to the right and left, while he insisted upon having the whole job to himself, literally, single-handed. He first drove the claws of the instrument well under the edge of the stone, then placed with his toe a small iron pin on the ground under the bar, and across its length, to act as a fulcrum, or shoulder. When all things were carefully adjusted to his mind, he slipped his hand to the upper end of the lever, and weighing it down, gave what he called "life" to the huge stone, which just before half a dozen strong men had not been able to disturb. Sure enough, however, it now moved, though only about half an inch, towards its intended resting-place. At each prise or hitch of the bar, the rock appeared to advance farther, till, after five or six similar shifts, it was finally lodged in the station prepared for it, where, I doubt not, it rests to this day, and may occupy for centuries to come.

I need scarcely say that the Admiral himself was delighted with his triumph, or that his provocation against the men subsided at each successful march of the stone, till, at length, when the operation was completed, he flung down the bar, and called out to the grinning party, but with infinite good humour, "There! you hay-making, tinkering, tailoring fellows, that's the way to move a stone—when you know how!"

In fact, no officer I have ever served with, better "knew how", not only himself to do everything "that might become a man," but how to stimulate others to do so likewise; or, if need should be, as in this instance of the corner-stone, to instruct them practically. What is interesting, however, and still more important in every way, he never lost sight of his own true dignity, or weakened his personal or his official authority, by any such condescensions. On the contrary, both appeared only to be enhanced by familiarities which such a mind alone could safely trust itself with, and which, from their being totally devoid of affectation, were always suitable to his character, and appropriate to the circumstances as well as persons in whose favour they were granted. This unreserved freedom of manner, an officer, less gifted by nature, or not so thoroughly master of his business in all its branches, could hardly have indulged in; but in Sir Samuel Hood's hands it became an instrument of great importance, and invariably turned the heartiest exertions of every officer and man under him to his purpose, which, I need scarcely add, was synonymous with the public good.

The loss of such a man to the country at large, and to the naval service in particular, was in many respects irreparable; for although his example must ever dwell deeply engraven on the minds of those who knew him personally, he carried away with him to his early grave very much which no instruction could impart, no memory supply, nor indeed, any eulogium do justice to. I allude chiefly to that rare combination of talent and professional experience welded together by the highest public spirit, animated to useful action by the most ardent zeal which perhaps ever possessed an officer. I have sometimes thought, that a professional sketch of this great commander's career, including, as it might readily and naturally be made to do, many of the most important incidents of the lives of his great contemporaries, Nelson, St. Vincent, and Collingwood, would prove a useful practical manual for the rising generation afloat.

In the meantime, for want of a better, I feel tempted to give a place here to a few words which I wrote in the Bombay *Courier*, in January 1815, [the first time I ever tried my hand in print,] on the day our excellent commander-in-chief's death was made known at that presidency.

"It is with the deepest regret we announce the death of Vice-admiral Sir Samuel Hood. This officer had raised himself so high in the public estimation by the number and importance of his services—had shewn himself so admirable in the conduct of every enterprise in which he had been engaged—was still so young in years and unbroken in spirit—so thoroughly possessed of the enthusiastic admiration and entire confidence of every man in his profession, that his loss cannot be considered otherwise than as a severe and irreparable misfortune to his country at large; while to those who have enjoyed a nearer view of his excellence, who have served under his command, or have lived in his society, his death is unspeakably afflicting.

"Sir Samuel Hood possessed in a peculiar degree the qualifications which form a great commander: to the calmest and most accurate judgment, he added a presence of mind and rapidity of perception, under all changes of situation, that enabled him to turn every event, which arose even out of unforeseen difficulties and dangers, to the purpose he had in view. In common with Nelson, he was anxious and impatient while there remained a doubt that the foe could be grappled with; but when the battle once began, his matchless intrepidity, his coolness, and the precision with which all his orders were given, diffused a confidence that was almost uniformly attended by victory.

"But it was not only on these great and trying occasions that he proved himself one of the best officers in the service; for he was eminently skilled in most branches of his profession, whether scientific or practical. He was intimately versed in astronomy, as far, at least, as it is connected with navigation. In geography, ship-building, and fortification, and in many branches of mechanical philosophy, he was also well skilled. He studied, without exception, the languages, and, as far as possible, the laws and customs, of every country he visited. His strong natural taste for scientific inquiry, and an unbounded curiosity to see things with his own eyes, were kept in perpetual action by the belief that these acquisitions of knowledge might one day prove useful to his country. That they did prove so, those who are acquainted wtih his life can amply testify. His surveys of the coasts in North America recommended him to early notice as an excellent hydrographer. The bold and original idea of fortifying the Diamond Rock at Martinique, and the immediate execution of that difficult undertaking, shewed him to be a skilful engineer. The extraordinary defence of Salerno, with a few marines opposed to an army—his capture of Tobago, St. Lucia, and Demerara—and his decision after the failure at Teneriffe—all exhibit him as an able general. His gallant capture of a Russian ship of the line, in presence of the Russian fleet; followed by his politic and conciliatory self-denial in sending the flag which he had just taken to the King of Sweden, as if it had been a trophy of that monarch's arms; and, some years before, his communications with the governors and pashas in Syria; together with innumerable other instances, place him high as a statesman and a negotiator.

"The unaffected modesty and simplicity of one who had filled so great a space in public admiration, was not the least remarkable part of his character: he had the rare felicity, even to his latest years, to preserve undiminished the vivacity of youth, and that taste for simple pleasures which so seldom survives a mixed and active intercourse with the world. The charm which this happy feeling communicated to his conversation and society, had something in it irresistibly pleasing. He was no less the delight of his friends than the pride of his country."

As it may possibly be imagined that the warmth of juvenile gratitude, combined with strong professional admiration, might have dictated some part of the above eulogium, which was written at a moment of high excitement, I have much satisfaction in adding the deliberate testimony of a perfectly competent authority. The following inscription, written by Sir James Mackintosh for a monument at Bath, is no less creditable to the sagacity and taste of its accomplished author, than it is honourable to the memory of his gallant friend.

SACRED TO THE MEMORY

OF

SIR SAMUEL HOOD, Bart.

Knight of the Most Honourable Order of the Bath,
And nominated Grand Cross thereof;
Knight of Saint Ferdinand and of Merit;
Knight Grand Cross of the Sword;
Vice-Admiral of the White;
And Commander-in-Chief of His Majesty's Fleet
In the East Indies.

An Officer of the highest distinction
Among the illustrious Men
Who rendered their own age the brightest period
In the Naval History of their Country:
In whom the same simplicity, calmness, and firmness,
Which gave him full command of his science and skill
In the midst of danger, secured also the rectitude
Of his judgment in its most rapid decisions,
Preserved the integrity and kindness of his nature
Undisturbed amidst the agitations of the world,
And diffused a graceful benignity
On the frank demeanour of his generous profession:

CAPTAIN BASIL HALL

Whose character was an example of the natural union
Of a gallant spirit with a gentle disposition,
And of private affection with public honour:
Whose native modesty was unchanged by renown.

This Column is erected
By the attachment and reverence of British Officers,
Of whom many were his admiring followers
In those awful scenes of war which, while
They called forth the grandest qualities of human nature,
In him, likewise gave occasion for the exercise of its
Most amiable virtues.

Fortunately for me, however, Sir Samuel Hood's death did not occur till more than two years after I reached India. Owing to his kindness, I was enabled to visit the interior of the peninsula of Hindoostan on two different occasions, and likewise to perform a journey of more than a thousand miles on the island of Java. Before touching on these extensive themes, I must give a short account of an alligator-hunt, at a place called Nellivelley, near Trincomalee, got up for the Admiral's express amusement, and performed by a corps of Malays in the British service, the 1st Ceylon Regiment.

Very early in the morning of the 22nd of September, the party, which consisted of several ladies and a large proportion of red coats and blue coats, were summoned from their beds to set forth on this expedition. The Admiral, as usual, was up, dressed, and on horseback, long before any of the rest of the company, whom he failed not to scold or to quiz, as they severally crept out of their holes, rubbing their eyes, and very much doubting whether the pleasures of the sport were likely to compensate for the horrible bore of early rising. In other countries the hour of getting up may be left to choice; in India, when anything active is to be done, it is a matter of necessity; for after the sun has gained even a few degrees of altitude, the heat and discomfort, as well as the danger of exposure, become so great, that all pleasure is at an end. This circumstance limits the hours of travelling and of exercise in the East very inconveniently, and introduces modifications which help in no slight degree to give a distinctive character to Indian manners.

As there was little risk of being too late on any party of which Sir Samuel Hood took the lead, the day had scarcely begun to dawn when we all cantered up to the scene of action. The ground lay as flat as a marsh for many leagues; here and there the plain was spotted with small stagnant lakes, connected together by sluggish streams, or canals, scarcely moving over beds of mud, between banks fringed with a rank crop of draggled weeds, and giving birth to clouds of mosquitoes. The chill atmosphere of the morning felt so thick and clammy, it was impossible for the most confident in his own strength and health not to think of agues, jungle fevers, and all the hopeful family of malaria. The hardy native soldiers, who had occupied the ground during the night in despite of the miasmata, were drawn up to receive the Admiral; and a very queer guard of honour they formed. The whole regiment had stripped off their uniform and every other stitch of clothing, save a pair of short trousers, and a kind of sandal. In place of a firelock each man bore in his hand a slender pole about six feet in length, to the extremity of which was attached the bayonet of his musket. His only other weapon was the formidable Malay Crease, a sort of dagger or small edition of the waving two-edged sword with which the angel Michael is armed in Raphael's picture of the Expulsion of our First Parents from Paradise.

Soon after the commander-in-chief came to the ground the regiment was divided into two main parties, and a body of reserves. The principal columns, facing, one to the right, the other to the left, proceeded to occupy different points in one of those sluggish canals I have already mentioned, connecting the lakes, or pools, scattered over the plain. These detachments, being stationed about a mile from one another, enclosed an interval where, from some peculiar cicumstances known only to the Malays [who are passionately fond of this sport], the alligators were sure to be found in great numbers. The troops formed themselves across the canal in three parallel lines, ten or twelve feet apart; but the men in each line stood side by side, merely leaving room enough to wield their pikes. The canal may have been about four or five feet deep in the middle of the stream, if stream it may be called, which scarcely moved at all. The colour of the water when undisturbed was a shade between ink and coffee; but no sooner had the triple line of Malays set themselves in motion, and the mud got stirred up, than the consistence and colour of the fluid became like those of pease-soup.

On everything being reported ready, the soldiers planted their pikes before them in the mud, and, if I recollect right, each man crossing his neighbour's weapon, and at the word "march" away they all started in full cry, sending forth a shout, or war-whoop sufficient to curdle the blood of those on land, whatever effect it may have had on the inhabitants of the deep. As the two divisions of the invading army, starting from opposite ends of the canal, gradually approached each other in pretty close column, screaming and yelling with all their souls, and striking their pikes deep in the slime before them, the startled animals naturally retired towards the unoccupied centre. Generally speaking, the alligators, or crocodiles [for I believe they are very nearly the same], had sense enough to turn their long tails upon their assailants, and to scuttle off as fast as they could towards the middle part of the canal. But every now and then, one of the terrified monsters, either confused by the sound, or provoked by the prick of a pike, or mystified by the turbid nature of the stream, floundered backwards, and, by retreating in the wrong direction, broke through the first, second, and even third line of pikes. This, which would have been anything but an amusement to unpractised hands, was the perfection of sport to the delighted Malays. A double circle of soldiers was speedily formed round the wretched aquatic who had presumed to pass the barrier. By means of well-directed thrusts with numberless bayonets, and the pressure of some dozens of feet, the poor brute was often fairly driven beneath his native mud. When once there, his enemies half choked and half spitted him, till at last they put an end to his miserable days in regions quite out of sight, and in a manner as inglorious as can well be conceived.

For the poor denizens of the pool, indeed, it was the choice between Scylla and Charybdis with a vengeance; and I am half ashamed to acknowledge the savage kind of delight with which we stood on the banks, and saw the distracted creatures rushing from one attack right into the jaws of another. The Malays, in their ecstasy, declared that the small fry from one side rushed down the throats of the big ones whom they met flying in the opposite direction. But this seems very questionable, though positively asserted by the enraptured natives, who redoubled their shouts as the plot thickened, and the two bodies of troops, marching from opposite quarters, drew within a hundred yars of each other. The intermediate space was now pretty well crowded with alligators, swimming about in the utmost terror; at times diving below, and anon shewing their noses well plastered with mud high above the surface of the dirty stream; or occasionally making a furious bolt in sheer despair right at the phalanx of Malays. On these occasions half a dozen of the soldiers were often upset, and their pikes either broken or twisted out of their hands, to the infinite amusement of their companions, who speedily closed up the broken ranks, as of their comrades had been shot down in battle. The killed were none, but the wounded many; yet no man flinchd in the least.

The perfection of the sport appeared to consist in detaching a single alligator from the rest, surrounding and attacking him separately, and spearing him till he was almost dead. The Malays then, by main strength, forked him aloft, over their heads, on the end of a dozen pikes, and, by a sudden jerk, pitched the conquered monster far on the shore. As the alligators are amphibious, they kept to the water no longer than they found they had an advantage in that element; but as the period of the final mélée approached, on the two columns of their enemy closing up, the monsters lost all discipline, floundered, and ploutered up the weedy banks, scuttling away to the right and left, helter-skelter. "Sauve qui peut!" seemed to be the fatal watch-word for their total rout. That prudent cry would, no doubt, have saved many of them, as it has saved other vanquished forces, had not the Malays judiciously placed beforehand their reserve on each side of the river to receive the distracted fugitives, who, bathed in mud, and half dead with terror, but still in a prodigious fury, dashed off at right angles from the canal, in hopes of gaining the shelter of a swampy pool overgrown with reeds and bulrushes, but which, alas for most of the poor beasts, they were never doomed to reach. The concluding battle between these retreating and desperate alligators and the Malays of the reserve was formidable enough. Indeed, had not the one party been fresh, the other exhausted, one confident, the other broken in spirit, it is quite possible that the crocodiles might have worsted the pirates, as the Malays are called in every other part of the world but the East, where they are generally admitted to be as good a set of people as any of their neighbours.

It is needless to say, that while all this was going on, our gallant Admiral, Sir Samuel Hood, was a pretty busy spectator. His eagle eye glanced along the canal and at a moment took in the whole purpose of the campaign. As the war advanced, and sundry small affairs of outposts took place, we could see his face flushing with delight. But when the first alligator was cast headlong and gasping at his feet, pierced with at least twenty pike wounds, and bristled with half a dozen fragments of these weapons fractured in the onslaught, the whole plain rung with his exclamation of boyish delight. When the detachment closed in upon their prey, and every moment gave birth to some new prodigy of valour, or laid a whole line of the Malay soldiers prostrate on the muddy stream, like so many nine-pins, I verily believe, that if none of his own people had been present, the Admiral would have seized a pike himself, and jumped into the thickest of the fight, boots, sword, cocked hat, and all! As it was, he kept himself close to the banks, and rivalled the best Malay amongst them in yelling and cheering on the forces to their duty. This intensity of eagerness had well nigh proved rather awkward for his Excellency's dignity, if not his safety; for, in spite of the repeated warnings of the English officers of the regiment, who knew from former hunts what was sure to happen eventually, the admiral persisted in approaching the edge of the canal as the final act of the alligators' tragedy commenced. And as we, his poor officers, were, of course, obliged to follow our chief into any danger, a considerable party of us found ourselves rather awkwardly placed between the reserve of Malays already spoken of and the canal, just as the grand rush took place at the close of the battle. If the infuriated crocodiles had only known what they were about, and had then brought their long sharp snouts, and still harder tails, into play, several of His Majesty's officers might have chanced to find themselves in a scrape. As it was we were extremely near being wedged in between the animals' noses and the pikes and creases of the wild Malays. It was difficult, indeed, to say which of the two looked at that moment the most savage—the triumphant natives or the flying troop of alligators wallopping away from the water. Many on both sides were wounded, and all, without exception, covered with slime and weeds. Some of our party were actually pushed over, and fell plump in the mud, to the very provoking and particular amusement of the delighted Admiral, whose superior adroitness enabled him to avoid such an undignified catastrophe, by jumping first on one side and then on the other, in a manner which excited both the mirth and the alarm of his company; though, of course, we took good care rather to laugh with our commander-in-chief than at him.

I forget the total number of alligators killed, but certainly there could not have been fewer than thirty or forty. The largest measured ten feet in length, and four feet girth, the head being exactly two feet long. Besides these great fellows, we caught, alive, a multitude of little ones, nine inches long, many of which we carried back to Trincomalee. Half-a-dozen of these were kept in tubs of water at the Admiralty House for many days; the rest being carried on board, became great favourites amongst the sailors, whose queer taste in the choice of pets has already been noticed.

CHAPTER III

Picnic Party in the Cave of Elephanta[1]

From Trincomalee we sailed back again to Bombay the only port in India possessing docks sufficiently capacious, and a harbour commodious enough for so large a ship as the *Illustrious*. This was the second visit I paid to that most interesting of all the presidencies. On two subsequent occasions I had even better opportunities of making myself acquainted with its merits; for I had by that time made two extensive journeys across the country, and, of course, become more or less familiar with various oriental topics. Nevertheless, Bombay continues to hold its ground as the place best worth seeing of any spot I have visited in India.

The fascinations of society at Bombay, in the particular circle to whose intimacy I had the happiness to be admitted on these occasions, were certainly very great; and, in a pretty extensive experience since, I have hardly found them matched. To think of studying, to any good purpose, the mouldering antiquities of the Hindoos, or of speculating with spirit on the manners and customs of the existing generation of the natives, while the conversation of such specimens of my own country folks lay within reach, was totally out of the question. And this feeling being shared by all the

1 [Elephanta is the Portuguese name for Gharpuri or Puri, the island in Bombay Harbour containing the wonderful Hindu cave temples, dating back to the 8th century after Christ. The stone elephant, which gave the place its name, was removed to Victoria Gardens in 1864. It was in an advanced stage of decay when Hall saw and measured it. (*Fragments*, II, III, Chap V.)]

party, it was considered a most brilliant idea to unite the two sources of interest in one expedition.

"Why should we not," said one of the ladies, [who, alas! is now no more,] "why should we not make a regular expedition in a body to Elephanta? Not for a mere visit of an hour or two, but to remain a week or ten days, during which we might examine the caves at leisure, draw them, describe them, and, in short, perform such a course of public antiquarian services as were never before undertaken?"

The notion was eagerly caught up by the company; one of whom, an officer of the engineers, called out:

"I'll send over a couple of tents, to be pitched before the mouth of the cave; one for the ladies, the other for the attendants and kitchen, while the gentlemen may pick out the softer bits of pavement within the cave to spread their beds on."

"I'll send cooks!" cried another.

"I'll be the caterer of our mess," shouted a third, "and take care of the commissariat department."

"And I," said a gentleman, who alone of all the party now lingers on the spot, though it is nearly twenty years since those merry days, "I shall see that you have wine enough, and plenty of Hodgson's pale ale."

All were eager to be of use, and nothing was thought of but making arrangements. We hired Bunder boats,[1] or native launches, to transport the heavy baggage, the tents, tables, and victuals; while it fell to my lot to provide smaller and faster-moving boats, called gigs, for the accommodation of the ladies. We passed over in detachments; some early in the morning; and others, whose business kept them in the fort, later in the afternoon; but in the course of a couple of days we were all established close to the scene of operations, and ready to commence working in earnest.

[1] [From Hind. *bandar*, a harbour.]

PICNIC PARTY

When I come to describe the method of travelling in India, it will not seem surprising how readily we made ourselves comfortably at home on the island of Elephanta. Most of the gentlemen slept actually within the cave, either boxed up in their palankeens, or on mattrasses, which they spread in the little niches or chapels carved out of the living rock on the sides of the cavern.

The first day was passed in rambling up and down the aisles, if they may be so called, of this wonderful cathedral, which the Hindoos of past ages had hewn out of the solid stone. The sculptures on the wall being varied in every possible way, within the fantastic limits of their extravagant theology, the effect was almost bewildering to those who viewed this wild scene for the first time. Even to those who had witnessed it once or twice before, it was impressive in a degree very difficult to describe. The imagination of a new-comer like myself was carried back irresistibly to dark periods of traditional history, where everything appeared nearly as vague and indistinct as the recollection of a fairy tale. To those, again, who had studied the subject long, and made themselves acquainted not only with the religion of the natives, but with their peculiar style of representing their gods, the cave of Elephanta offered a rich feast of research; and there could be heard from time to time, loud expressions of delight from these adepts in the science of oriental antiquarianism, when they lighted upon any group particularly fertile in characteristic attributes of the deities they were in quest of.

Towards the end of the day, the party, which had hung together more or less during the morning, fell to pieces. Some of the gentlemen straggled into the jungle to catch a shot at a parrot or a monkey; while others, exhausted with the closeness of the cave, and the labour of climbing up to examine the details, stretched themselves in the shade, under the fly, as it is called [or roof], of a large tent, beneath which the air passed freely along, in consequence of the canvass walls being removed. For my own part, I could hardly detach myself for more than a few minutes at a time from the temple, but wandered backwards and forwards, with a restless kind of impatience of my own ignorance, which was rather aggravated than relieved by the snatches of explanation won from more experienced orientalists. During the whole time of dinner I could think of nothing but the indistinct figures on the dark walls which enclosed us on three sides; and I stole away from table as soon as I could, to regale myself with this antiquarian banquet, till the night closed in. I then tried a walk in the open air, but felt the chill land-wind breathing through the damp underwood afford only a deceitful kind of refreshment which soon passed away, and left my brow throbbing and feverish with the intense excitement of the day. My companions declared themselves sick of the cave; and as I could talk of nothing else, I was no society for them, nor they for me, so off I slipped very early to my cot, spread in one of the little recesses already mentioned, lying on the left or eastern side of the principal excavation. Without taking off my clothes, I threw myself down, and in the course of a few minutes, as I imagined, fell asleep.

It is the fashion in India to burn a lamp in every sleeping apartment; not a vulgar rushlight, enclosed as in England, in a wretched case of perforated tin, like a stable lantern, but a small bright flame rising from a classical-shaped bronze vessel, worthy of Etruria, filled with oil expressed either from the cocoanut or the sesamé, and as clear as crystal. What is the origin of this oriental custom of burning a light in the bedchamber, I could never learn exactly. Some persons allege that it affords a protection from the snakes which are said to prevail in those regions; though I never had the fortune to see a single one of them in all the different journeys I made across the continent and islands of India. Whatever be the cause, the practice is so universal, that our servants, who in that country are the most perfect machines imaginable, continued, even in the cave, to place lights by our bed-sides, as a matter of course. A thousand such lamps, however, as were flickering on the stone floor of our huge apartment, would have served very feebly to illuminate even the small portion of the gorgeous temple which I then occupied.

After lying asleep for some time, as I thought, I either awoke, or believed I did, and, on looking round, was not a little startled to find myself alone in such a strange place, of the real nature of which I had but an obscure recollection. The solitary lamp appeared to have gained far more power, for the whole cave now seemed as light as if the sun had been shining into it. On turning round to discover where I could possibly have got to, and looking up, I beheld, with a feeling of indistinct alarm, and of much uncertainty as to the reality or visionary nature of what I was gazing upon, a huge figure, half male and half female. I remembered, that during the morning we had been told by one of the learned folks of our party, that in the Hindoo mythology such a monster was to be found, with the jaw-breaking name of Ardhanar-Ishwar.[1] As I strained my eyes to examine this fantastic figure, I asked myself over and over again whether I could be awake or was still asleep. The foaming cups of Hodgson's pale ale, and the ruby-coloured nectar of Château Margaux, at a pretty late dinner, may possibly have helped this mystification, while they certainly took nothing from the interest of the dream, if dream it were. The

[1] [*Ardhanareshvara:* The androgynous god, *i.e.*, combination of Siva and his consort Parvati in a single form. Skt *ardha nara*, "half-man".]

gigantic image at which I was looking, though at first it seemed detached and in motion, appeared, on closer examination, to be sculptured in high relief on the hard rock of the mountain. This strange hermaphrodite seemed gifted with four arms [which is one of those clumsy devices by which the Hindoo artists seek to convey an idea of power], and standing not quite erect, but inclining a little, with the foremost of its right arms resting on the hump of the famous Nundi,[1] the bull of Shiva, on which it is the fancy of this double-sexed god occasionally to ride. The right side of the figure appeared to be male, the left female; and it is singular how much this distinction was preserved in all respects. The two sides of the cap seemed different, the right presenting the crescent of Shiva, and the female side of the cap being trimmed with curls rising over it, while the male side appeared to be ornamented by a string of knobs, or beads. The ear-rings were different, and on the left, or female side, there hung two; one of them a *bali*, or jewel for the upper part of the ear, the other a large ring; while the male side carried one only, and the ear being lengthened and stretched downwards towards the shoulder. The armlets, also, appeared different, the two right or male arms being both encompassed by a thin metal bar, unjoined at the ends [a common ornament in the East], and the left, or female arms, encircled by a broader ornament. Each of the right-hand wrists was clasped by one ornament, the left by two bracelets. The inner right hand, which was in good preservation, bore a ring on the little finger. The inner left hand, which was also unbroken, carried two rings; one on the little finger, the other on the middle finger. The inner·right hand held the snake called *cobra di capella*, the head of which rose aloft as if listening to the figure. The outer right hand rested on the

[1] [Nandi, the bull, the *vahan* or vehicle of Siva, stands facing the doorway of every Saivite temple.]

horn of the bull, while the elbow was placed on the hump. Both the serpent and the bull Nundi marked out the god Shiva. From the left breast of this curious figure being that of a female, and from its being single, the idea has arisen that the intention was to represent an Amazon. But this is clearly a mistake. And indeed the same distinction of the sexes observed between the appearance of the right and left sides of the principal figure extend to all the others in this very curious compartment of the cave; those attendants on the right hand of Ardnari belonging to Shiva, those on the left to his wife Parvati. Long before I could get half through this catalogue of attributes of the celebrated double-sexed Hindoo deity, the lamp began once more to burn blue, the figures on the wall faded gradually away from my sight, and, in spite of every effort to continue the observations, I dropped again on my pillow fast asleep. During the whole of our stay at Elephanta, I was never afterwards troubled with such visions, for the labours and amusements, to say nothing of the festivities of our glorious and patent picnic, disposed all the party to good sound sleep.

At first we set rather confusedly to work, without much discipline in our examination of the cave; but as the task was extensive, and we had undertaken to do it properly, some systematic arrangement became absolutely necessary. Mr. William Erskine[1] had agreed, with the assistance of his friends, to draw up the account of the cave, and we placed ourselves under his orders as the captain, or chief. The description which was produced by this united service, is by far

[1] ["I had a long and interesting conversation with Mr. Erskine, a gentleman distinguished for his talents and oriental learning. He has studied the Hindoo Mythology at its source, in the sacred language, and has sent home, for publication in the first volume of the Researches of the Bombay Literary Society, an account of the Cave of Elephanta."

Fitzclarence, *Journal of a Route Across India*, 1819, *p*. 331.]

the most exact and minute that has ever been made of Elephanta, and was afterwards published in the Bombay *Transactions*, vol. I. These details undoubtedly owe most of their interest to the skill and taste with which the accomplished writer has arranged them; but as he always very disinterestedly considered his account as the joint property of the party who aided his researches, I have not scrupled, in speaking of the caves, to borrow freely from materials which I helped to collect.

His first assistant [the original proposer of the scheme] was a lady[1] of high qualifications as an artist; not a mere fashionable screen-sketcher and murderer of the picturesque, but a regular painter, trained by long study, and under the influence of good taste. It is grievous to think that so much worth, and beauty, and talents, and such extensive knowledge, should so soon have sunk into the grave; and the smart is, indeed very bitter which accompanies such recollections, when we feel that they are taken away from us for ever. Perhaps there has very seldom existed any person whose loss has been so truly regretted by the circle of her friends, on account of the hopeless difficulty of supplying her place. As it was at all times a piece of good fortune to find one's self in the same party with this charming person, even when it was left to the chapter of accidents to provide opportunities of conversation, it was considered the greatest of all possible catches to secure her companionship for so many days, and in such a place as Elephanta.

Our master of the ceremonies very judiciously fixed his principal hand and eye before the celebrated triple

[1] [Mrs. Ashburner. This lady was well known in Bombay society for her wit, beauty and artistic talents, and her charitable undertakings. She was an accomplished artist, and illustrated Erskine's paper on the Elephanta Caves in the *Transactions of the Literary Society*. She lived at Bhandup, about 20 miles out of Bombay, where her husband had a distillery. See Maria Graham, *Journal of a Residence in India*, p. 115ff.]

head, the most remarkable by far in all the cave. A large mat was spread on the ground, with a table and drawing apparatus in the middle of it, near which there was left ample room for the fair artist's host of merry children to romp and roll about on. Near this spot was also placed the easy chair of her eccentric, but accomplished and highly-informed husband, who refused to undertake any part of the hard work, but quizzed the whole of us unmercifully, for the useless, or, as he called it, idle labour we were bestowing on the cave. This gentleman, who was a great experimental agriculturist, as well as theoretical political economist, in short, what may be called a philosopher of all work, was worth any money on such a picnic as this. His knowledge of the world, and his talents in the art of conversation, though of the first order, were still subordinate to the boundless ingenuity of his fancy, by which anything and everything could be made to fit the most incongruous phases of his arguments. If in his whole composition there had been a spark of ill-nature, such singular powers of adapting facts to fancies, and such earnestness in driving his points home, would have rendered him the most supreme of all bores, in or out of a cave; but, fortunately for the Elephanta company, the matchless sweetness of his disposition, his thorough good-breeding, his delight in all the amiable parts of our nature, and his constant readiness to oblige and be obliged, carved him out as the beau idéal of an ally on such an occasion. Many a time and oft the old cavern rang with peals of jolly mirth, and called us from our various holes and corners, to enjoy the witty sallies of this most amusing of persons, whose endless good-humoured jokes, and queer views of things, were always cracking and sparkling round the drawing party before the principal compartment of the temple.

We took our breakfast and dinner at a long table, spread much nearer the mouth of the cave, that we might enjoy, not only the light of day, and the cool clear air of the sea-breeze, but such peeps of the distant ghauts and other parts of the landscape, seen across the upper parts of the beautiful bay, as we could catch through the foliage. Of course, we kept far enough back to escape the fierce glare of the sky, which in those climates sends down, especially when it is clouded, the treacherous influence of the sun's indirect rays in a manner almost as troublesome, though not quite so fatal, as his full blaze of light. It may be worth while to mention, that we never allowed beef in any shape or way to approach our board; for although the temple of Elephanta has for centuries been desecrated, and, consequently, is no longer used by the Hindoos, there still hangs about this splendid monument a certain degree of sanctity in the eyes of the poor natives, which it would be cruel not to respect. Accordingly, one of the most beautiful rounds of beef that ever was pickled, received orders to march off the island, without any consideration for the wants and wishes of two or three gourmands of the party, whose self-denial proved no match for their appetite, and whose respect for these imaginary feelings of the natives became equal to zero, as the algebraists say. It afforded some consolation, however, to these disappointed members of the picnic, to observe the boundless delight with which our native attendants carried away the unspeakable abomination of the round of beef. The cow and bull, in every shape, are held sacred by the Hindoos; and even those castes who object to no other meat, would much rather die than taste that of an ox.

I was once gravely assured, that in the penal codes of Hindoostan, it is set down as a crime of greater magnitude for a man to jump over a cow than to kill his own mother!—a strangely fantastic classification, surely. Until I heard of this singular law, I certainly had no more thoughts of committing one of these crimes than the other; but, ever after receiving this curious piece of information, I could never see a cow reposing in a meadow without feeling a perverse desire to make a run and leap over her. I actually ventured to try the experiment once in the Green Park, and was very nearly paying the penalty of my Hindoo sacrilege, for the good lady [I mean the cow], astonished at the proceeding, tossed up her head, and all but spitted me on her horns.

Since the above statement was written, I have discovered that I was entirely in error as to the Hindoo superstition above alluded to. Nevertheless, I let the paragraph stand, as it affords a pretty fair specimen of the manner in which a raw traveller, poking about greedily and indiscreetly in search of what he calls characteristic information, may sometimes manage to be taken in. A quizzical friend of mine at Bombay, observing my head half-turned with the glare of Oriental novelties, and bewildered in the intricacies of the Hindoo mythology, thought he would experiment on the traveller's credulity, by inventing and palming off upon me the above fiction about the crime of leaping over a cow. Before presenting to the public, however, so very curious a piece of superstition, I thought it but prudent to make further inquiries as to the fact, and only then discovered that, for the last twenty years, I have been going on relating, with all the confidence imaginable—as a solemn point of Hindoo law—the mere figment of a mercurial cadet's imagination. Verily, if the cow in the Green Park had given me a graze with her horn, it would have served me right!

Our antiquarian commander-in-chief, after a cabinet council held daily at the breakfast-table, distributed us in different parts of the cave; one gentleman being appointed to count and measure the columns, another to ascertain the height of the ceiling, while a third, a very exact and trustworthy assistant, was ordered to construct a ground-plan of the whole excavation. The gentleman named as the chief engineer in this important department of our researches was a medical man in the Company's establishment, who had recently come down to the presidency from the interior, where he had been stationed for some years. He was a single man at the period in question; but most of his associates in this delightful Elephanta picnic had the pleasure of attending his marriage-feast not long afterwards.

The fair damsel of his choice had come out to India to join the family of a married sister; but on reaching Bombay, it appeared that both that lady and her husband had died; and although she knew of several other relations in India, they either resided at remote, up-country stations, or were not known to the people at the presidency. On learning these particulars, the captain of the ship in which the lady had taken her passage found himself in a strange puzzle. All his other passengers had landed, and were safe and snug in the bosoms of their respective families, while the disconsolate young woman alluded to remained alone in the empty cabin. The captain could hardly land her like a bale of goods on the beach, neither could he keep her on board; while the poor girl herself, totally ignorant of the ways of the East, could give no opinion as to what ought to be done. The captain, therefore, as in other cases of difficulty, held a consultation with his chief officer, a rough-spun business-like person, who at once said:

"Go to the governor, sir; he's as good-hearted an old gentleman as ever stepped, and it is his proper business to give directions in such a case. At all events, if you report it regularly to his excellency, the affair cannot rest, and it will be off your shoulders."

"Man the boat! man the boat!" exclaimed the delighted skipper; then turning to the "maiden all forlorn", and assuring her that everything would soon be settled to her satisfaction, he hurried on shore.

The governor, Sir Evan Nepean,[1] though he had been many years secretary of the Admiralty [a tolerably puzzling berth, I guess!], was yet rather taken aback by the captain's communication.

"I'll see about it," he said, though not knowing for the life of him what on earth to do with the lady, who, being young, pretty, and accomplished, might have felt herself rather awkward in the government-house—for Lady Nepean had remained in England. The captain made his escape as soon as he heard the governor adopt the responsibility, by declaring he would think of it.

"You'll see," said the mate to the captain, "that it will all go right by and by; this is not a country in which young ladies, so good and so bonny as our poor passenger, are likely to be left long adrift."

He was right in his conjecture; for the governor, having pondered a little on the matter, sent for a gentleman, not of the East India Company's service, but a resident merchant, at the head of a great house of agency in Bombay, one of the most benevolent of mortal men, and certainly one of the kindest and most generally useful in that country of kind offices and long purses.

"Mr. Money," said Sir Evan to the man of rupees, "will you oblige me by taking a young lady to live with your family till she can hear from, or be heard of by some of her friends, as those to whom she has come out are either dead or not forthcoming."

"I shall be delighted to be of use to any friend of yours, Sir Evan," was, of course, the ready and sincere reply; and in less than half an hour the mate and the captain of the ship were congratulating each other on having got a clear ship at last!

[1] [Governor of Bombay (1812-19). He came out with Hall as a passenger in the *Volage*. *Vide supra*, p. 17.]

What might have been this very interesting young person's fate had she, on her first arrival, found all things as she expected, I cannot pretend to say. Fortune regulates these matters in such queer ways, that our calculations are often sadly put out; but nothing could have been more agreeable than the issue of this apparently untoward adventure. Our engineer of the cave was a friend of the wealthy citizen with whom the governor had deposited the fair lady who had been thrown on his hands by the captain of the ship, and he happened to be asked to dinner there one day. He likewise happened to sit down next the pretty damsel in question; and all this [though, I presume, purely the work of chance] seemed natural enough. The worthy doctor, however, was what is called a "determined bachelor", one of those knowing personages who, for reasons of their own, seem resolved never to marry, and yet who, perchance, may be just on the verge of that awful catastrophe, though little dreaming that the noose which is dangling in festoons on their neck will, by the fall of some unexpected "drop", become in a moment as tight as any rib of steel in the frame-work of their fate. So, at least, it proved with our Elephanta Benedict. In a happy hour he sat down to dinner, but, it is said, did not even look at his neighbour; for he had accidentally caught a glimpse of her figure and drapery, which, though he knew not why, had somewhat shaken his antimatrimonial fortitude, and made his pulse beat five or six throbs faster in the minute than when he first entered the room. Nothing was said by either party; for, by some accident, no regular introduction had taken place between the gentleman and the pretty stranger, and even their names were respectively unknown. At length, the master of the house, recollecting this omission, introduced them to each other, and then called out:

"Doctor, won't you ask your neighbour to take a glass of wine?"

Both names were very remarkable, and might, perhaps, under any circumstances, have engaged notice; but upon this occasion the effect was striking enough; for the lady's father had been a great friend and patron of the doctor some years before, and she had often heard him spoken of at home, as a person in whom the family were much interested. On hearing their names mentioned, therefore, both the lady and the gentleman started—turned quickly round—their eyes met—the little god laughed—and on that day three weeks they were man and wife!

"But this," to use the words of dear old Robinson Crusoe, "is a digression, and I must not crowd this part of my story with an account of lesser things, but return to the main thread." Our party, then, in the Elephanta cave, consisted, besides our chief artist and her spouse, of two or three other ladies and gentlemen, extremely agreeable persons, one of these being a perfect treasure on such an expedition, from the extent and variety of her resources, and the delightful simplicity with which the whole were placed at the disposal of the company. There was one gentleman particularly well versed in Indian, as well as European astronomy, if we may distinguish these things, and our investigations in the cave often rendered his interpretations of much value. We had also with us a very learned person who had come to India as a missionary, but whose zeal in the cause of conversion had gradually evaporated, while in its place there grew up an intense curiosity to investigate the literature and antiquities of the Hindoos. He was just the hand for us, and formed a good pendant to another and still more agreeable companion, who took an equal interest in the modern customs of the natives, chiefly in what related to their religious ceremonies, their costumes, and their domestic amusements. His knowledge of details we found of great use in deciphering and describing the groups of figures sculptured on the face of the rock, in the different compartments of the cave.

Lastly, we enjoyed the society of a gentleman of the civil service, high in office under the East India Company; and the only drawback which we experienced in his case, was the necessity he was under of going across after breakfast to Bombay, where his business kept him till an hour or so before dinner. A shout of joy from old and young always hailed his most welcome return; and as the time approached, many an anxious eye was turned towards the mouth of the cave, happy to be the first to catch a glimpse of his tall figure on the bright sky. As I name no names, and make no allusions but such as will be understood by those only whom they will not offend, I may be allowed to say, in passing, that in beating up the world since, pretty briskly, I have rarely, if ever, met, even separately, persons so estimable in all respects, as many of those who were here collected in the Elephanta cave, expressly to make themselves agreeable to one another. There can be no doubt, in most cases, and little doubt in any case, that time, distance, and totally different duties and occupations in life, estrange man from man, and by gradually diluting friendships into acquaintances, eventually obliterate, or nearly so, all recollection of the closest intimacies. But there are instances, and this Elephanta picnic is one of them, in which, by a strange and pleasing mental process, the recollection is not only kept warm, but is even improved in its temperature by time. At all events, the more I have seen of the rest of the world, the more sensible I have become to the merits of the delightful friendships of that day, and the more truly I have felt attached to them, although the correspondence which has since passed between us hardly deserves the name.

It makes me sigh, indeed, to think how busy death has been with some of the members of that party, whom the survivors could least have spared, and to look round and see how widely all the rest are now scattered over the different quarters of the globe. In the course of my wandering life, indeed, it has happened to me to meet most of them again, and several of them more than once. The extent, indeed, as well as variety of opportunities I have enjoyed of forming valuable acquaintances has been so great, and the loss of friends by death so frequent, that I now find, to whatever direction I turn, or to whatever fragment of my life I apply myself for topics of interest, or however brilliant the scene was at the time, the view is now almost always sobered, or mellowed, I will not call it "sicklied o'er" with the pale cast of thought, consequent upon the remembrance of these losses. So much is this the case, that I should certainly feel some reluctance in thus disturbing the ashes of my early expectations, if there had not happily arisen out of these promises, in most cases, a far more enduring performance than even I, sanguine as I have ever been, had ventured to hope for. I have read much and heard more of the disappointments to which all men are subjected in this matter; but I can only say, for myself, that in this much-abused lottery of human life I never drew a false friend.

Of the Elephanta party, one only of the whole number still hovers round the neighbourhood of the cave; another has been settled for nearly twenty years at Calcutta, and I had the pleasure of beating up his quarters on returning from China some years afterwards; a third took flight, strangely enough, exactly in the opposite direction, and exchanged the luxuries of the glorious and graceful eastern world for the raw materials of the west, and actually "located" himself and his family in North America. I had an opportunity of visiting him, too; but such a contrast! "Every man to his liking," certainly; but how any mortal that has enjoyed the pleasures of an old country, and possesses taste enough to appreciate its innumerable advantages, can permanently reside in a new one, is to me absolutely marvellous! Most of those clever transatlantic writers, who delight us so much by their works of fancy, and who cry up with increasing emphasis the charms of their own country, seem to take exceeding good care, I observe, rarely to verify their theories on this score by any considerable touch of their practice. They affect to scorn the testimony of travellers who report different things of their country, while they themselves [just as we Scotchmen—I must confess—are apt enough to do, in a similar case,] take the best possible means of substantiating the fidelity of such depreciating statements, by seldom returning home again!

The method we adopted for investigating and describing the cave, was to divide the labour in some cases, and in others to combine our exertions, but, in all parts of the task, to make the work as amusing as possible. While our principal artist was engaged at the proper distance in making the beautiful and accurate sketches which have since been engraved for the *Transactions* of the Bombay Society, the chronicler of the cave proceeded, with one or two of the party as his aides-de-camp, to examine the sculptures more narrowly; and having continued his investigation till he was satisfied that nothing had been passed over, he sat down at a little table, carried about for that purpose from place to place, and there, on the very spot, wrote an account of what was before him. When the description was completed, a kind of general council, or "committee of the whole cave," were assembled, to report upon the result. Some of the party, including of course, the ladies, sat round the writer, while others, assisted by ladders, climbed up to the top of the carvings, in order to detect any inaccuracy in the description. Mr. Erskine then commenced reading his own account, while the rest stood by in readiness to check whatever might seem to require correction. On the occurrence of any remark in the description which, to some of us, did not appear to be borne out by the facts, an immediate halt was requested; and the point being diligently re-examined, the writing was either confirmed, or altered till it met the approbation of the whole host of critics. This method of proceeding gave wonderful animation to what, under ordinary circumstances, might have been considered dry details. It also put all the investigating detachments to their mettle; generally furnished abundant matter for discussion; and often set us off upon fresh and amusing courses of inquiry.

It likewise not infrequently happened, that where a piece of sculpture was unfortunately much decayed by time, or injured by the hands of wanton heretics, or chanced to be placed far back in the cave, there arose no small difficulty in coming to any rational conclusion about the matter. Where the cruel hammer of some meddling geological or antiquarian traveller had driven away two or three out of half-a-dozen of a poor Hindoo god's arms, or crushed down his sacred nose, there remained for us little or no resource except that atrabilarious process of soundly anathematising the delinquent or delinquents unknown. But where there existed any remedy within reach, we spared no pains to throw light on the subject. This, in fact, [without any pun], was our chief desideratum; and the scientific heads of the company were put in requisition, to devise methods for illuminating the dark parts of the temple. The first and most obvious plan was to stick a number of little bits of wax taper all over and round those portions of the sculptures which were under immediate investigation. But this was found to be troublesome, in more respects than one. The wax melted and ran down, and the corner of the cave in which we were working either became too choky by the smoke and heat, or the lights burned down and required to be shifted. This plan, therefore, was only resorted to when the other methods I am about to describe failed in effecting the purpose.

The sun at no time of the day shone full into the cave, which faces due north, but we found that by borrowing the looking-glasses from the ladies' tent we could catch his rays, and send them to the very back of the excavation, and thence, by means of other mirrors, could polarise our light in such a way as even to make it turn corners, and fall on spots where, probably, never sunlight rested before. The ecstasy of the natives on beholding the success of this manœuvre was so great, that some of them expressed themselves highly flattered by the honours paid to their long-degraded deities. On hearing this stated by the Hindoos, one of the wits of our party remarked, that if these said gods, Messrs. Vishnu, Shiva, and Brahma, should get their heads above water again, they could, of course, do no less than remember that we noticed them in their adversity; a stale Joe Miller, indeed, as everyone must remember who has kissed the bronze toe of St. Peter in the Vatican —erst old Jupiter of the Capitol; but it made the natives laugh heartily when it was interpreted to them.

Another device of the same kind assisted our researches not a little, and was of still greater service to us in dissipating nearly all the gloom of the cave, thus helping to keep up that air of cheerfulness which is of such vast importance to the success of every undertaking in this world, great or small. The tea-urn having been capsized on the breakfast-table one morning, the servants naturally spread the tablecloth in the sun on the shrubs before the cave. The immediate effect of this mass of white was to lighten up everything within; and the hint once given, we lost no time in expanding it, by hoisting half a dozen other cloths, at the proper angles, till a bright yet soft glow of light was thrown upon the principal figure of all, at the top of the great division of the cave. As soon as this effect was perceived, all other work was suspended, and everyone flocked round the commander of the party while he drew forth his scroll, and, without any flourish of trumpets, proceeded nearly as follows:

"The figure that faces the principal entrance is the most remarkable in this excavation, and has given rise to numberless conjectures and theories. It is a gigantic bust, representing some three-headed being, or three heads of some being to whom the temple may be supposed to be dedicated. Dr. William Hunter, in the *Archæologia*, Vol. VII. p. 292, describes this bust as having four heads, one being hid behind. It is to be observed, however, that no traces of the fourth head appear, it being left entirely to the imagination to supply it, as well as the fifth on the top, if the bust be Shiva's. Some writers have imagined that it is what they have called the Hindu Trinity of Bramha, Vishnu, and Shiva, and very strange historical conclusions have been drawn from this hypothesis. The Hindu Trimurti, or Trinity, as it has been called, does not occupy a very remarkable place in the theology of the Brahmins. The word Trimurti means *three-forms*.

"The three-headed figure at Elephanta represents the deity only down to the breast, or a third-length. One head faces the spectator, another looks to the right, and a third to the left; the fourth may be imagined to be concealed behind. It will give some idea of its bulk to mention, that from the top of the cap of the middle figure to the bottom of the image is seventeen feet ten inches, while the horizontal curved line, embracing the three heads at the height of the eyes and touching the eyes, is twenty-two feet nine inches. All these figures, it may be mentioned, are carved out of the solid rock, which is a coarse-grained dark-grey basaltic formation, called by the geologists trachyte."

When the describer had written so far, he paused, and asked our opinion; upon which there was a general demand upon him to insert something by which his future readers might be informed who, as well as what, this extraordinary figure was?—which of the various Hindoo gods it was intended to represent? Thus prompted, he went on again.

"All the Hindu deities have particular symbols by which they may be distinguished; much as the family of an European may be discovered by its armorial bearings. Unfortunately, many of the figures of Elephanta are too much mutilated to allow us to resort with certainty to this criterion for distinguishing them; and this is particularly the case with the principal figure. The face which looks to the east, or right hand [the spectator's left], is evidently Shiva or Mahadeo, whose principal face, by the rules laid down for fixing images in Hindu temples, must always face the east, while Yoni generally turns to the north. In his hand he holds the cobra di capella, which twists itself round his arm, and rears its head so as to look him in the face. His countenance seems to bear the marks of habitual passion."

While our accomplished antiquary was writing, the rest of the picnickers were scrambling about the heads, like schoolboys on a haystack, till once more called upon to listen. The above lines [now quoted, as I may mention once for all, from the *Transactions of the Bombay Literary Society*,] were read, and agreed to, except some remarks towards the end. One of the company, whose name will appear by and by, and who was perched on the top of a ladder resting on the tip of Shiva's handsome Roman nose, called out that these last words were a scandalous libel on the worthy god, whose expression was eminently placid, evincing anything but habitual passion.

"Well," said the narrator, "what do you make of that

swelling between the eye-brows? Surely that indicates the corrugator muscle in action, or, in other words, shews that your friend Mr. Shiva is in a rage?"

"I admit no such thing," said the objector, who from his garb appeared to be nautical, "I see no wrinkling of the brow: after a long examination, I cannot help thinking that the protuberance on this brow is intended for the third eye of the god: it is entirely raised above the general surface of the brow without any indenture, such as that which occurs on the wrinkled forehead of Passion. The whole skin of this figure's brow is smooth, except this oval protuberance, which nowise resembles that of Bhyrava, as you called the figure we were examining yesterday in the north-east compartment north of the Lingam, where the brow is marked by deep furrows highly expressive of passion."

Upon this objection being started, the whole expedition assembled as near the disputed point as possible; a temporary scaffold was rigged up for the ladies on a level with Shiva's eyes; and no Lilliputians ever investigated the countenance of honest Gulliver with more interest than we did that of the no less wonderful Trimurti. A couple of additional mirrors were put in requisition to fling a strong light into the cave, and a fresh supply of candles ordered up from the tents. The more the parties examined the matter, the less they were agreed; and the controversy began at last to assume that positive and rather warmish character which so often belongs to inquiries in which the data are few and obscure. It is then we find the imaginative or guessing process most vivid, exactly in proportion as the reasoning or matter-of-fact process becomes dull. The interest also, which people take in any such discussion is generally inversely as its importance; and the hope of agreement becomes less and less as the inquiry proceeds. In all probability such might have been the result of this battle in the cave touching poor

Shiva's third eye, had not one of our periodical absentees arrived just at that moment. He wiped his spectacles, held a candle to the image, and declared that, until the dirt was washed away, we might go on disputing till doomsday without getting nearer the mark.

Before those eager combatants, "the eyes" and the "no eyes", had recovered from the oily pause cast upon the troubled waves of the controversy by this dictum, our head-servant came forward to announce the ever-welcome fact that dinner was on the table! The communication was received with a cheer that made the bats fly out of their holes in dismay.

It is, perhaps, needless to observe, that on each succeeding day the wine appeared to become more racy, the water cooler, the coffee more fragrant, the tea more refreshing, and, above all, the conversation more animated, gossipy, and instructive. I ought to have mentioned before, that although, unfortunately, there were no singers of the party, one gentleman played beautifully on the violoncello; the effect of which, in the solemn stillness of the cave, was singularly pleasing. We had also a great store of books; and happening to have some good readers [a rare catch], our evenings slipped away so merrily amongst the olden gods and goddesses of the eastern world, that we often sighed to think how soon we must return to the ordinary business of modern life.

I lay awake half the night of the controversy about Shiva's eye, thinking how we could best settle this great question; and at last bethought me of a scheme, which with the earliest dawn I put in practice. When my coxswain came in the morning for orders, I sent him back to the *Theban*, a frigate of which I had then the acting command, and bade him return as speedily as possible with the ship's fire-engine. Accordingly, before breakfast was well over, we had the hose led along and the pump in full action. The deluge which was now poured over the celebrated Trimurti, must have enchanted the thirsty shades of the "water-loving Mahadeo." The Hindoos, assembled to see what was going on, were astonished and delighted, and so, in fact, were we, to discover how clear, sharp, and beautiful the sculptures stood out, after being played upon for a couple of hours, and well scrubbed with hard brushes in every corner. This service certainly had not been performed upon them for three centuries at the least, and possibly not for a thousand years.

At the next sitting of our grand committee on Shiva's well-washed countenance, the following notes were made by Mr. Erskine. "The face looking east has a fine Roman nose, and its brow is swollen, and protruded between the eyes. This was at first regarded as only the swelling protuberance between and above the eyelids, which is remarked by physiognomists to be indicative of passion; but having been led to more careful examination of it by Captain Basil Hall, to whose unwearied curiosity the present account owes much of the accuracy that it may possess; and, from comparing it with similar protuberances on the brow of other figures in the cave, I have little doubt that it represents the third eye of Shiva, from which flame is supposed to issue, and fire by which the world is finally to be destroyed. As Shiva had five heads, though he had only one such eye, it is represented on his principal head alone, which, of course, is that looking eastward." [As the centre head faces the north, this observation refers to that which is turned to the right hand, or is looking towards the spectator's left.] "He has mustachios," adds the writer, "on his upper lip; and he and one other figure in the eastern wing are the only figures in the cave that have them. At the corner of each of his lips a tusk projects over the under lip. The lower lip of all the figures at Elephanta seems thickish, and more African than Asiatic. His tongue is thrust out between his lips; his eyebrows are not regularly arched, rather irregularly twisted, and depressed on each side towards the nose, as in those of a person habitually passionate."

So far the historian; but it would seem, from the printed account in the Bombay *Transactions*, that the party were not yet unanimous; for in a note, or protest which I gave to Mr. Erskine for publication along with his account, the following words occur:

"This head seems to be speaking to the snake; and I would rather say that the tongue is protruded in doing so, than that it is indicative of anger: nor can I quite agree to the account of the eyebrows. They are certainly not arched; but the deviation is not much, nor does it convey to me any idea of agitation, but rather of mirth, as if he were singing to the snake, and gratified to see its pleasure. The dimples at the corner of the mouth, too, strike me as resembling the approach to a smile much more than the distortion of habitual passion; and the corners of the mouth are, if anything, turned upwards. The mustachios, also, lend their aid in giving a fiercer look to Shiva than I can allow is intended by the sculptor."

Thus it will be perceived that travellers, as well as doctors, can differ, even when the subject of examination is under their eye. In what follows relating to this beautiful head we were all quite agreed; and I add these few lines, more to complete the account, than from any particular interest they contain. Indeed, I question much if it be possible without numerous drawings to engage the attention agreeably or usefully towards any class of Hindoo antiquities. There are, indeed, some other specimens of ancient Indian sculpture which may form an exception, particularly an immense statue of solid granite, upwards of sixty feet high, in the centre of southern India, which I visited on crossing the peninsula.

Mr. Erskine concluded his account of the eastern head of the Trimurti in Elephanta, in these words:

"His cap is richly adorned with variegated figures, branches, and flowers; among others may be distinguished a skull, or death's head; a serpent, with various folds and branches of the bilva-tree, the leaves of which issue three from a point, like the trefoil; and nirgûndi, a sort of shrub, which are symbols that belong peculiarly to Shiva; a few curls run along below his cap. Behind his cap the stone is excavated into two narrow parallel slips, [not seen in the drawing], the one higher than the other, in which two persons might lie stretched at length, without being observed from below; but there are no steps up to them."

The description given in the Bombay *Transactions* of the two other heads is equally minute, graphic, and strictly accurate; and nobody should visit the cave without that account to guide them. At this distance from the spot, however, those details, so peculiarly interesting when present, are apt to become tiresome.

This magnificent triad lies in a recess cut in the rock to the depth of thirteen feet, including the thickness of the doorway screen, or wall, which is about two feet and a half. The basement is raised about two feet nine inches from the ground. In the corners of the threshold are two holes, as if doorposts had been inserted in them; and in the floor is a groove, as if for receiving a screen, which may have been occasionally let down to conceal the group. The vignette at the beginning of this volume, carefully copied from Mrs. Ashburner's drawing, gives a good idea of this singular work of art.

The occurrence of a triple head of such magnitude, and of such skill and beauty in the workmanship, in a spot so much within the range of observation, has naturally led travellers into various speculations as to its origin and the object of its sculptors. On this subject, the following remarks of Mr. Erskine are possessed of considerable interest, not only with reference to this particular section of the Elephanta cave, but as they relate to a curious branch of the fantastic mythology of the Hindoos.

"Such, then, is the remarkable figure that occupies the most conspicuous place in the temple, and which of late has generally been regarded as the Hindoo Trinity: but it appears that, if our opinions be guided by a general examination of this figure compared with the others in the excavation, and with the apparent design of the cave, little doubt will be left that the whole excavation is a temple dedicated to Shiva alone, who is also singly represented by the three-headed bust. The impression made on Christians, however, by the view of this triple figure, has had more influence than any regard to genuine Hindu doctrines, or to the legends in the sacred books of the Brahmins, in fixing the opinions most prevalent on the subject of this mysterious bust. To account for the appearance of a many-headed monster in a mythology like that of the Hindus, which swarms with gods of every description, it does not seem necessary to resort to the doctrine of the Trinity, which cannot be correctly said to have a place in the theology of the Hindoos."[1]

[1] Bombay *Transactions* vol. i.

CHAPTER IV

Excursion to Candelay Lake in Ceylon[1]

The fervid activy of our excellent Admiral, Sir Samuel Hood, in whose flag-ship I served as lieutenant, from 1812 to 1815, on the Indian station, furnished abundant materials for journal-writing, had we only known how to profit by them. There was ever observable a boyish hilarity about this great officer, which made it equally delightful to serve officially under him, and to enjoy his friendly companionship; in either case, we always felt certain of making the most of our opportunities.

Scarcely, therefore, had we returned from the alligator hunt, near Trincomalee,[2] which I have already described, when Sir Samuel applied himself to the collector of the district, who was chief civilian of the place, and begged to know what he would recommend us to see next.

"Do you care about antiquities?" said the collector.

"Of course," replied the Admiral, "provided they be genuine and worth seeing. What have you got to show us in that way? I thought this part of the country had been a wild jungle from all time, and that the English were only now bringing it into cultivation."

[1] [Kantalai is on the mainroad from Trincomalee to Kandy, twelve miles from the former place. It is celebrated for its beautiful tank, which was constructed by the old Sinbalese Kings of Ceylon.]

[2] [This once famous naval station, the former headquarter of the East India Squadron, lies on the North-East coast of Ceylon and has one of the finest harbours in the world. It was taken by the Portuguese in 1622. It was successively captured and recaptured by the Dutch, French, and lastly the English, in 1795, after a siege of three weeks by the fleet.]

"On the contrary," observed our intelligent friend, "there are manifest traces, not very far off, of a dense and wealthy population. At all events, the inhabitants appear to have understood some of the arts of life, for they formed a huge tank or pond for the purpose of irrigation; so large, indeed, that there still exists, in one corner of it, a sheet of water extensive enough to deserve the name of a lake."

"Let us go and see it," exclaimed the Admiral. "Can we ride? Order the horses; who minds the heat of the sun?" for, like almost all newcomers, Sir Samuel cared nothing for exposure, and laughed at the precautions of more experienced residents. It was this habitual indifference which, I believe, two years after the period I am now speaking of, cost him his life. When travelling in the interior of India, near Seringapatam, he reached a station at which a fresh set of palankeen-bearers were to have met him, but where, owing to some accident, they had not been posted. "It matters not," cried the energetic chief, "let us walk." And sure enough he set off, to perform on foot a stage which even on horseback it might have been dangerous to undertake; for the sun had risen nearly to the meridian, and there was hardly a breath of wind. Possibly no mischief might have ensued from this fatal march, had not the Admiral been previously residing for some days in Tippoo Sultan's palace on the island of Seringapatam, the most unhealthy spot in Mysore; and it appears to be a curious circumstance connected with the malaria of that noxious district, that its effects frequently lie dormant till some time after the traveller has quitted the region in which he breathed it. Sir Samuel Hood did not escape; but he felt no inconvenience till after he descended the Ghauts and entered the Carnatic. At Madras, the jungle fever, of which the fatal seeds had been sown at Seringapatam, and quickened into growth by subsequent exposure, attacked our noble friend, and in a few days carried him off.

The collector of Trincomalee soon satisfied the Admiral that an expedition to Candelay Lake, as the ancient tank of the natives was called, could not be undertaken quite so speedily. Boats and horses indeed were all ready, and tents could easily be procured; but it was likewise necessary to prepare provisions, to pack up clothes, and to send forward a set of native pioneers to clear the way through brushwood otherwise impenetrable. The Admiral was in such ecstasies at the prospect of an adventure which was to cost some trouble, that he allowed nobody rest till everything had been put in train. Early in the morning of the next day but one, we accordingly set out in several of the flag-ship's boats, accompanied by a mosquito fleet of native canoes to pilot and assist us. Lady Hood, whom no difficulties could daunt, accompanied Sir Samuel; the captain of his ship, and his flag-lieutenant, with the collector as pilot, and one or two others, made up the party; and our excursion, though nearly destitute of adventures vulgarly so called, proved one of the most interesting possible.

The early part of our course lay over the smooth and beautiful harbour of Trincomalee, after which we passed through a series of coves, forming what is called the lake of Tamblegam,[1] a connecting bay or arm of the sea, though far out of sight of the main ocean We soon lost ourselves amid innumerable little islands clad thickly in the richest mantles of tropical foliage down to the water's edge, and at many places even into the water; so that, as not a stone or the least bit of ground could be seen, these fairy islets appeared actually to float on the surface. This kind of scenery was not

[1] [The actual name of the lake is Tampalakamam. It is famous for the "window-pane oyster" *placuna placenta*, so named from the use formerly made of its flat, translucent shells.]

altogether new to many of our party, who had been in the West Indies and at Bermuda; but it belonged to that class which the eye of a traveller never becomes tired of. The scene which followed, however, proved new enough to us all. We had to row our boats through a dense aquatic forest of mangroves for nearly a mile, along a narrow lane cut through the wood expressly for us the day before by the natives. These fantastical trees, which grow actually in the water, often recall to the imagination those villages one sees in countries liable to frequent inundation, where each house is perched on the top of piles. We saw with astonishment clusters of oysters and other shell-fish clinging to the trunks and branches, as well as to the roots of these trees, which proves that the early voyagers were not such inventors of facts as folks suppose them, nor far wrong in reporting that they had seen fish growing, like fruit, on trees!

Shortly before entering this watery wilderness, we encountered a party of native pearl-divers; and the Admiral, who was at all times most provokingly sceptical as to reported wonderful exploits, pulled out his watch, and insisted on timing the best diver amongst them, to see how long he could remain under water. In no case did the poor fellow make out a minute complete; upon which, the admiral held up his watch exultingly in his triumph, and laughing to scorn the assurances that at other parts of the island divers might be found who could remain five minutes at the bottom. "Show me them! show me them!" cried he, "and then, but not till then—begging your pardon—I shall believe it."

This challenge, I am sorry to say, was never answered. The method used by these divers is to place between their feet a basket loaded with one or two large lumps of coral, the weight of which carries them rapidly to the bottom. The oysters being then substituted for the stones, the diver disengages his feet, and shoots up to the surface again, either bringing the full basket with him, or leaving it to be drawn up by a line.

Nothing could be imagined more wild and Arabian-Night-like than the mangrove avenue through which we rowed, or rather paddled, for the strait was so narrow that there was no room for the oars when pushed out to their full length. The sailors, therefore, were often obliged to catch hold of the branches and roots of the trees, to draw the boats along. The foliage as may be supposed, where perennial heat and moisture occur in abundance, spread overhead in such extraordinary luxuriance, that few of the sun's rays could penetrate the massy network of leaves and branches forming the roof of our fairy passage. Not a single bird could be seen, either seated or on the wing; nor was even a chirp distinguishable above the dreamy hum of millions of mosquitoes floating about in a calm so profound, that it seemed as if the surface of the water had never been disturbed since the creation. The air, though cool, felt so heavy and choky, that by the time we had scrambled to the end of this strange tunnel or watery lane, we could scarcely breathe, and were rejoiced to enter the open air again,—although, when we came out, the sun "flamed in the forehead of the morning sky," and beat fiercely and hotly upon the parched ground, from which every blade of grass had been scorched away.

The village of Tamblegam, to which we soon came, is inhabited by a colony of Hindoo emigrants from the coast of Malabar. It is a neat little place, of which the huts, formed chiefly of branches of the tamarind tree and leaves of the plantain, standing under prodigiously high cocoanuts, are so very diminutive, that the whole looks more like a child's toy-box village than the residence of grown people. The principal edifice, which we failed not to visit forthwith, is a pagoda[1] built of stone, exactly ten feet square. Not fancying there could be any harm in taking such a liberty, we entered the pagoda unceremoniously, and one of our artists set to work sketching the bronze image which the natives worship as a deity. This strange figure is in pretty good keeping with the rest of the establishment, being not quite three inches in height. But the Hindoos were shocked at our impiety, and soon ousted the Admiral and his party, who then turned towards a little tank or pool of water, beautifully spangled over with the leaves and flowers of the water-lily, or lotus, so celebrated in Persian poetry. In the midst of these, several elegant groups of Indian girls had assembled themselves, and appeared to be enjoying the coolness of the water in a style which we envied not a little.

The eastern fashion of bathing differs much from ours. Instead of plunging in and swimming about, one person sits down, while others pour pitchers of water over the head. We took notice also of one particularly interesting party of young and most beautifully formed damsels, who waded in till the water reached nearly to their breasts. Each of these girls held in her hands a chatty or water-pot, shaped somewhat like an Etruscan vase, the top of which barely showed itself above the level of the pool. Upon a signal being given by one of the party, all the girls ducked out of sight, and at the same time raised their water-jars high in the air. In the next instant, just as their heads began to re-appear above the surface, the vessels were simultaneously inclined so that the water might pour out gradually, and in such measure that by the time the bathers again stood erect, the inverted jars might be quite empty. Nothing could be more graceful than the whole proceedings; and we sat in the shade of the pagoda looking at these nymphs for half

[1] [See p. 24, note 1, and p. 183, note 2.]

an hour in great admiration, and thinking what a fine subject such beautiful figures would have formed for sculpture.

In the meantime, a slender pole, forty feet in height, had been erected by a set of native tumblers, who presently exhibited before us various feats of extraordinary agility and strength—some of these are almost too curious to be believed by those who are not aware of the flexibility and dexterity of the Hindoos. We were most surprised and amused by the exploits of a lady of forty, which is considered a very old age in that climate, who ran up the pole more like a monkey than a human being, and then sticking herself on the top horizontally like a weathercock, whirled herself round to the great astonishment of the European beholders. What tickled us particularly on this occasion was the good lady accompanying her strange movements with a noise so exactly like that of our old and respected friend Punch, when drubbed by his faithful wife Judy, that we all burst out a-laughing. Our shout occasioned a momentary embarrassment to the tumbler, who little guessed, poor old soul, how far off the point of the joke lay. Every traveller, I am sure, must have remarked that it is these chance touches of home interest which most strongly excite his feelings when wandering in distant countries, and where he least expects to have his national sympathies awakened.

As the sun had by this time fallen past that particular angle in the sky above which it is considered by the bearers inexpedient to travel, we nestled ourselves into our respective palankeens, and proceeded on the journey through what seemed to us a very respectable forest, growing on lands which had once been under the plough, but apparently very long ago. To our inexperienced eyes and European associations, it seemed as if a century at least must have elapsed from the time such a matting of wood first supplanted the labours of the husbandman; but our friend the collector, soon explained to us, that if any spot of ground in that rich district were neglected for a very few years, natural trees, as tall as those we now admired so much, would soon shoot up spontaneously and occupy all the soil. We shook our heads at this with the confident scepticism of ignorance, and exchanged glances amongst ourselves at the expense of our official companion; but, in the course of an hour we were compelled, by the evidence of our own senses, to alter our note of disbelief. On coming to the real untouched virgin forest of the climate, we beheld a most noble spectacle indeed, in the way of scenery, such as I at least had never seen before, and I have but rarely met with since. I do not recollect the names of the principal trees, though they were mentioned to us over and over again, nor does it matter much, for these would not help the description. The grand banyan, however, with which European eyes have become so correctly familiar through the pencil of Daniell,[1] [which is quite matchless in the representation of the scenery, people, and animals of India] rose on every side, and made us feel, even more decidedly than the cocoanut trees had done in the morning, that we were indeed in another world. I may remark, that the cocoanut, as far as I know, flourishes only near the shore. It seems, indeed, to delight in holding out its slender and feathery arms to embrace the sea-breeze as it passes. All my associations, at least, connected with the appearance of this graceful tree, are mingled up with the cheerful sound of the surf breaking along interminable lines of snow-

[1] [There were three members of the Daniell family, Thomas (1749-1840), and his two nephews, William (1769-1837) and Samuel (1775-1811), who were famous for their landscapes of India, Ceylon and Egypt. Thomas Daniell's most famous work is *Oriental Scenery*, in six volumes, completed in 1808. William is best known for his panoramas, the earliest being one of Madras, painted in 1832. Samuel published a volume of *The Scenery, Animals and Natives of Ceylon* in 1806.]

white beaches, formed of coral sand and pebbles, torn by the waves from the ledges almost everywhere fringing the coasts of the ever-delicious islands of the east.

Shortly after we had left the Indian village, the night fell, and, while we were threading the gigantic forest by the light of torches, the only thing at all like an adventure promised to occur to us; but it ended in nothing. The party consisted of six palankeens, each attended by eight bearers, though only four at a time, or at most six, supported the poles; these trotted along by the side of the bearers, between two and three dozen coolies or porters carrying provisions and torches.

With a mixture of vague alarm and curiosity we now listened to the accounts of wild elephants in these woods, though in the morning we had heard the same stories with indifference and incredulity; while the old hands of the party, who had felt rather piqued at our distrust of their narrations pointed out with malicious satisfaction the recent foot-marks of these undisputed and formidable lords of the manor.

Sir Samuel and Lady Hood, with some of their staff, had left their palankeens and walked forward on the path, which barely admitted two people abreast, in order to enjoy the exceeding beauty of the Indian jungle, lighted up with the blaze of our torches. Suddenly the headmost musalgee[1] or torch-bearer paused, listened, and then retreated precipitately upon the hinder ranks. Nothing was said by them, and nothing could we hear in the woods to explain the cause of this panic, which, however, soon became general amongst the natives. The bearers set down the palankeens, and in an instant they, as well as all the coolies, took to their heels, while the torches flitted about in the forest in a style which, had there been no apprehension, might have been acknowledged as very picturesque. Sir Samuel not only stood fast himself,

[1] [Masalchi, a link-boy.]

but ordered all of us to do so likewise—remarking, that until we knew what to fly from, we might only be making matters worse by moving. Presently the loud crashing of the underwood of the forest, and a heavy thumping on the ground, gave abundant evidence that a wild elephant was close to us.

Some of the natives told us afterwards, that they had seen the monster, but although we peered into the forest with all our eyes, none of us could honestly take upon us to say we actually saw him—though assuredly we heard his footsteps as he broke his way through the jungle. Robinson Crusoe and his wolves in Tartary came to our recollection; and upon our asking the natives what effect fires really had on wild beasts, they all assured us that hardly an animal, however ferocious, would come up to a light, and that we were safe so long as we kept near a torch. This might be consolatory reasoning for the musalgees, each of whom carried a light, but it afforded little security to us, who, it was evident, would again be left in the dark should an elephant cross our path a second time. The Admiral therefore, and by his desire all of us, made an attempt to carry the torches ourselves. But we were soon so plaguily smoked and scorched for our pains, that we rested contented with the risk, and the bearers having gradually crept back to the palankeens, we once more moved on. In spite of all that had passed, some of the party remained so doggedly sceptical, from being habitually distrustful of all things wonderful, that they declared the whole affair a mere matter of panic, and dared to swear there could not be found an elephant within fifty miles of us. Scarcely had this opinion, so injurious to the honours and glories of our late adventure, been uttered, when the commander-in-chief, who, as usual, was leading the way, snatched a light from one of the men's hands, and waved it over what the geologists call a "recent deposit", half the size of a wheel-barrow, and out-rivalling in its column of smoke the muggiest torch in the line.

"There!" exclaimed the Admiral, better pleased than if he had found a pile of rupees, instead of Album Græcum. "Will that evidence satisfy you? How many hundred yards off do you think can the fellow be who left this trace of his proximity?"

It was past ten o'clock when we reached our tents, which had been pitched in the morning on the borders of the celebrated lake we came to visit. All the party were well fagged, and so ravenously hungry, that we shouted for joy on seeing supper enter just as we came to the ground. It is the greatest mistake possible to suppose that people, when they are very hungry, are indifferent or insensible to the merits of good cookery. It is true that they will then eat, and even relish things which at other seasons they might not choose to touch; but I have invariably observed, that is it when the appetite is keenest that the perception of choice viands becomes the most acute—exactly as a really good bed is most enjoyed when we are most fatigued.

"This," said our excellent caterer the collector, "is the dish upon which we pride ourselves most at Trincomalee. It is the true Malay curry—rich, as you perceive, in flavour, and more than half of it gravy—which gravy, I beg of you particularly to take notice, is full of minced vegetables, while the whole is softened with some of the youngest kind of cocoanut, plucked this very evening since the sun went down. The capital 'artiste', as I suppose they would call him in Paris, who dressed this superb mess, served many years as master-cook to the Sultan of Djocjocatra, in the interior of Java. The rogue was captured with a stew-pan in his hand when the brave General Gillespie[1]

[1] [General Gillespie was the hero of the brilliant victory over the French troops outside Batavia (1811), and was killed, three years later, in the Gurkha War.]

stormed the lines round the palace. That rice, which fills the dishes flanking the curry, comes from India—one kind from Patna, the other from Pillibeet."

These praises fell far short of the merits of this glorious supper; nor can I remember anything in the way of gourmandise in any part of the world comparable to this exquisite midnight feast.

While we are on the subject of curry, a word or two on the history of this most delicious of all the varieties of the family of stews may prove acceptable to true lovers of good eating. In the first place, I daresay it will surprise most people—old Indians inclusive—to learn that the dish we call curry[1]—pronounced Kari by the natives—is not of India, nor, indeed, of Asiatic origin at all. It is not known to the Persians, Arabs, Chinese, Burmans, Siamese, or to any of the Indian Islanders. Neither is it known, even to this day, to the inhabitants of Hindustan itself, except to such as are in frequent communication with Europeans. Even the word curry, or kari, is not supposed to be of genuine Indian origin—in short, there is reason to believe that curries were first introduced into India by the Portuguese; and this view is in some degree supported by the consideration that chilies or capsicums, so invariably one of the most important ingredients, are known to be natives not of Asia, but of America.

I have so often watched the palankeen-bearers and other natives preparing their supper, which, after the fashion of the Romans, is their great meal, that I think, upon a pinch, I could make a tolerable curry myself. I would set about it thus:—I would first pound together twelve parts of coriander seed, two of black pepper, one of cayenne, three of cummin, and five of pale turmeric; then add a few cloves, a bit of cinnamon, half a nutmeg,

[1][From the Tamil-*Kari*, sauce. The dish is a very old one: it is mentioned by Athenæus (c. 400 A.D.). Hall is therefore wrong in his conclusions.]

and two or three onions. In India—I mean on the continent of Hundustan—the liquid or gravy which is added to these spiceries, before the fish or meat is put in, consists generally of ghee, which is boiled or clarified butter. This ghee, which is a considerable article of commerce in India, is preferred to butter in making curries, and that which is formed from the milk of the buffalo is considered superior to that made from cow's milk. In the northern provinces of India it is common to add a little milk or cream, and still more frequently a little curdled and acidulated milk, called dhye. The Malays generally make the gravy of their curries of the ground kernel of the fresh cocoanut, instead of using butter or ghee.

As to the kinds of rice which are eaten with curry, they are innumerable. They differ in almost every province of India, in each of which, also, there are upwards of a dozen varieties. What is curious enough, the inhabitants are so attached to the particular kinds of rice produced amongst themselves, that it is with extreme difficulty they can be made to eat any other kind. Thus, at the first establishment of our new settlement of Singapore—at the extreme or southern end of the Malay peninsula—the native troops or sepoys would not touch a grain of the beautiful rice of Java, Siam, and Cochin China, although the Europeans preferred it greatly to that of Bengal. Mr. Crawfurd, the governor of Singapore, from whom I have procured most of these details, had the greatest difficulty in prevailing on the Bengal convicts to eat the fine rice of China—just as if the superintendent of the hulks in the Thames were to find coercive measures necessary to induce the Pats and Sanderses of their gangs to eat the wheaten bread of Kent, instead of the potatoes and oaten cakes of their native land!

The finest rice in Hindustan, in the opinion of many persons is produced in the province of Behar, commonly called, from the capital, Patna rice. This is cultivated in about the latitude of 26° north. But the finest of all is grown considerably further north in the province of Rohilcund, and called, from its principal market, Pillibeet, a town lying between the 28th and 29th degrees of north latitude. And it is a singular fact that these, which are undoubtedly the two best kinds of rice, should be produced in countries and in latitudes where it is only an occasional object of culture. Rice is not the staple corn in any country lying beyond the tropic.

At the door and windows of our supper tent were hung up by the neck sundry well-bedewed goglets of spring water, cheek by jowl with a jolly string of long-necked bottles of Lafitte and Château Margaux, joyously fanning themselves in the thorough draught of the cool night breeze, breathing so gently along, that we could just hear it whispering through the leaves of the damp forest, and sweeping towards the lake past the tents, the curtains of which it scarcely stirred.

The wine perhaps was almost more chilled than a fastidious wine-fancier might have directed; nevertheless, it flowed over our parched palates with an intensity of zest which I do not believe it is in mortals to be conscious of enjoying till they have toiled a whole day in the sun within half-a-dozen degrees of the equator. Bottle after bottle—each one more rich and racy than its valued and lamented predecessor—vanished so fast, that, ere an hour had elapsed, we felt as if a hundred wild elephants would have stood no chance with us!

As we straggled off to our respective beds, made up in the palankeens, according to the custom of the country, we became sensible of a serious annoyance, of which we had taken but little notice while baling in the hot curries and cool clarets within the tent. A most potent and offensive smell was brought to us by the land-wind; and the Admiral, who was not a man to submit to any evil capable of remedy, insisted on an immediate investigation into the cause of this annoyance.

After hunting about in the wind's eye for a short time in the jungle, with torches in our hands, we came upon a huge dead buffalo, swollen almost to double his natural size. Upon seeing this, the bearers and servants shrugged their shoulders, as if the case had been hopeless. Not so the gallant Admiral, who, in his usual style of prompt resource, called out, "Let us bury this monster before we go to bed." And, sure enough, under his directions, and by his assistance, [for, though he had but one hand, he plied it better than most other men's two] we contrived, in a quarter of an hour, to throw sand, earth, and leaves enough over the huge carcase to cover it completely. "There's a cairn for you!" exclaimed the Admiral, throwing down his spade, "and now let us turn in; for by the first peep of the morning we must have a touch at the wild ducks and peacocks on the sides of the lake, and perhaps we may contrive to have a shot at a buffalo, or a stray elephant."

Accordingly, next morning, actually before it was light, I felt the indefatigable Admiral tugging at my ear, and bidding me get up, to accompany him on a shooting excursion, and as he said, "maybe we shall get sight of some of those elephants, the existence of which you presumed to doubt last night. Come, Mr. Officer, shew a leg! I know you are a bit of a philosopher, and curious in natural history; so rouse up and come along with me."

Most cordially did I then anathematise all philosophy and wish I had never expressed any curiosity on the score of wild beasts, peacocks, or ancient tanks; but as the Admiral was not a person to be trifled with, I made a most reluctant move, and exchanged the delightful dream of hot curries and cool sherbet for the raw reality of a shooting match, up to the knees in water, at five in the morning. At one place, such was his excellency's anxiety to secure a good shot at some ducks, that he literally crawled for a couple of hundred yards along the muddy shore of the lake on his knees, and at the end expressing himself fully repaid by getting a single capital shot at a wild peacock! He was also gratified by bringing down a magnificent jungle-cock—a bird which resembles our barn-door fowl in form, but its plumage is vastly more brilliant, and its flight more lofty and sustained, than any of which the bird can boast in its tame state. Our scramble in the mud brought us within sight of a drove of several hundred buffaloes. We saw also several troops of wild deer; but, to our great disappointment, not a single elephant could we catch even a glimpse of. We counted, at one time, several dozens of peacocks—some perched on the trees, some high in the air; we fired at them repeatedly, but, conscientiously, I do not believe any came within shot. Their plumage exceeded that of our tame peacocks less in the brilliancy of the colour than in the wonderful fineness of the gloss—a characteristic of animals of all kinds in their native state. We scarcely saw one small bird during our whole excursion, or heard a single note but the hideous screams of the peacock and parrot—tones which dame Nature, in her evenhanded style of doing things, has probably bestowed upon these dandies of the woods, to counterbalance the magnificence of their apparel.

Perhaps this absence of smaller birds may be accounted for at the time of our visit by the unusually long drought which had occurred, with the consequent failure in the paddy, or rice-crop. While discussing this point, the collector took occasion to point out to us the great importance of such artificial means of irrigating a country as the ancient lake of Candelay, by the side of which we were now encamped, must have furnished to agriculturists of those forgotten days, when its precious waters were not allowed to run to waste, but were husbanded and drawn off by careful means to fertilise the surrounding country.

This stupendous monument of the wealth and industry of some former race, is placed on ground slightly elevated above the districts lying between it and the sea, which, in a direct line, may be distant about twelve or fourteen miles. We could not ascertain exactly what was the precise elevation, but, from the remains of trenches, sluices, and other contrivances for drawing off and distributing the water, it appeared that the fall in the ground must have been sufficient to enable the husbandmen to irrigate the fields at pleasure; though, to our eyes, no inclination could be perceived. The lake itself is now greatly diminished in extent from the dilapidations in its "bund", or retaining embankment, but still it stretches over many square miles of area. On three sides it is confined by the swelling nature of the ground, and it is only on the fourth that any extensive artificial means have been resorted to for confining the water. At this place, across a flat broad valley, there has been thrown a huge embankment, constructed chiefly of oblong stones, many of them as big as a sofa, extending in a zig-zag line for several miles. At some places it rises to the height of thirty or forty feet, and the courses of stone being laid above one another with considerable regularity, this great retaining wall assumes the appearance of a gigantic flight of steps, and being crowned at top by an irregular line of tall trees, it breaks the sky-line beyond the lake in a manner extremely picturesque. Here and there lateral gaps between the hills occur in the other sides, all of which are filled up with similar embankments.

Near one end of the principal wall we could distinctly trace the ruins of a considerable tower, beneath which the great tunnel or outlet used for tapping the lake most probably passed. It is said that some early European settlers, a century or two ago, impressed with an idea that treasure was hid in this building, had torn it down to get at the gold beneath. I remember believing this at the time, and abusing the Dutch accordingly, although nothing like evidence had been adduced to substantiate the charge.

I found afterwards, in travelling over India, and other countries which had changed hands repeatedly, that the poor predecessors of the existing rulers were very convenient persons upon whose shoulders to rest the extra blame of deeds which would not bear the light. It is possible enough, that the early Dutch settlers may have demolished the tower in question, but they could hardly be so silly as to expect to find treasure in the foundation. The true treasure at that spot—and hence, probably, the report and misconception—consisted in the enriching property of the water, judiciously saved and applied to the grounds on a lower level. All this appears so obvious, that one is lost in conjecturing what motives could induce any people to take the trouble to destroy so noble a work.

Nothing appears to be known of the age in which the work in question was raised; and, indeed, the course of vegetation is there so rapid, that, without considerable care and many allowances, no safe inference can be drawn from external appearances. The exposed faces of the stones seemed greatly weathered; but on turning one of them round by means of poles, we could distinguish the marks of a sharp-pointed chisel—a sight which, while it really told nothing of dates, was enough to carry the imagination far back into the depths of time lying beyond tradition, and respecting which we know nothing except what these feeble, but distinct evidences, afford us of the hand of man having actually been there.

On beholding these ancient chisel marks at Candelay in Ceylon, at Pæstum in Italy, or at Stonehenge in England, of whose origin and history all trace is lost, we experience a sensation akin to what we feel on examining the fossil remains of animals in the strata of the earth. There is no need of further evidence than that of our senses to satisfy us that the birds, beasts, and fishes, which we see imbedded in the rocks, must once have been alive and merry; but when, and where and under what circumstances, are questions which baffle the boldest fancy. It may have been a million years ago, or ten hundred millions of years—that is to say, we know nothing precisely about the matter! Such, no doubt, is the case at present. We know well, that the date of these phenomena must lie beyond certain periods, as we know that the fixed stars lie beyond certain distances from the earth. But I am willing to believe, that both in geology and in astronomy the investigating powers of man will eventually penetrate many secrets which are now hid even deeper than these; and that the time may possibly one day come, when the rise, progress, and relative dates and intervals between the remotest and the most recent geological phenomena shall be ascertained with as much precision as the velocity of light, or the complicated motions of the moon. The precise epochs of these occurrences may, indeed, like the actual distance of the fixed stars, very long continue to baffle human investigation; but even these will probably yield at last to the researches of laborious man, and become as simple, and as easy of practical applications, as the law of gravitation, or the perplexing theory of the tides.

CHAPTER V

GRIFFINS IN INDIA—SINBAD'S VALLEY OF DIAMONDS —A MOSQUITO HUNT

ON the evening of the 18th of November, 1812, we sailed, in his majesty's ship *Illustrious*, from the magnificent harbour of Trincomalee. In attempting to get out we were sadly baffled by light shifting winds, which knocked us about from side to side of the entrance, in which, unfortunately, no good anchorage is to be found, owing to the great depth of water and the rocky nature of the ground. This serious evil of a rocky bottom is now almost entirely obviated by the admirable invention of iron cables, when the water is not too deep. The links of the chain merely acquire a polish by their friction against the coral reefs and other sharp ledges, by which the best hempen cables of past times would be cut through in ten minutes.

The chain cable, however, is difficult of management in deep water, that is to say, when the soundings are more than twenty or twenty-five fathoms. Nothing is so easy as getting the anchor to the bottom in such cases; it is the "facilis descensus", with a vengeance! But when the anchor is to be pulled up again, then comes the tug. I once let go my anchor with a chain cable bent to it in forty-five fathoms, without having calculated on the probable effects of the momentum. Though the cable was bitted, all the stoppers snapped like packthread; and the anchor, not content with shooting to the bottom with an accelerated velocity, drew after it more than a hundred fathoms of chain, in such fearful style that we thought the poor ship must have been shaken to pieces. The noise was like that of rattling thunder, and so loud that it was impossible to hear a word; indeed it was even difficult to speak, from the excessive tremor caused by the rapid and violent passage of the links, as the chain leaped, or rather flew, up the hatchway, flashing round the bits, and giving out sparks like a fire-work. Finally, it tore its way out at the hause-hole, till the whole cable had probably piled itself on the anchor in a pyramid of iron at the bottom of the sea. The inner end of the cable had of course been securely shackled round the heel of the mainmast, but the jerk with which it was brought up, made the ship shake from end to end as if she had bumped on a rock, and everyone fully expected to see the links fly in pieces about the deck, like chain-shot fired from a cannon. It cost not many seconds of time for the cable to run out, but it occupied several hours of hard labour to heave it in again. The ordinary power of the capstan, full manned, scarcely stirred it; and at the last, when to the weight of chain hanging from the bows there came to be added that of the anchor, it was necessary to apply purchase upon purchase, in order to drag the ponderous mass once more to the bows.

When we got fairly clear of the harbour of Trincomalee, and caught the monsoon, we dashed along shore briskly enough; and having rounded the south point of Ceylon, well-named or called Dondra Head, or thunder cape, we paid a visit to Point de Galle, celebrated for its bread-fruit and cocoanuts. We then passed on to Columbo, the capital, or seat of government of the island. Ceylon, I may take occasion to mention, is not considered by our countrymen of the East to be in India.[1] We stared with all our eyes when this unexpected information was first given us, and fancied our merry friends were quizzing us. But we soon learned that in the technical language of that

[1] [Ceylon, of course, is under the Colonial Office.]

country, Ceylon does not form a part of India; still less does Sumatra, Java, or any, indeed, of the islands in the great tropical Archipelago; and far less still is China talked of as constituting a part of India. New-comers are, of course, a good deal perplexed by these and sundry other local peculiarities in language and manners, which they at first laugh at as a good joke, then ridicule as affected, and lastly conform to as quite natural and proper, because universally understood amongst those whom it most concerns.

The same thing takes place, I believe, in the technicalities of every profession as much contradistinguished from ordinary life as that of the British in India. I have seen a party of tourists from the inland counties of England prodigiously tickled at Portsmouth, on going afloat to find a rope called a sheet, to see gigs moving about without wheels, and to hear the people on board ship talking of saddles, bridles, bits, and martingales! But to return to the East: I may mention that the term India is confined, amongst the English residents there, to the peninsula of Hindustan, and does not include Ceylon, probably from that island being immediately under the King's government, and not a part of the Company's possessions. The straits of Malacca, Sunda, and so on, together with the China sea, and those magnificent groups of islands, the Philippines and Moluccas, are all included in the sweeping term—"To the eastward."

At almost every part of this immense range I found further local distinctions, of greater or less peculiarity and extent according to circumstances. At one place I was puzzled by hearing the name of a whole country appropriated to a single spot. At Bombay, for example, I remember it was the custom, at a certain season of the year, to talk of going to the Deccan, which word properly includes an immense region consisting of many provinces; whereas those who used this expression meant, and were understood to express only one point in it—a little watering-place.[1] Mere local words, in like manner, come to have a much more expanded signification. The word Ghaut, I believe, means, in strictness, a pass between hills—and hence, some bold etymologists pretend, comes our word gate! The term, however, is now applied to the whole range of mountains which fringe the western coast of India, just as the more gigantic Cordilleras of the Andes guard the shores of the Pacific.

I remember well, that one of the most striking peculiarities to a stranger's ear on landing in India, was the appropriation of all Europe when speaking exclusively of England—as if in England we were to speak of Asia when we meant only Calcutta or Madras. If you ask a man whether that is a "Europe"[2] newspaper which he is reading, he may reply, "No—it is the *Frankfort Journal.*" The word England, or English, is hardly ever used. Were anyone inadvertently to talk of having on a pair of English shoes, in contradistinction we shall suppose, to "country shoes", or those made in India, the mistake in language would at once betray his being a griffin. He ought to say "Europe shoes". The use of the word "employment", I remember also thinking quite strange for a time. In other countries it signifies occupation or actual work; but in India it means exclusively being in office under government. I have seen some very busy fellows, overwhelmed with business from morning till night, but complaining all the while that they had "no employment".

But whether Ceylon be in India or not, all the world

[1] [The reference is, apparently, to the annual migration of the Bombay Government to Poona for the "monsoon", June to October.]

[2] [The use of the adjective "Europe" as the equivalent for "Western", as opposed to "Country", was common a century ago, but is now obsolescent.]

knows that this island is celebrated for precious stones; indeed, there are writers who believe that Mount Ophir of the Scripture is Adam's Peak of Ceylon.[1] Be this, also, as it may, our ever-enterprising and active-minded Admiral, Sir Samuel Hood, determined to bring this reputation to the proof, and, one day at dinner at the governor's table, actually announced his intention of having a hunt for the sapphires, rubies, tourmalines, chrysoberyls, corundums, and so on, for which the island has been long celebrated. His excellency, with the suavity of a courteous host, smiled, and wished the Admiral success. Her excellency, the governor's lady, smiled, too, at this vain fancy of the Admiral's, and exacted a promise of a ring set with the stones which the proposed expedition was to yield. Even the well-bred aides-de-camp and the knowing secretaries exchanged quizzical glances at the Admiral's expense. The company at large scarcely knew, as yet, whether to treat so queer a proposal as a joke or as a serious affair. Sir Samuel, however, was not a man to be quizzed out of his purposes; and he therefore begged to have a party of workmen sent to him next morning to accompany him to a river not far off, along the banks of which, he had somewhere heard it reported, most of the finest stones in Ceylon had been found. He begged also that each of the men might be furnished with a basket, a request which naturally produced a second titter; for it was made in such a tone as led us to fancy the worthy Admiral expected to collect the rubies and garnets in as great profusion as his far-famed predecessor, Sinbad the sailor, found them in the Valley of Diamonds.

His precise plan he kept to himself till he reached

[1] [This is wrong. Ophir has been looked for in many directions, from East Africa to Burma, but it is almost certainly not in Ceylon. Ophir was famous for its gold. The most plausible identification is the ancient Buddhist port of Suppara, near Bombay.]

the river, the alluvial strip of ground bordering which was formed chiefly of fine gravel, mixed with sand, leaves, and mud. He then desired the men to fill their baskets, and to carry the whole mass, just as they picked it up, to one of the ship's boats, which he had directed to meet him at the landing-place. This cargo of dirt and rubbish, on its reaching the ship, was put into a large sack, and carefully stowed away, as the Admiral's poulterer reported, and the whole ship's company believed, for the benefit of the inhabitants of the hen-coops—an idea not unnaturally conceived, for it is precisely with such gravel that fowls, as everyone knows, are supplied at sea, as regularly as with food.

Not a word more was said on the subject at Government-house, nor on board the ship, till a couple of days after we had left Columbo, when the Admiral ordered the bag of gravel into his cabin, along with a great tub of water and half-a-dozen wash-deck buckets. The whole stuff collected on shore was now thoroughly cleaned, and when only the gravel remained, it was divided into a number of small portions, and laid on plates and dishes on the table of the fore-cabin. As soon as all was arranged, the Admiral, who superintended the operation, called out:

"Send for all the young gentlemen in the ship, and let everyone take a plateful of gravel before him, to catch what jewels he can."

Before the party had time to assemble, the delighted Admiral had himself discovered in his own dish three or four small garnets, one ruby, and several small crystals of corundum. By the aid of his young friends, to the astonishment of everyone, a collection was soon made, which afterwards not only furnished the promised ring to the governor's lady, but made half-a-dozen others of equal beauty and perfect purity of materials. These precious stones were certainly not of the largest dimensions; but, for all that, the Admiral, as he was wont in everything he attempted, completely established his point.

It was the fashion at Columbo to dine early, say at half-past three or four, in order to command the whole evening for riding or lounging about in the open air. The grand place of resort in those days was a sort of esplanade looking to the south, and called, if I recollect right, the "Galle Face", from being turned towards Point de Galle. The collection of people in the evenings at this spot afforded pleasing studies for every eye. All ranks and parties, from the governor to the lowest cooly, appeared to be assembled to see the sun go down upon the western waters, at an hour, when the sea breeze having died away, the surface scarcely shewed a ripple. Multitudes of the natives, too, not only of the island, but of many parts of India, and of the eastern archipelago, drove about in their peculiar conveyances, hackeries[1] and bandies, or chose to be carried in palankeens. Later in the night came the governor's parties and balls, where only the Europeans were assembled, and where, contrary to expectation, we generally found the coolest and most airy apartments. Indeed, it is only in cold countries that one meets with over-heated ballrooms. In India, every door and window being thrown open, a thorough draught sweeps through the house; or, if it be calm, an artificial breeze is produced by the waving of a dozen punkahs overhead, and everything is kept fresh and agreeable. Instead, therefore of the ballrooms in that country being choky and unwholesome, as they almost invariably are in cold climates, they are as airy as if they were erected on the open esplanade.

It is a curious fact, that this admirable contrivance of the punkah, which is merely a large fan suspended to the roof, and extending nearly the whole length of the

[1] ["Hackery", perhaps a corruption of the Portuguese *a carreta*, is a bullock-carriage; "bandy" is the Tamil *bandi*, a cart.]

rooms in India, is not only a purely English invention, but is very modern. It was first devised and introduced by the Bengal officers who served with Lord Cornwallis in the war of Mysore against Tippoo in 1791-92. The punkah afterwards became general under the Madras and Bombay presidencies, but not for some time; and it was only in 1811 they were introduced by the English into Java, on the conquest of that island. I believe the natives of India have not, as yet, anywhere adopted the fashion. But indeed the Hindoos are wretchedly behind the Europeans in every article of real luxury, for which all their noisy pomp and tinselly shew is but a poor substitute.[1]

This and many other devices which have been fallen upon by the ingenious, wealthy, and luxurious Europeans, to counteract the heat of the climate, are so successful, that, with a very few exceptions, I have hardly ever felt the temperature of India seriously oppressive. It is true, that some people delight in hot weather, and suffer so much from cold, that they consider it almost a point of honour and conscience not to complain, however high the thermometer rises. I cordially sympathise with these chilly folks, so that my testimony on this matter is not the best. I do own, indeed, that I have very often experienced a most disagreeable allowance of heat when exposed to the sun's rays on duty, either in a boat, or when keeping watch in a calm on the burning quarter-deck of a line-of-battle ship. In spite of the awnings spread fore and aft, the fierce sun of those climates will make his power felt. But as the evil effects of such exposure are very great, every discreet commanding officer will take the utmost pains to avoid employing his officers or people unneces-

[1] [Hall is wrong here. A reference to Yule's Hobson Jobson will shew that punkahs were known to the Arabs in the 8th century, and are mentioned by a large number of early travellers, the earliest, apparently, being Linschoten (1596).]

sarily during the heat of the day, a period when the hardiest are the most apt to suffer, and the most experienced [paradoxical as it may appear] generally among the least fitted to stand the sun with impunity.

It is very strange, that during the first year, and in some cases longer, most new-comers are hardly conscious of any ill effects arising from the influence of the sun's direct rays; and, accordingly, they walk and ride about, go to the marshes for snipe-shooting, bathe in the surf, and commit all sorts of folly, not only without inconvenience, but with much real enjoyment; while the older hands make themselves hoarse with preaching to these griffins[1] that they are guilty of suicide. The ruddy-cheeked griffin, in his turn, laughs and quizzes the yellow-visaged Indian, and having trudged off to the swamps, passes the whole morning up to the knees in water so industriously, after a snipe, that he is brought home at three or four o'clock with a *coup de soleil!* Even if he escapes this sudden fate, he is pretty sure to feel, about a year and a day after his arrival, a severe twinge in his right shoulder, a pain in his side, and all the horrid symptoms of the fatal liver complaint.

"I tell you what it is, young fellows," said a venerable sun-dried officer to some of these gay Johnny Newcomes, "you shoot all day, you walk, and ride about in the sun; you poke along the streets without your palankeens; you play cricket on the esplanade at noon; you swill Hodgson's pale ale, claret, and sangaree,[2] till you drive yourselves into the liver complaint, of which you die; and then, forsooth, we have the trouble of

[1] [*Griffin*, a new-comer; ".Johnny Raw". The word was apparently first used in Madras. It has been traced back as far as Beaumont and Fletcher, and Prof. Skeat thinks it may be a corruption of *Griffith*, "a raw Welshman". Vide p. 180-2.]

[2] [A once-famous Anglo-Indian beverage, a kind of punch made of 'lemon-water and red wine".]

writing home to your friends that the climate did not agree with you!"

The fact is simply this: the climate of India will certainly not agree with those who are utterly careless about it, as too many are, and will give it no fair play; or who, from peculiar temperament, are predisposed to diseases incident to great heat; or, lastly, whose duties are of such a nature, that whether they will or not, they must be much exposed to the sun, without having the power of changing their place of residence frequently. The constant shifting about is, I believe, one of the chief causes of the superior healthiness of seamen in India over fixed residents on shore, though apparently of equal constitutional strength. This idea seems to be confirmed by the fact of most European troops employed in the wars of India being comparatively healthy, however much exposed to the sun, when in active service, and constantly moving from one encampment to another.

But whether on shore or afloat, it seems admitted to be of the greatest importance not to employ soldiers or sailors in the sun more than is absolutely necessary for the public service. It is a most painful thing, therefore, and exceedingly destructive to the health of a ship's crew, who have been for some time in that country, when she falls under the command of an inexperienced officer, just arrived from Europe, and who, from being himself at first almost entirely insensible to the disagreeable effect of the heat, considers the objections which other people make to exposure as mere fancies. Under this impression, he admits of no difference being made in the hours of work, but employs his people aloft, and in the boats, when sailing through the straits of Sunda, or moored in Madras roads, with as much unconcern as if he were navigating the British Channel, or lying snug at Spithead. The officers, and especially the surgeon, remonstrate in vain; poor Jack of course can say nothing; but in a few months, or it may be in a few weeks or days, half the ship's company find themselves in the doctor's list. Many die of dysentery, others sink under the liver complaint, and the slightest cuts often produce locked jaw, while many more, broken down by the climate, are invalided and sent home, having become useless to the service and to themselves for life! A judicious captain, under exactly similar circumstances, will not, perhaps, lose a man, nor need his crew be broken up and his ship rendered unserviceable.

From half-past nine or ten, till two or three o'clock, an officer of experience and consideration, if he can help it, will never allow a seaman's head to appear above the hammock-railing, but will discover some employment for the men on the main and lower decks. If the ship be at anchor, he will lay out a line, and warp the ship broadside to the sea breeze, that the cool air may sweep freely through all parts of the decks, and render everything fresh, sweet, and wholesome. No boats will be sent away from the ship during that fiery interval; or, if any duty absolutely requires exposure, it will be got over with the utmost expedition. In the event of the men getting wet by a shower of rain, it is always right to make them shift their clothes instantly, and to muster them afterwards, to see that their things are dry and clean. These, and a hundred other little precautions, all of which are well-known to old stagers, ought to be industriously sought after by new-comers, and adopted implicitly and at once with scrupulous attention. At all events, the officer who has the means of enforcing these precautions, and yet does not choose to adopt them, has much to answer for if any of his crew die in consequence of needless exposure. He may rely upon it, that the fatal effects of a hot climate on the European constitution, unless very carefully watched, are inevitable. When I have seen regiments reduced to mere skeletons, and ships so weakened in their crews that they could scarcely weigh the anchor, I have often thought of Dr. Johnson's graphic description, in his paper on the Falkland Islands, of those unseen evils of war in uncongenial regions, of which so few people in high latitudes take any account: "By which," says he, "fleets are silently dispeopled, and armies sluggishly melted away!"

Persons living on shore, however, and who possess the means of purchasing the ordinary luxuries of an oriental life, need scarcely ever suffer much inconvenience from the heat. The dress of Europeans, which consists of the lightest and whitest materials, reflects a great part of the heat. The rooms are always large and airy, without carpets, and stuck so full of open doors and windows, that when there comes the slightest breath of wind from the sea, it is sure to be felt; but all these are carefully closed up when the air is hot. The sun is excluded by various contrivances, chiefly by a shady verandah, ten or twelve feet wide, which generally runs quite round the house, so that no direct rays can strike into the apartments. And the painful glare of the lower sky, or, which is nearly as distressing to the eyes, the dazzling reflection from bright objects on the ground, is cut off by painted mats made of split rattan imported from China. These devices, which scarcely intercept the wind, effectually prevent the admission of more light than is absolutely required. In some parts of India, a large open frame-work is placed in a sloping position against the top of the verandah, and resting on the ground on the windward side of the house. This frame being covered over thickly, but loosely, with a layer of a peculiar kind of sweet-scented grass, called, I think, "cuscus,"[1] is kept well drenched

[1] [The *khaskas* is a grass used for making tatties or thermantidotes, a mat which is hung before the open window in hot weather: the wind causes evaporation, which greatly reduces the temperature.]

with water. The process of evaporation caused by the hot and arid wind passing through the wet matting, produces a more considerable degree of cold than any one who has not enjoyed the surpassing luxury of these coolers, or tatties, can form any conception of. I have heard it said, indeed, that the damp, cool air which streams through this wall of grass, though the most delightful thing in the world at the time, is apt to give colds, stiff necks, and the whole family of rheumatic twitches, to those who are in the habit of catching cold readily. But I will believe none of these stories against the exquisite tatties, under the lee of which I have seen people so often sitting, gasping for breath and praying for a breeze; for I need not remark, that during a calm they are useless.

Persons long accustomed to watch those periodical changes in the wind, which occur in hot climates with such wonderful regularity every day, can often tell, by some intuitive consciousness, not capable of communication to inexperienced senses, almost the very moment when the long looked-for sea breeze is coming. I remember, at Madras, sitting one day in the inner room of a friend's house, who had been my schoolfellow a dozen years before—now, alas! nearly twenty years in his grave. He was telling me of his quickness of perception in this matter, as we sat baking and stewing in what is called a garden-house on the far-famed Choultry Plain.[1] My friend's quickness of sight beat that of the pig's, [who, everyone knows, can see the wind] for he declared he could see the calm, and, calling me to the verandah, pointed out this wonderful sight. The whole landscape appeared to have given way, like molten silver, under the heat, and to be moving past more like a troubled stream than the solid ground.

[1] [The open plain or *maidan*, once existing to the S.W. of Madras. It was a residential site, and H.Q. of the Madras Army. *Choultry*, in Tamil, signifies a rest-house or traveller's bungalow.]

The trees and shrubs, seen under a variety of refractions through differently heated strata of air, seemed all in violent motion, though probably not one leaf of the highest cocoa-nut tree, nor a single blade of the lowest grass, stirred in reality. The buildings in the distance looked as if their foundations had been removed, while the shattered and broken walls danced to and fro, as if under the influence of some magical principles of attraction and repulsion; whilst many patches of imaginary water—the celebrated "mirage" of the desert—floating where no water could have existed mocked our sight in this fantastic landscape.

Not a human being was then to be seen. The blue-skinned buffaloes, and the queer-looking Indian bullocks with humps on their shoulders, squeezed themselves under the skirts of the aloe and bamboo hedges. Others, pre-eminently happy, poor beasts! in order to escape the intolerable misery of the mosquitoes, immersed themselves in the muddy tanks or ponds, beneath the surface of which they contrived to hide every part of their bodies except the top of their nostrils, with just as much of their eyes as they could keep clear by the brush of their eyelids. Even our native bearers, who in general seem marvellously indifferent to the sun, had lifted the palankeens into the shade, and with their wrappers over their heads, lay sleeping about the steps of the verandah in the coolest corners they could find. I tried first one chair, then another; then flung myself on a cane-bottomed sofa, seeking for rest, but all in vain. I next stretched myself flat on my back on the polished chunam[1] floor, directly under the punkah, with my white jacket thrown open, neckcloth cast away, and collar unbuttoned. It was still to no purpose! The more moves I made, the worse became the oppression of the heat; and, for once in my life, I had very nearly confessed that it might

[1] [Plaster.]

possibly be rather too hot—when, just in time to save my credit for consistency, my friend clapped his hands and exclaimed, "Here comes the sea breeze! I see it! I feel it! I hear it! Huzza for your life." I, however, could see nothing, nor feel anything; yet it was evident that all the experienced men of the party did. The bearers stationed to cast water on the tatties had already commenced their operations, and a slight touch of the aromatic perfume of the delicious cuscus began to pervade the room. On walking towards the opening between two of the tatties, and looking towards the sea, I could distinctly perceive the intermediate scenery settling into its natural position by the more uniform arrangement of the various strata of air forming the medium through which the objects were viewed.

I believe all the curious phenomena of the mirage are easily explained, upon the supposition, that under certain circumstances, the lower stratum of air may become actually lighter than those which are next above it. The effect of this will be obvious to those who have attended to the subject of atmospherical refraction, the usual effect of which, as everyone knows, is to elevate objects, or make them seem higher than they really are. But the unusual effect, or that caused by the contact of hot ground rendering the lowest portion of the air specifically lighter than the superincumbent layers, is to make high objects seem to the eye lower than they really are. Thus, what we fancy to be water between two ridges of sand highly heated, is nothing more than a portion of the clear sky, the rays from which, in passing through the intermediate atmosphere, having entered the warm and rarefied stratum in contact with the sand, are refracted to the eye in a manner which impresses on the sense of vision an image of the sky; and this so closely resembles the surface of still water, that the deception becomes at times quite complete. The tendency of the colder and heavier air above to mix with that which is hotter and lighter beneath it, is of course very considerable: the consequence is, that near the line of contact of the two media, there occurs an intermixture of air differing in density, and therefore in refractive power. Hence every object viewed through this troubled or heterogeneous part of the atmosphere must inevitably seem broken, distorted, and in motion.

Dr. Wollaston, who was, I conceive, the first to explain all these, and many other attendant phenomena, has also, with his usual ingenuity, suggested several popular experiments to prove the truth of his theory. [See the *Philosophical Transactions* for 1800]. One is, to place some water, or clear syrup, in a square phial, and then add spirits of wine, or any other fluid of a different specific gravity, taking care not to allow them to intermix too suddenly, but to arrange matters so that the adjustment may take place gradually. Objects viewed through the phial, as the intermixture takes place, will undergo inversions and other variations in form and position similar to those of the mirage.

In the sleeping apartments of India, great care is taken to secure coolness. The beds, which are always large and hard, are generally placed as nearly as may be in the very middle of the apartment, in the line of the freest thorough draught which open doors and open windows can command. I speak now, of course, of the beds of men who live in single blessedness. In other cases, a simple contrivance has been devised, which, if it does render the sleeping-room a little less airy than that of the free and solitary bachelor, nevertheless accomplishes a good deal, and secures all the proprieties. The door, which is shut, has its upper half cut away, so that the air enters freely above; and the windows, also, being high, are always left open.

Round each bed is suspended a gauze curtain, without which sleep would be as effectually murdered as ever it was by any tragedy king. For, if even one villainous mosquito contrives to gain admission into your fortress, you may, for that night, bid good-bye, not only to sleep, but to temper, and almost to health. I defy the most resolute, the most serene, or the most robust person that ever lived between the tropics, to pass a whole night in bed, within the curtain of which a single invader has entered, and not to be found, when the morning comes, in a high fever, with every atom of his patience exhausted. Temper, under such circumstances, is really out of the question; the most placid creature on earth, even old Uncle Toby himself, would be driven into a rage!

The process of getting into bed in India is one requiring great dexterity, and not a little scientific engineering. As the curtains are carefully tucked in close under the mattress, all round, you must decide at what part of the bed you choose to make your entry. Having surveyed the ground, and clearly made up your mind on this point, you take in your right hand a kind of brush, or switch, generally made of a horse's tail; or, if you be tolerably expert, a towel may answer the purpose. With your left hand you then seize that part of the skirt of the curtain which is thrust under the bedding at the place you intend to enter, and, by the light of the cocoa-nut oil lamp, [which burns on the floor of every bed-room in Hindustan] you first drive away the mosquitoes from your immediate neighbourhood, by whisking round your horse-tail; and, before proceeding further, you must be sure you have effectually driven the enemy back. If you fail in this matter your repose is effectually dashed for that night; for these confounded animals—it is really difficult to keep from swearing, even at the recollection of the villains, though at the distance of ten thousand miles from them—these well-cursed animals, then, appear to know perfectly well what is going to happen, and assemble with the vigour and bravery of the flank companies appointed to head a storming party, ready in one instant to rush into the breach, careless alike of horse-tails and towels. Let it be supposed, however, that you have successfully beaten back the enemy. You next promptly form an opening, not a hair's breadth larger than your own person, into which you leap, like harlequin through a hoop, or, to borrow Jack's phrase, "as if the devil kicked you on end!" Of course, with all the speed of intense fear, you close up the gap through which you have shot yourself into your sleeping quarters.

If all these arrangements have been well managed, you may amuse yourself for a while by scoffing at, and triumphing over the clouds of baffled mosquitoes outside, who dash themselves against the meshes of the net, in vain attempts to enter your sanctum. If, however, for your sins, any one of their number has succeeded in entering the place along with yourself, he is not such an ass as to betray his presence while you are flushed with victory, wide awake, and armed with the means of his destruction. Far from this, the scoundrel allows you to chuckle over your fancied great doings, and to lie down with all the complacency and fallacious security of your conquest, and under the entire assurance of enjoying a tranquil night's rest. Alas for such presumptuous hopes! Scarcely have you dropped gradually from these visions of the day to the yet more blessed visions of the night, and the last faint effort of your eyelids has been quite overcome by the gentle pressure of sleep, when, in deceitful slumber, you hear something like the sound of trumpets.

Straightway your imagination is kindled, and you fancy yourself in the midst of a fierce fight, and struggling, not against petty insects, but against armed men and thundering cannon! In the excitement of the mortal conflict of your dream, you awake, not displeased mayhap, to find that you are safe and snug in bed. But in the next instant what is your dismay, when you are again saluted by the odious notes of a mosquito close at your ear! The perilous fight of the previous dream, in which your honour had become pledged, and your life at hazard, is all forgotten in the pressing reality of this waking calamity. You resolve to do or die, and not to sleep, or even attempt to sleep, till you have finally overcome the enemy. Just as you have made this manly resolve, and, in order to deceive the foe, have pretended to be fast asleep, the wary mosquito is again heard, circling over you at a distance, but gradually coming nearer and nearer in a spiral descent, and at each turn gaining upon you one inch, till, at length, he almost touches your ear, and, as you suppose, is just about to settle upon it. With a sudden jerk, and full of wrath, you bring up your hand, and give yourself such a box on the ear as would have staggered the best friend you have in the world, and might have crushed twenty thousand mosquitoes, had they been there congregated. Being convinced that you have now done for him, you mutter between your teeth one of those satisfactory little apologies for an oath which indicate gratified revenge, and down you lie again.

In less than ten seconds, however, the very same felon whom you fondly hoped you had executed, is again within hail of you, and you can almost fancy there is scorn in the tone of his abominable hum. You, of course, watch his motions still more intently than before, but only by the ear, for you can never see him. We shall suppose that you fancy he is aiming at your left hand; indeed, as you are almost sure of it, you wait till he has ceased his song, and then you give yourself another smack, which, I need not say, proves quite as fruitless as the first. About this stage of the action you discover, to your horror, that you have been suddenly bit in one ear and in both heels, but when or how you cannot tell. These wounds, of course, put you into a fine rage, partly from the pain, and partly from the insidious manner in which they have been inflicted. Up you spring on your knees—not to pray, heaven knows!—but to fight. You seize your horse's tail with spiteful rage, and after whisking it round and round, and cracking it in every corner of the bed, you feel pretty certain you must at last have demolished your friend.

In this unequal warfare you pass the live-long night, alternately scratching and cuffing yourself—fretting and fuming to no purpose—feverish, angry, sleepy, provoked, and wounded in twenty different places!

At last, just as the long-expected day begins to dawn, you drop off, quite exhausted, into an unsatisfactory, heavy slumber, during which your triumphant enemy banquets upon your carcase at his convenient leisure. As the sun is rising, the barber enters the room to remove your beard before you step into the bath, and you awaken only to discover the bloated and satiated monster clinging to the top of your bed, an easy, but useless, and inglorious prey!

CHAPTER VI

Ceylonese Canoes[1]—Peruvian Balsas—the Floating Windlass of the Coromandel Fishermen

The canoes of Ceylon, as far as I remember, are not described by any writer, nor have I met with any professional men who are aware of their peculiar construction, and of the advantages of the extremely elegant principle upon which they are contrived, though capable, I am persuaded, of being applied to various purposes of navigation.

Among the lesser circumstances which appear to form characteristic points of distinction between country and country, may be mentioned the head-dress of the men, and the form and rig of their boats. An endless variety of turbans, sheep-skin caps, and conical bonnets, distinguish the Asiatics from the "Topee Wallas" or hat-wearers of Europe; and a still greater variety exists amongst the boats of different nations. My purpose just now, however, is to speak of boats and canoes alone; and it is really most curious to observe, that their size, form, cut of sails, description of oar and rudder, length of mast, and so on, are not always entirely regulated by the peculiar climate of the locality, but made to depend on a caprice which it is difficult to account for. The boats of some countries are so extremely ticklish, or unstable, and altogether without bearings, that the smallest weight on one side more than on the other upsets them. This applies to the canoes of the North American Indian, which require considerable practice, even in the smoothest water, to keep them upright; and yet the Indians cross immense lakes in them, although the surface of those vast sheets of fresh

[1] [These *catamarans*, to use the Tamil term, are not really canoes at all, but rafts made of lashed logs.]

water is often as rough as that of any salt sea. The waves, it is true, are not so long and high; but they are very awkward to deal with, from their abruptness, and the rapidity with which they get up when a breeze sets in.

On those parts of the coast of the United States where the seasons are alternately very fine and very rough, our ingenious friends, the Americans, have contrived a set of pilot boats, which are the delight of every sailor. This description of vessel, as the name implies, must always be at sea, as it is impossible to tell when her services may be required by ships steering in for the harbour's mouth. Accordingly, the Baltimore clippers and the New York pilots defy the elements in a style which it requires a long apprenticeship to the difficulties and discomforts of a wintry navigation in a stormy latitude, duly to appreciate. In the fine weather, smooth waters, and light winds of summer, these pilot-boats skim over the surface with the ease and swiftness of a swallow, apparently just touching the water with their prettily formed hulls, which seem too small to bear the immense load of snow-white canvas swelling above them, and shooting them along as if by magic, when every other vessel is lost in the calm, and when even taut-masted ships can barely catch a breath of air to fill their sky-sails and royal studding-sails. They are truly "water witches;" for, while they look so delicate and fragile that one feels at first as if the most moderate breeze must brush them from the face of the ocean, and scatter to the winds all their gay drapery, they can and do defy, as a matter of habit and choice, the most furious gales with which the rugged "sea-board" of America is visited in February and March.

I have seen a pilot-boat off New York, in the morning, in a calm, with all her sails set, lying asleep on the water, which had subsided into such perfect stillness that we could count the seam of each cloth in the mirror beneath her, and it became difficult to tell which was the reflected image, which the true vessel. And yet, within a few hours, I have observed the same boat, with only her close-reefed foresail set—no one visible on her decks—and the sea running mountains high—threatening to swallow her up. Nevertheless, the beautiful craft rose as buoyantly on the back of the waves as any duck, and, moreover, glanced along their surface, and kept so good a wind, that, ere long, she shot a-head and weathered our ship. Before the day was done, she could scarcely be distinguished from the mast-head to windward, though we had been labouring in the interval under every sail we could possibly carry without risk of the masts!

The balsas of Peru, the catamarans and masullah[1] boats of the Coromandel coast, and the flying proas of the South Sea Islands, have all been described before, and their respective merits dwelt upon by Cook, Vancouver, Ulloa, and others. Each in its way, and on its proper spot, seems to possess qualities which it is difficult to communicate to vessels similarly constructed at a distance. The boats of each country, indeed, may be said to possess a peculiar language, understood only by the natives of the countries to which they belong; and truly, the manner in which the vessels of some regions behave under the guidance of their respective masters, seems almost to imply that the boats themselves are gifted with animal intelligence. At all events, their performance never fails to excite the highest professional admiration of those whom experience has rendered familiar with the difficulties to be overcome.

Long acquaintance with the local tides, winds, currents, and other circumstances of the pilotage, and the constant pressure of necessity, enable the inhabitants of each particular spot to acquire such masterly command over their machinery, that no new comer, how-

[1] [Surf-boat.]

ever well provided, or however skilful generally, can expect to cope with them. Hence it arises, that boats of a man-of-war are found almost invariably inferior, in some respects, to those of the port at which she touches. The effect of seeking to adapt our boats to any one particular place would be to render them less serviceable upon the whole. After remaining some time at a place we might succeed in occasionally outsailing or outrowing the natives; but what sort of a figure would our boats cut at the next point to which the ship might be ordered—say a thousand miles farther from, or nearer to, the equator, where all the circumstances would inevitably be found totally different from what they were at the last port? We should have to change again and again, losing time at each place, and probably not gaining, after all, any of the real advantages which the natives long resident on the spot alone know the art of applying to practice.

It has been somewhere remarked, that when the human frame is compared with that of the inferior animals, it is found that, while in swiftness it is beaten by one, in scent by another, in strength by a third, yet does it contain by far the most admirable and varied combination of all those qualities severally possessed by the unintellectual animals. Thus man, upon the whole, is far better fitted than any of them for enduring the boundless varieties of climate which distinguish the different quarters of the globe, and for bringing into useful effort those inherent energies both of body and mind with which he is gifted, and which in the end render him the undisputed master of all other living things. So it is [to compare great things with small] in the case of the boats of ships of war which are most ingeniously contrived to be useful in all climates, in all seas, on every coast, and at all times and seasons. It is true they seldom, if ever, match the boats of the ports at which they anchor, either in sailing or in rowing. But they are invariably found to accomplish these purposes well enough for real service, besides securing many other advantages which the local boats cannot command. They are likewise sufficiently well adapted to all seas and all weathers, and can either carry heavy loads or sail quite light. They are so strongly built that they can take the ground without injury, and yet are not so heavy as to be troublesome in handling. While they are strong enough to bear the firing of a cannon in their bow, they are capacious enough to carry water casks or provisions, or to disembark troops without being inconveniently cumbersome when stowed on the booms, or suspended from the quarters. Like the hardy sailors who man them, they are rough and ready for any service, in any part of the world, at any moment they may be required.

It is not likely that we shall ever essentially improve the build or equipment of our boats; but it must always be useful to seafaring men to become acquainted with such practical devices in seamanship as have been found to answer well; especially if they seem capable of being appropriated upon occasions which may possibly arise in the course of a service so infinitely varied as that of the navy. It is partly on this account, and partly as a matter of general curiosity, that I think some mention of the canoes of Ceylon, and the balsas of Peru, may interest many persons for whom ordinary technicalities possess no charm. At least there appears to be an originality and neatness about both these contrivances, and a correctness of principle, which we are surprised to find in connection with perfect simplicity, and an absence of that collateral knowledge which we are so apt to fancy belongs only to more advanced stages of civilisation and philosophical instruction.

The hull or body of the Ceylonese canoe is formed, like that of Robinson Crusoe's, out of the trunk of a single tree, wrought in its middle part into a perfectly smooth cylinder, but slightly flattened and turned up at both ends, which are made exactly alike. It is hollowed out in the usual way, but not cut so much open at top as we see in other canoes, for considerably more than half of the outside part of the cylinder or barrel is left entire, with only a narrow slit, eight or ten inches wide, above. If such a vessel were placed in the water it would possess very little stability, even when not loaded with any weight on its upper edges. But there is built upon it a set of wooden upper works, in the shape of a long trough, extending from end to end; and the top-heaviness of this addition to the hull would instantly overturn the vessel, unless some device were applied to preserve its upright position. This purpose is accomplished by means of an out-rigger on one side, consisting of two curved poles, or slender but tough spars, laid across the canoe at right angles to its length, and extending to the distance of twelve, fifteen, or even twenty feet, where they join a small log of buoyant wood, about half as long as the canoe, and lying parallel to it, with both its ends turned up like the toe of a slipper, to prevent its dipping into the waves. The inner ends of these transverse poles are securely bound by thongs to the raised gunwales of the canoe. The out-rigger—which, it may be useful to bear in mind, is always kept to windward—acting by its weight at the end of so long a lever, prevents the vessel from turning over by the pressure of the sail; or, should the wind shift suddenly, so as to bring the sail a-back, the buoyancy of the floating log would prevent the canoe from upsetting on that side by retaining the out-rigger horizontal.

So far the ordinary purpose of an out-rigger is answered; but there are other ingenious things about these most graceful of all boats which seem worthy of the attention of professional men. The mast, which is very taut, or lofty, supports a lug-sail of immense size, and is stepped exactly in midships, that is, at the same distance from both ends of the canoe. The yard, also, is slung precisely in the middle; and while the tack of the sail is made fast at one extremity of the hull, the opposite corner, or clew, to which the sheet is attached, hauls aft to the other end. Shrouds extend from the mast-head, to the gunwale of the canoe; besides which, slender backstays are carried to the extremity of the out-rigger; and these ropes, by reason of their great spread, give such powerful support to the mast, though loaded with a prodigious sail, that a very slender spar is sufficient. If I am not mistaken, some of these canoes are fitted with two slender masts, between which the sail is triced up, without a yard.

In the vignette title-page to this volume, the canoes are taken from a drawing by the late Mr. Daniell. The background of Ceylon, with Adam's Peak in the centre, distant upwards of seventy miles, is from a sketch I made on board his Majesty's ship *Minden*.

The method of working the sails of these canoes is as follows. They proceed in one direction as far as may be deemed convenient, and then, without going about, or turning completely round as we do, they merely change the stern of the canoe into the head, by shifting the tack of the sail over to leeward, and so converting it into the sheet—while the other clew, being shifted up to windward, becomes the tack. As soon as these changes have been made, away spins the little fairy bark on her new course, but always keeping the same side, or that on which the out-rigger is placed to windward. It will be easily understood that the pressure of the sail has a tendency to lift the weight at the extremity of the out-rigger above the surface of the water. In sailing along, therefore, the log just skims the tops of the waves, but scarcely ever buries itself in them, so that little or no interruption to the velocity of the canoe is caused by the out-rigger. When the breeze freshens so much as to lift the weight higher than the natives like, one, and sometimes two of them, walk out on the horizontal spars, so as to add their weight to that of the out-rigger. In order to enable them to accomplish this purpose in safety, a "man rope," about breast high, extends over each of the spars from the mast to the backstays.

Of all the ingenious native contrivances for turning small means to good account, one of the most curious, and, under the circumstances, perhaps the most useful, is the balsa, or raft of South America, or, as it is called on some parts of the coast, the catamaran. This singular vessel is not only very curious in the eyes of persons who have attended at all to such things as amateurs, but is calculated also to furnish some useful hints to professional seamen. The simplest form of the raft, or balsa, is that of five, seven, or nine large beams of a very light wood—say from fifty to sixty feet long—arranged side by side, with the longest spar placed in the centre. These logs are firmly held together by cross bars, lashings, and stout planking near the ends. They vary from fifteen to twenty, and even thirty feet in width. I have seen some at Guayaquil of an immense size, formed of logs as large as a frigate's fore-mast. These are intended for conveying goods to Paita, and other places along shore. The balsa generally carries only one large sail, which is hoisted to what we call a pair of shears, formed by two poles crossing at the top, where they are lashed together. It is obvious, that it would be difficult to step a mast securely to a raft in the manner it is done in a ship. It is truly astonishing to see how fast these singular vessels go through the water; but it is still more curious to observe how accurately they can be steered, and how effectively they may be handled in all respects like any ordinary vessel.

The method by which the balsas are directed in their course is extremely ingenious, and is that to which I should wish to call the attention of sailors, not merely as a matter of curiosity, [although on this score, too, it certainly has great interest] but chiefly from its practical utility in seamanship. No officer can tell how soon he may be called upon to place his crew on a raft, should his ship be wrecked; and yet, unless he has been previously made aware of some method of steering it, no purpose may be answered but that of protracting the misery of the people under his charge. We all recollect the horrid scenes which took place on the raft which left the French frigate Méduse, on the coast of Africa, in 1816; and yet it is perfectly obvious, from the state of the wind and weather, that if anyone of that ill-fated party had been aware of the principle on which the South American balsas are steered, they might easily have reached the land in a few hours, and all the lives, so horribly sacrificed, might have been saved.

Nothing can be conceived more simple, or more easy of application, than the South American contrivance. Near both ends of the centre spar there is cut a perpendicular slit, about a couple of inches wide by one or two feet in length. Into each of these holes a broad plank, called guaras by the natives, is inserted in such a way that it may be thrust down to the depth of ten or twelve feet; or, at pleasure, it may be drawn up entirely. The slits are so cut, that, when the raft is in motion, the edges of these planks shall meet the water; or, in mathematical language, their planes are parallel with the length of the spars. It is clear, that if both the guaras be thrust quite down, and there held fast in a perpendicular direction, they will offer a broad surface towards the side, and thus, by acting like the leeboards of a river barge, or the keel of a ship, prevent the balsa from drifting sidewise or dead to leeward. But while these guaras serve the purpose of a keel, they also perform the important duty of a rudder, the rationale of which every sailor will understand, upon considering the effect which must follow upon pulling either up the guara in the bow or that in the stern. Suppose when the wind is on the beam, the foremost one drawn up; that end of the raft will instantly have a tendency to drift to leeward from the absence of the lateral support it previously received from its guara or keel at the bow; or, in sea language, the balsa will immediately "fall off," and in time she will come right before the wind. On the other hand, if the foremost guara be kept down while the sternmost one is drawn up, the balsa's head, or bow, will gradually come up towards the wind, in consequence of that end retaining its hold of the water by reason of its guara, while the stern end, being relieved from its lateral support, drifts to leeward. Thus, by judiciously raising or lowering one or both the guaras, the raft may not only be steered with the greatest nicety, but may be tacked or wore, or otherwise directed, with a degree of precision which appears truly wonderful to those who see it for the first time; nor is this contrivance less a subject of admiration after the principles have been studied.

I never shall forget the sensation produced in a ship I commanded one evening on the coast of Peru, as we steered towards the roadstead of Payta, so celebrated in Anson's voyage, and beheld an immense balsa dashing out before the land wind, and sending a snowy wreath of foam before her like that which curls up before the bow of a frigate in chase. As long as she was kept before the wind, we could understand this in some degree; but when she hauled up in order to round the point, and having made a stretch along shore, proceeded to tack, we could scarcely believe our eyes. Had the celebrated Flying Dutchman sailed past us, our wonder could hardly have been excited more.

In Ulloa's interesting voyage to South America, a minute account is given of the balsa, which I recommend to the attention of professional men. He winds up in these words:—

"Had this method of steering been sooner known in Europe, it might have alleviated the distress of many a shipwreck, by saving numbers of lives; as, in 1730, the *Genoesa*, one of his Majesty's frigates, being lost on the Vibora, the ship's company made a raft; but, committing themselves to the waves without any means of directing their course, they only added some melancholy minutes to their existence."—*Ulloa*, Book IV, Chap. 9.

I have lately seen a model of a raft devised some years ago, expressly in imitation of the South American balsa, by Rear-Admiral Sir Frederick Maitland, K.C.B., to be made out of the spare spars with which every ship of war is supplied. He proposes to form each of the guaras, or steering boards, of two of the ship's company's mess tables joined together by gratings and planks. But he sees no reason why these should be limited in number, and thinks that they might perhaps be usefully distributed along the entire length of the centre spar, so as effectually to prevent leeway or drift. In this manner, Sir Frederick is of opinion that a raft, capable of carrying a whole ship's crew, might be navigated for a considerable distance with ease and security. And I am glad to find myself anticipated by an authority deservedly so high with the profession, in this practical illustration of an idea that has appeared to me extremely feasible, from the first moment I saw the Peruvian balsas.

It will generally be found well worth an officer's attention to remark in what manner the natives of any coast, however rude they may be, contrive to perform difficult tasks. Such things may be very simple and easy for us to execute, when we have all the appliances and means of our full equipment at command; but, as circumstances may often occur to deprive us of many of those means, and thus, virtually, to reduce us to the condition of the natives, it becomes of consequence to ascertain how necessity, the venerable mother of invention, has taught people so situated to do the required work. For example, it is generally easy for a ship of war to pick up her anchor with her own boats; but, it will sometimes happen, that the launch and other large boats may be stove, and then it may prove of consequence to know how a heavy anchor can be weighed without a boat at all.

We happened, in his Majesty's ship *Minden*,[1] to run upon the Coleroon shoal, off the mouth of the great river of that name, about a hundred miles south of Madras. After laying out a bower anchor, and hauling the ship off, we set about preparing the boats to weigh it in the usual way. But the master-attendant of Porto Novo, who had come off to our assistance with a fleet of canoes and rafts, suggested to Sir Samuel Hood, that it might be a good opportunity to try the skill of the natives, who were celebrated for their expertness in raising great weights from the bottom. The proposal was one which delighted the Admiral, who enjoyed everything that was new. He posted himself accordingly in his barge near the spot, but he allowed the task to be turned over entirely to the black fellows, whom he ordered to be supplied with ropes, spars, and anything else they required from the ship. The officers and sailors, in imitation of their chief, clustered themselves in wondering groups in the rigging, in the chains, and in the boats, to witness the strange spectacle of a huge bower anchor, weighing nearly

[1] [H.M.S. *Minden*, a 74, was the first ship of its size to be built in the Bombay dockyards. Its builder, the famous Jamsetjee Bomanjee, was presented with a cup by the Admiralty, who were delighted with its beautiful lines. Bombay dockyard, under the Lowjee Wadia family, earned a great reputation during the 18th century for the fine battleships and frigates built there. Being of teak, they resisted gunfire better than oak, and were less liable to rot. Another fine Bombay vessel was the *Cornwallis*, p. 168.]

four tons, raised off the ground by a set of native fishermen, possessed of no canoe larger than the smallest gig on board.[1]

The master-attendant stood interpreter, and passed backwards and forwards between the ship and the scene of operations—not to direct, but merely to signify what things the natives required for their purpose. They first begged us to have a couple of spare topmasts and topsail-yards, with a number of smaller spars, such as top-gallant-masts and studding-sail booms. Out of these they formed, with wonderful speed, an exceedingly neat cylindrical raft, between two and three feet in diameter. They next bound the whole closely together by lashings, and filled up all its inequalities with capstanbars, handspikes, and other small spars, so as to make it a compact, smooth, and uniform cylinder from end to end. Nothing could be more dextrous or seaman-like, than the style in which these fellows swam about and passed the lashings; in fact, they appeared to be as much at home in the water as our sailors were in the boats or in the rigging.

A stout seven-inch hawser was now sent down by the buoy-rope, and the running clinch or noose formed on its end, placed over the flue of the anchor in the usual way. A couple of round turns were then taken with the hawser at the middle part of the cylindrical raft, after it had been drawn up as tight as possible from the anchor. A number of slew ropes, I think about sixty or seventy in all, were next passed round the cylinder several times, in the oppòsite direction to the round turns taken with the hawser.

Upwards of a hundred of the natives now mounted

[1] [A similar story is told of the huge bell at the N.E. corner of the Shwe Dagon Pagoda at Rangoon. After the second Burmese War, the English tried to carry it off to Calcutta, but by accident it was sunk to the bottom of the river. The Burmese got permission to raise it, and did so in a marvellous manner, by means of lashed bamboos.]

the raft, and, after dividing themselves into pairs, and taking hold of the slew ropes in their hands, pulled them up as tight as they could. By this effort they caused the cylinder to turn round till its further revolutions were stopped by the increasing tightness of the hawser, which was wound on the cylinder as fast as the slew ropes were wound off it. When all the ropes had been drawn equally tight, and the whole party of men had been ranged along the top in an erect posture, with their faces all turned one way, a signal was given by one of the principal natives. At this moment the men, one and all, still grasping their respective slew ropes firmly in their hands, and, without bending a joint in their whole bodies, fell simultaneously on their backs, flat on the water! The effect of this sudden movement was to turn the cylinder a full quadrant, or one quarter of a revolution. This, of course, brought a considerable strain on the hawser fixed to the anchor. On a second signal being given, every alternate pair of men gradually crept up the spars by means of their slew ropes, till one-half of the number stood once more along the top of the cylinder, while the other half of the party still lay flat on the water, and by their weight prevented the cylinder rolling back again.

When the next signal was given, those natives, who had regained their original position on the top of the cylinder, threw themselves down once more, while those who already lay prostrate, gathered in the slack of their slew ropes with the utmost eagerness as the cylinder revolved another quarter of a turn. It soon became evident, that the anchor had fairly begun to rise off the ground, for the buoy-rope, which at first had been bowsed taut over the stern of our launch, became quite slack. But Sir Samuel would not allow his people in the launch to assist the natives, as he felt anxious to see whether or not they could accomplish single-handed what they had undertaken. Accordingly, the slack of the buoy-rope merely was taken in by the launch's crew.

I forget how many successive efforts were made by the natives before the anchor was lifted; but, in the end, it certainly was raised completely off the ground by their exertions alone. The natives, however, complained of the difficulty being much greater than they had expected or had ever encountered before, in consequence of the great size of our anchor. In fact, when at length they had wound the hawser on the cylinder so far that it carried the full weight, the whole number of the natives lay stretched on the water in a horizontal position, apparently afraid to move, lest the weight, if not uniformly distributed amongst them, might prove too great, and the anchor drop again to the bottom, by the returning revolutions of the cylinder.

When this was explained to Sir Samuel Hood, he ordered the people in the launch to bowse away at the buoy-rope. This proved a most seasonable relief to the poor natives, who, however, declared, that if it were required, they would go on, and bring up the anchor fairly to the water's edge. As the good-natured Admiral would not permit this, the huge anchor, cylinder, natives, launch, and all, were drawn into deep water where the ship lay. The master-attendant now explained to the natives, that they had nothing more to do than to continue lying flat and still on the water, till the people on board the ship, by heaving in the cable, should bring the anchor to the bows, and thus relieve them of their burden. The officer of the launch also was instructed not to slack the buoy-rope till the cable had got the full weight of the anchor, and the natives required no farther help.

Nothing could be more distinctly given than these orders, so that I cannot account for the panic which seized some of the natives when close to the ship. Whatever was the cause, its effect was such that many of them let go their slew-ropes, and thus cast a disproportionate share of burden on the others, whose strength or rather weight, proving unequal to counterpoise the load, the cylinder began to turn back again. This soon brought the whole strain, or nearly the whole, on the stern of the launch, and had not the tackle been smartly let go, she must have been drawn under water and swamped. The terrified natives now lost all self-possession, as the mighty anchor shot rapidly to the bottom. The cylinder, of course, whirled round with prodigious velocity as the hawser unwound itself, and so suddenly had the catastrophe occurred, that many of the natives, not having presence of mind to let go their slew-ropes, held fast and were, of course, whisked round and round several times, alternately under water beneath the cylinder and on the top of it, not unlike the spokes of a coach-wheel wanting the rim.

The Admiral was in the greatest alarm, lest some of these poor fellows should get entangled with the ropes and be drowned, or be dashed against one another, and beaten to pieces against the cylinder. It was a great relief, therefore, to find that no one was in the least degree hurt, though some of the natives had been soused most soundly, or, as the Jacks said, who grinned at the whole affair, "keel-hauled in proper style."

In a certain sense, then, this experiment may be said to have failed; but enough was done to shew the feasibility of the method, which, under the following modifications proposed by our great commander—who was one of the best sailors that ever swam the ocean—I have no doubt might be rendered exceedingly effective on many occasions.

"In the first place," said Sir Samuel, "you must observe, youngsters, that this device of the natives is neither more nor less than a floating windlass, where the buoyant power of the timber serves the purpose of a support to the axis. The men fixed by the slew-ropes to the cylinder, represent the hand-spikes or bars by which the windlass is turned round, and the hawser takes the place of the cable. But," continued he, "therc appears to be no reason why the cylinder should be made equally large along its whole length; and were I to repeat this experiment, I would make the middle part, round which the hawser was to be passed, of a single topmast, while I would swell out the ends of my cylinder or raft to three or four feet in diameter. In this way a great increase of power would evidently be gained by those who worked the slew-ropes. In the next place," said the Admiral, "it is clear that either the buoy-rope, or another hawser also fastened to the anchor, as a 'preventer,' ought to be carried round the middle part of the cylinder, but in the opposite direction to that of the weighing hawser. This second hawser should be hauled tight round at the end of each successive quarter turn gained by the men. If this were done, all tendency in the cylinder to turn one way more than the other would be prevented; for each of the hawsers would bear an equal share of the weight of the anchor, and being wound upon the raft in opposite directions, would, of course, counteract each other's tendency to slew it round. The whole party of men, instead of only one-half of them, might then mount the spars; and thus their united strength could be exerted at each effort, and in perfect security, against the formidable danger of the cylinder whirling back by the anchor gaining the mastery over them, and dropping again to the bottom. But without using their clumsy, though certainly very ingenious, machinery of turning men into handspikes, I think," said he, "we might construct oui floating windlass in such a way that a set of small spars, studding-sail booms, for instance, might be inserted at right angles to its length, like the bars of a capstan, and these, if swifted together, could be worked from the boats, without the necessity of anyone going into the water."

While speaking of the dexterity of the natives of India, I may mention a feat which interested us very much. A strong party of hands from the ship were sent one day to remove an anchor, weighing seventy-five hundred-weight, from one part of Bombay dock-yard to another, but, from the want of some place to attach their tackle to, they could not readily transport it along the wharf. Various devices were tried in vain by the sailors, whose strength, if it could have been brought to bear, would have proved much more than enough for the task. In process of time, no doubt, they would have fallen upon some method of accomplishing their purpose; but while they were discussing various projects, one of the superintendents said he thought his party of native coolies or labourers could lift the anchor and carry it to any part of the yard. This proposal was received by our Johnnies with a loud laugh; for the numbers of the natives did not much exceed their own, and the least powerful of the seamen could readily, at least in his own estimation, have demolished half a dozen of the strongest of these slender limbed Hindoos.

To work they went, however, while Jack looked on with great attention. Their first operation was to lay a jib-boom horizontally, and nearly along the shank of the anchor. This being securely lashed to the shank, and also to the stock, the whole length of the spar was crossed at right angles by capstan bars, to the ends of which as many handspikes as there was room for were lashed also at right angles. In this way, every coolie of the party could obtain a good hold, and exert his strength to the greatest purpose. I forget how many natives were applied to this service; but in the course of a very few minutes, their preparations being completed, the ponderous anchor was lifted a few inches from the ground, to the wonder and admiration of the British seamen, who cheered the black fellows, and patted them on the back as they trotted along the wharf with their load, which appeared to oppress them no more than if it had been the jolly-boat's grapnel!

A VIEW OF THE GOVERNMENT HOUSE AND COUNCIL CHAMBER, MADRAS

[*face p.* 141

CHAPTER VII

THE SURF AT MADRAS

FROM Ceylon we proceeded after a time to Madras roads, where we soon became well acquainted with all the outs and ins of the celebrated surf of that place. This surf, after all, is not really higher than many which one meets with in other countries; but certainly it is the highest and most troublesome which exists as a permanent obstruction in front of a great commercial city. The restless ingenuity and perseverance of man, however, have gone far to surmount this difficulty; and now the passage to and from the beach at Madras offers hardly any serious interruption to the intercourse. Still, it is by no means an agreeable operation to pass through the surf under any circumstances; and occasionally, during the north-east monsoon, it is attended with some degree of danger. For the first two or three times, I remember thinking it very good sport to cross the surf, and sympathised but little with the anxious expressions of some older hands who accompanied me. The boat, the boatmen, their curious oars, the strange noises they made, and the attendant catamarans to pick up the passengers if the boat upsets being all new to my eyes, and particularly odd in themselves, so strongly engaged my attention, that I had no leisure to think of the danger till the boat was cast violently on the beach. The very first time I landed, the whole party were pitched out heels over head on the shore. I thought it a mighty odd way of landing; but supposing it to be all regular and proper, I merely muttered with the sailor whom the raree showman blew into the air,—"What the devil will the fellows do next?" and scrambled up the wet sand as best I might.

The nature of this risk, and the methods adopted by the natives to prevent accidents, are easily described. The surf at Madras consists of two distinct lines of breakers on the beach, running parallel to each other and to the shore. These foaming ridges are caused by a succession of waves curling over and breaking upon bars or banks, formed probably by the reflux action of the sea carrying the sand outwards. The surf itself, unquestionably, owes its origin to the long send of the ocean-swell coming across the Bay of Bengal, a sweep of nearly five hundred miles, from the coasts of Arracan, the Malay peninsula, and the island of Sumatra—itself a continent. This huge swell is scarcely perceptible far off in the fathomless Indian sea; but when the mighty oscillation—for it is nothing more—reaches the shelving shores of Coromandel, its vibrations are checked by the bottom. The mass of waters, which up to this point had merely sunk and risen, that is, vibrated without any real progressive motion, is then driven forwards to the land, where from the increasing shallowness, it finds less and less room for its "wild waves' play," and finally rises above the general level of the sea in threatening ridges. I know few things more alarming to nautical nerves than the sudden and mysterious "lift of the swell," which hurries a ship upwards when she had chanced to get too near the shore, and when, in consequence of the deadness of the calm, she can make no way to seaward, but is gradually hove nearer and nearer to the roaring surge.

At last, when the great ocean wave approaches the beach, and the depth of water is much diminished, the velocity of so vast a mass sweeping along the bottom, though greatly accelerated, becomes inadequate to fulfil the conditions of the oscillation; and it has no resource but to curl into a high and toppling wave.

So that this moving ridge of waters, after careering forwards with a front high in proportion to the impulse behind, and, for a length of time regulated by the degree of abruptness in the rise of the shore, at last dashes its monstrous head with a noise extremely like thunder along the endless coast.

Often, indeed, when on shore at Madras, have I lain in bed awake, with open windows, for hours together, listening, at the distance of many a league, to the sound of these waves, and almost fancying I could still feel the tremor of the ground, always distinctly perceptible near the beach. When the distance is great, and the actual moment at which the sea breaks ceases to be distinguishable, and when a long range of coast is within hearing, the unceasing roar of the surf in a serene night, heard over the level plains of the Carnatic shore, is wonderfully interesting.

Long afterwards, when within about five miles in a direct line from the Falls of Niagara, I remember thinking the continuous sound of the cataract not unlike that produced by the surf at Madras. What rendered the similarity greater, was the occasional variation in the depth of the note, caused by the fitful nature of the intervening flaws of wind, just as the occasional coincidence in the dash of a number of waves, or their discordance as to the time of their occurrence, or finally, some variation in the strength of the land-breeze, broke the continuity of sound from the shore.

But it must fairly be owned, that there is nothing either picturesque or beautiful—though there may be a touch of the sublime—in the surf, when viewed from a boat tossing about in the middle of its deafening clamour, and when the spectator is threatened every instant to be sent sprawling and helpless amongst the expectant sharks which accompany the masullah boats with as much regularity, though for a very different purpose, as the catamarans. These primitive little life-preservers, which are a sort of satellites attending upon the great masullah or passage-boat, consist of two or three small logs of light wood fastened together, and capable of supporting several persons. In general, however, there is but one man upon each, though on many there are two. Although the professed purpose of these rafts is to pick up the passengers of such boats as may be unfortunate enough to get upset in the surf, newcomers from Europe are by no means comforted in their alarm on passing through the foam, to be assured that, in the possible event of their boat being capsized, the catamaran men may probably succeed in picking them up before the sharks can find time to nip off their legs! I grievously suspect that it is the cue both of the boatmen and of these wreckers to augment the fears of all Johnny Raws ; and possibly the sly rogues occasionally produce slight accidents, in order to enhance the value of their services, and thereby to strengthen their claim to the two or three fanams which they are enchanted to receive from you as a toll.

Any attempt to pass the surf in an ordinary boat is seldom thought of. I remember hearing of a naval officer who crossed in his jolly-boat once in safety, but on a second trial he was swamped, and both he and his crew well-nigh drowned. The masullah boats of the country resemble nothing to be seen elsewhere.

They are distinguished by flat bottoms, perpendicular sides, and abruptly pointed ends, being twelve or fourteen feet long by five or six broad, and four to five feet high. Not a single nail enters into their construction, all the planks being held together by cords or lacings, which are applied in the following manner: —Along the planks, at a short distance from the edge, are bored a set of holes, through which the lacing or cord is to pass. A layer of cotton is then interposed between the planks, and along the seam is laid a flat narrow strip of a fibry and tough kind of wood. The cord is next rove through the holes and passed over the strip, so that when it is pulled tight the planks are not only drawn into as close contact as the interposed cotton will allow of, but the long strip is pressed against the seam so effectually as to exclude the water. The wood of which these boats are constructed is so elastic and tough, that when they take the ground, either by accident or in regular course of service, the part which touches yields to the pressure without breaking, and bulges inwards almost as readily as if it were made of shoe-leather. Under similar circumstances, an ordinary boat, fitted with a keel, timbers, and planks nailed together, not being pliable, would be shivered to pieces.

At the after or sternmost end, a sort of high poop-deck passes from side to side, on which the steersman takes his post. He holds in his hand an oar or paddle, which consists of a pole ten or twelve feet long, carrying at its extremity a circular disc of wood about a foot or a foot and a half in diameter. The oars used by the six hands who pull the masullah boat are similar to that held by the steersman, who is always a person of long experience and known skill, as well as courage and coolness—qualities indispensable to the safety of the passage when the surf is high. The rowers sit upon high thwarts and their oars are held by grummets, or rings made of rope, to pins inserted in the gunwale, so that they can be let go and resumed at pleasure, without risk of being lost. The passengers, wretched victims! seat themselves on a cross bench about a foot lower than the seats of the rowers, and close in front of the raised poop or steersman's deck which is nearly on a level with the gunwale.

The whole process of landing, from the moment of leaving the ship till you feel yourself safe on the crown of the beach, is as disagreeable as can be; and I can only say for myself, that every time I crossed the surf it rose in my respect. At the eight or tenth transit I began really to feel uncomfortable; at the twentieth I felt considerable apprehension of being well ducked; and at about the thirtieth time of crossing, I almost fancied there was but little chance of escaping a watery grave, with sharks for sextons, and the wild surf for a dirge. The truth is, that at each successive time of passing this formidable barrier of surf, we become better and better acquainted with the dangers and possibilities of accident—somewhat on the principle, I suppose, that a veteran soldier is said to be by no means so indifferent as a raw recruit is to the whizzing of shot about his ears.

However this may be, as all persons intending to go ashore at Madras must pass through the surf, they step with what courage they can muster into their boat alongside the ship, anchored in the roads a couple of miles off, in consequence of the water being too shallow for large vessels. The boat then shoves off, and rows to the "back of the surf," where it is usual to let go a grapnel, or to lie on the oars till the masullah boat comes out. The back of the surf is that part of the road-stead lying immediately beyond the place where the first indication is given of the tendency in the swell to rise into a wave; and no boat not expressly fitted for the purpose ever goes nearer to the shore, but lies off till the "bar-boat" makes her way through the surf, and lays herself alongside the ship's boat. A scrambling kind of boarding operation now takes place, to the last degree inconvenient to ladies and other shore-going persons not accustomed to climbing. As the gunwale of the masullah boat rises three or four feet above the water, the step is a long and troublesome one to make, even by those who are not encumbered with petticoats—those sad impediments to locomotion—devised by the men, as I heard a Chinaman remark, expressly to check the rambling propensities of the softer sex, always too prone, he alleged, to yield to wandering impulses!

Be this, also, as it is ordained, I know to my cost, in the shape of many a broken shin, that even gentlemen bred afloat may contrive to slip in removing from one boat to the other, especially if the breeze be fresh, and there be what mariners call a "bubble of a sea"—a term redolent in most imaginations with squeamishness and instability of stomach and footing. In a little while, however, all the party are tumbled, or hoisted into the masullah boat, where they seat themselves on the cross bench, marvellously like so many culprits on a hurdle on their way to execution! Ahead of them roars and boils a furious ridge of terrific breakers, while close at their ears behind, stamps and bawls, or rather yells, the steersman, who takes this method of communicating his wishes to his fellow-boatmen, not in the calm language of an officer entrusted with the lives of so many harmless and helpless individuals, but in the most extravagant variety of screams that ever startled the timorous ear of ignorance. In truth, no length of experience can ever reconcile any man, woman, or child, to these most alarming noises, which, if they do not really augment the danger, certainly aggravate the alarm, and add grievously to their feeling of insecurity on the part of the devoted passengers.

I need scarcely say, that the steersman is the absolute master for the time being, as every skipper ought to be, whether he wear a coat and epaulettes, or be limited in his vestments, as these poor masullah boatmen are, to the very minimum allowance of inexpressibles. This not-absolutely-naked steersman, then, as I have before mentioned, stands on his poop, or quarter-deck, just behind the miserable passengers, whose heads reach not quite so high as his knees. His oar rests in a crutch on the top of the stern-post, and not only serves as a rudder, but gives him the power to slew or twist the boat round with considerable rapidity, when aided by the efforts of the rowers. It is necessary for the steersman to wait for a favourable moment to enter the surf, otherwise the chances are that the boat will be upset, in the manner I shall describe presently. People are frequently kept waiting in this way for ten or twenty minutes, at the back of the surf, before a proper opportunity presents itself.

During all this while, the experienced eye of the veteran skipper abaft glances backwards and forwards from the swell rolling in from the open sea, to the surf which is breaking close to him. From time to time he utters a half word to his crew, with that kind of faint interrogative tone in which a commanding officer indulges when he is sure of acquiescence on the part of those under him, and is careless whether they answer or not. In general, however, he remains quite silent during this first stage of the passage, as do also the rowers, who either rest the paddles horizontally, or allow their circular blades to float on the surface of the water. Meanwhile, the boat rolls from side to side, or is heaved smartly upwards as the swell, just on the eve of breaking, lifts her into the air, and then drops her again into the hollow with the most sea-sickening velocity. I should state, that during this woefully unpleasant interval, the masullah boat is placed sideways to the line of surf, parallel to the shore, and, of course, exactly in the trough of the sea.

I have often watched with the closest attention to discover what were the technical indications by which these experienced boatmen inferred that the true moment was arrived when it was safe to enter the surf, but I could never make out enough to be of much professional utility. It was clear, indeed, that the proper instant for making the grand push occurred when one of the highest waves was about to break—for the greater the dash, the greater the lull after it.

But how these fellows managed to discover, beforehand, that the wave, upon the back of which they chose to ride in, was of that exact description, I could never discover. On the approach of a swell which he knows will answer his purpose, the steersman, suddenly changing his quiet and almost contemplative air for a look of intense anxiety, grasps his oar with double firmness, and exerting his utmost strength of muscle, forces the boat's stern round, so that her head may point to the shore. At the same time he urges his crew to exert themselves, partly by violent stampings with his feet, partly by loud and vehement exhortations, and partly by a succession of horrid yells, in which the sounds Yarry! Yarry!! Yarry!!! predominate—indicating to the ears of a stranger the very reverse of self-confidence, and filling the soul of a nervous passenger with infinite alarm.

These fearful noises are loudly re-echoed, in notes of the most ominous import, by all the other men, who strain themselves so vigorously at the oars, that the boat, flying forwards, almost keeps way with the wave, on the back of which it is the object of the steersman to keep her. As she is swept impetuously towards the bar, a person seated in the boat can distinctly feel the sea under him gradually rising into a sheer wave, and lifting the boat up—and up—and up, in a manner exceedingly startling. At length the ridge, near the summit of which the boat is placed, begins to curl, and its edge just breaks into a line of white fringe along the upper edge of the perpendicular face presented to the shore, towards which it is advancing, with vast rapidity. The grand object of the boatmen now appears to consist in maintaining their position, not on the very crown of the wave, but a little further to seaward, down the slope, so as to ride upon its shoulders, as it were. The importance of this precaution becomes apparent, when the curling surge, no longer able to maintain its elevation, is dashed furiously forwards, and dispersed into an immense sheet of foam, broken by innumerable eddies and whirlpools, into a confused sea of irregular waves rushing tumultuously together, and casting the spray high into the air by impinging one against the other. This furious turmoil often whirls the masullah boat round and round, in spite of the despairing outcries of the steersman, and the redoubled exertions of his screaming crew, half of whom back their oars, while the other half tug away in vain endeavours to keep her head in the right direction.

I have endeavoured to describe the correct and safe method of riding over the surf on the outer bar upon the back of a wave, a feat in all conscience sufficiently ticklish; but woe betide the poor masullah boat which shall be a little too far in advance of her proper place, so that, when the wave curls over and breaks, she may be pitched head foremost over the brink of the watery precipice, and strike her nose on the sand-bank. Even then, if there happen, by good luck, to be depth of water over the bar sufficient to float her, she may still escape; but, should the sand be left bare, or nearly so, as happens sometimes, the boat is almost sure to strike, if, instead of keeping on the back or shoulder of the wave, she incautiously precedes it. In that unhappy case, she is instantly tumbled forwards, heels over head, while the crew and passengers are sent sprawling amongst the foam.

Between the sharks and the catamaran men a race then takes place—the one to save, the other to destroy—the very Brahmas and Shivas of the surf! It is right, however, to mention, that these accidents are so very rare, that during all the time I was in India I never witnessed one.

There is still a second surf to pass, which breaks on the inner bar, about forty or fifty yards nearer to the shore. I forget, however, exactly the method by which this is encountered. All I recollect is, that the boatmen try to cross it, and to approach so near the beach, that, when the next wave breaks, they shall be so far ahead of it that it may not dash into the boat and swamp her, and yet not so far out as to prevent their profiting by its impulse to drive them up the steep face of sand forming the long-wished for shore. The rapidity with which the masullah boat is at last cast on the beach is sometimes quite fearful, and the moment she thumps on the ground, as the wave recedes, most startling. I have frequently seen persons pitched completely off their seats, and more than once I have myself been fairly turned over, and with all the party, like a parcel of fish cast out of a basket! In general, no such untoward events take place, and the boat at length rests on the sand, with her stern to the sea. But as yet she is by no means far enough up the beach to enable the passengers to get out with comfort or safety. Before the next wave breaks, the bow and sides of the boat have been seized by numbers of the natives on the shore, who greatly assist the impulse when the wave comes, both by keeping her in a straight course, and likewise by preventing her upsetting. These last stages of the process are sometimes very disagreeable, for every time the surf reaches the boat, it raises her up and lets her fall again, plump on the ground, with a violent jerk. When at last she is high enough to remain beyond the wash of the surf, you either jump out, or more frequently descend by means of a ladder, as you would get off the top of a stage-coach; and, turning about, you look with astonishment at what you have gone through, and thank Heaven you are safe!

The return passage from the shore to a ship, in a masullah boat, is more tedious, but less dangerous than the process of landing. This difference will easily be understood, when it is recollected that in one case the boat is carried impetuously forward by the waves, and that all power of retarding her progress on the part of the boatmen ceases after a particular moment. In going from the shore, however, the boat is kept continually under management, and the talents and experience of the steersman regulate the affair throughout. He watches, just inside the surf, till a smooth moment occurs, generally after a high sea has broken, and then he endeavours, by great exertions, to avail himself of the moment of comparative tranquillity which follows, to force his way across the bar before another sea comes. If he detects, as he is supposed to have it always in his power to do, that another sea is on the rise, which will, in all probability, curl up and break over him before he can row over its crest and slide down its back, his duty is, to order his men to back their oars with their utmost speed and strength. This retrograde movement withdraws her from the blow, or, at all events, allows the wave to strike her with diminished violence at the safest point, and in water of sufficient depth to prevent the boat taking the ground injuriously, to the risk of her being turned topsy-turvy. I have, in fact, often been in these masullah boats when they have struck violently on the bar, and have seen their flat and elastic bottoms bulge inwards in the most alarming manner, but I never saw any of the planks break or the seams open so as to admit the water.

It is very interesting to watch the progress of those honest catamaran-fellows, who live almost entirely in the surf, and who, independently of their chief purpose of attending the masullah boats, are much employed as messengers to the ships in the roads, even in the worst weather. Strange as it may seem, they contrive, in all seasons, to carry letters off quite dry, though, in getting across the surf, they may be overwhelmed by the waves a dozen times. I know of nothing to be compared to their industry and perseverance, except the pertinacity with which an ant carries a grain of corn up a wall, though tumbled down again and again.

I remember one day being sent with a note for the commanding officer of the flagship, which Sir Samuel Hood was very desirious should be sent on board; but as the weather was too tempestuous to allow even a masullah boat to pass the surf, I was obliged to give it to a catamaran-man. The poor fellow drew off his head a small skull-cap made apparently of some kind of skin, or oil-cloth, or bladder, and having deposited his despatches therein, proceeded to execute his task.

We really thought, at first, that our messenger must have been drowned even in crossing the inner bar, for we well nigh lost sight of him in the hissing yeast of waves in which he and his catamaran appeared only at intervals, tossing about like a cork in a pot of boiling water. But by far the most difficult part of his task remained after he had reached the comparatively smooth space between the two lines of surf, where we could observe him paddling to and fro as if in search of an opening in the moving wall of water raging between him and the roadstead. In fact, he was watching for a favourable moment, when, after the dash of some high wave, he might hope to make good his transit in safety.

After allowing a great many seas to break before he attempted to cross the outer bar, he at length seized the proper moment, and turning his little bark to seaward, paddled out at fast as he could. Just as the gallant fellow, however, reached the shallowest part of the bar, and we fancied him safely across, a huge wave, which had risen with unusual quickness, elevated its foaming crest right before him, curling upwards many feet higher than his shoulders. In a moment he cast away his paddle, and leaping to his feet, he stood erect on his catamaran, watching with a bold front the advancing bank of water. He kept his position, quite undaunted, till the steep face of the breaker came within a couple of yards of him, and then leaping head foremost, he pierced the wave in a horizontal direction with the agility and confidence of a dolphin. We had scarcely lost sight of his feet, as he shot through the heart of the wave, when such a dash took place as must have crushed him to pieces had he stuck by his catamaran, which was whisked, instantly afterwards, by a kind of somerset, completely out of the water by its rebounding off the sand bank. On casting our eyes beyond the surf, we felt much relieved by seeing our shipwrecked friend merrily dancing on the waves at the back of the surf, leaping more than breast-high above the surface, and looking in all directions, first for his paddle, and then for his catamaran. Having recovered his oar, he next swam, as he best could, through the broken surf, to his raft, mounted it like a hero, and once more addressed himself to his task.

By this time, as the current always runs fast along the shore, he had drifted several hundred yards to the northward farther from his point. At the second attempt to penetrate the surf, he seemed to have made a small miscalculation, for the sea broke so very nearly over him, before he had time to quit his catamaran and dive into still water, that we thought he must certainly have been drowned. Not a whit, however, did he appear to have suffered, for we soon saw him again swimming to his rude vessel. Many times in succession was he thus washed off and sent whirling towards the beach, and as often obliged to dive head foremost through the waves. But at last, after very nearly an hour of incessant struggling, and the loss of more than a mile of distance, he succeeded, for the first time, in reaching the back of the surf, without having parted company either with his paddle or with his catamaran. After this it became all plain sailing; he soon paddled off to the Roads, and placed the Admiral's letter in the first lieutenant's hands as dry as if it had been borne in a despatch-box across the court-yard of the Admiralty, in the careful custody of my worthy friend Mr. Nutland.

I remember one day, when on board the *Minden*, receiving a note from the shore by a catamaran lad, whom I told to wait for an answer. Upon this he asked for a rope, with which, as soon as it was given him, he made his little vessel fast, and lay down to sleep in the full blaze of a July sun. One of his arms and one of his feet hung in the water, though a dozen sharks had been seen cruising round the ship. A tacit contract, indeed, appears to exist between the sharks and these people, for I never saw, nor can I remember ever having heard of any injury done by one to the other. By the time my answer was written, the sun had dried up the spray on the poor fellow's body, leaving such a coating of salt, that he looked as if he had been dusted with flour. A few fanams[1]—a small copper coin—were all his charge, and three or four broken biscuits in addition, sent him away the happiest of mortals.

It has sometimes occurred to me, that professional men, both in the army and in the navy, ought to study all the tactics of these masullah boats, and to make themselves acquainted with the principle of their construction. Of what infinite importance to the army, for instance, might not fifty or a hundred of these boats have proved when our troops were landed, through the surf, at the mouth of the Adour in 1814? [2]

It is matter of considerable surprise to everyone who has seen how well the chain pier at Brighton stands the worst weather, that no similar work has been devised at Madras. The water is shallow, the surf does not extend very far from the beach, and there seems really no reason why a chain pier should not be erected, which

[1] [A tiny gold or silver coin of great antiquity, still in circulation on the West Coast. A Madras fanam is worth about 2d. Tamil *panam*, money, from *pan*, to barter. Vide p. 183, infra.]

[2] [At the end of the Peninsular Campaign.]

might answer not only for the accommodation of passengers, but for the transit of goods to and from the shore.

Before quitting this subject, I think it may be useful to mention, that by far the best representation of this celebrated surf which I have ever seen, is given in the noble Panorama of Madras, painted by Mr. W. Daniell[1], and exhibited last year. I rejoice to learn that this highly characteristic work will again be open to the public, in a more accessible situation than that in which it formerly stood.

[1] [*Vide supra*, p. 90.]

CHAPTER VIII

THE SUNNYASSES[1]

IF, by means of any contrivance, a man were to visit the moon, and afterwards, on returning to the earth, to set about giving us an account of his trip, the chances are, if he adhered to strict truth, that his narrative would prove a mighty dull one. A similar fate, and probably for the same reason, but too often attends those books about India which have nothing but bald and naked matter of fact to recommend them. It is not that in the East there are no objects of eminent curiosity in themselves, and well worthy of observation and record; but, unfortunately, they are generally not such as we in England can sympathise with. From wanting this link in the chain, the topic is deprived of that familiarity which alone can render distant descriptions either amusing or instructive; for we all know, that the nearer we approach to our own firesides, the more vivid the interest of any narrative becomes.

We read, for example, with the utmost avidity, the account of a riot in Piccadilly, in which a policeman of the C division is killed, while we skip carelessly over the adjacent paragraph in the same newspaper, giving the details of a battle in Syria, between the Pacha of Egypt, and the Grand Seignor, in which five thousand men on each side have left their bones to whiten in the wilderness. The solitary death of the poor constable affects us not only from its proximity, but from all its localities being familiar to us. We can readily imagine ourselves on the identical spot, and can even fancy the

[1] [From the Sanskrit *Sannyasi*, a Hindu religious mendicant.]

angle of the brickbat which did the mischief coming in contact with our own sconce. Those prime ministers to our curiosity, the reporters, have merely to touch in a light, or a shade, or a tint of exaggeration here and there, and the picture of all that passed stands as palpably before our mind's eye, as if Teniers,[1] or Ostade, or, better still, our own inimitable Wilkie, had drawn the whole affray from the life.

In short, it matters not much whether recorded incidents be great or small—their interest in our eyes will ever be measured either by their actual geographical distance, or by that moral approximation in the sentiment belonging to them which at once brings home to our feelings the workings of the most remote relations between man and man. Nothing, indeed, can so effectually awaken our attention, or keep it permanently alive, as that which engages our familiar sympathies.

Of these truths we have a striking example in the case of Bishop Heber,[2] who, evidently without study, but merely by giving the reins to his own exquisite taste, fancy and learning, describes to us Indian scenery and manners, in a way of which we possess no other example. He wastes none of our thoughts by claiming attention to dry descriptions of fact, but trusting, unconsciously, to that artless simplicity both of thought and expression, and to that entire singleness of purpose which distinguished this most benevolent of men, he touches those chords only which are in unison with our most habitual and domestic feelings. It will be recollected that the unceasing object of this accomplished writer's labours

[1] [The two Teniers, father and son, and the brothers Adrian and Isaac Ostade were famous 17th century Dutch painters. Sir David Wilkie, R.A. (1785-1841) was a friend of the Hall family.]

[2] [Bishop Reginald Heber, who died at Trichinopoly in 1826 at the early age of 38, was made Bishop of Calcutta in 1823, and a fine statue of him stands in the Cathedral. He is famous for several hymns, but most of all for his *Journal*, which is a classic of Anglo-Indian literature.]

was to fulfil the solemn injunctions of his Divine Master, "Go ye into all the world, and preach the Gospel to every creature." And as Bishop Heber probably considered that he possessed far higher opportunities for the accomplishment of this glorious end than perhaps any other man has enjoyed since the days of the Apostles, so we at home feel our brightest hopes kindle under the inspiration of such an example. Without much exaggeration, we may be said to follow his footsteps with almost as much confidence in his truth as we should to those of an angel sent to administer peace on earth, and good-will towards men. Every thing which he touches partakes of the brilliant colouring of his own glowing but well-regulated imagination; and, what is still more important and useful, everything he says is modified into practical application by the business-like sagacity of his most ordinary reflections upon what he describes. At the same time, the heartiest and most devout zeal may be traced in every line he writes; and as there never occurs anything wild or over-enthusiastic, we go along with him cheerfully and unreservedly, and travel in his company not only without fatigue, but with perpetual and varying delight in the companionship. Thus, step by step, we are taught to take a new and unexpected interest in things from which heretofore we have often turned with indifference or distaste.

It certainly is very fortunate that we possess Bishop Heber's journal, fresh and entire as it was written on the spot; for had the press been corrected by himself, though we might have obtained something very good, we should hardly have been allowed to peruse the unpremeditated expression of those sentiments and opinions which appear to have crowded to the surface in the unbounded fulness of his topic. Many of these must have been irretrievably chilled by the sober touch of subsequent reflection.

I remember, even on the spot itself, at Madras, being frequently made sensible how exceedingly small the interest of some of the most extraordinary of the native customs appeared, in comparison to that of the common-place usages in the Bungaloes of my own countrymen. A game at brag; a very moderate flirtation; even a sober cup of tea with an old friend; an evening drive along the Mount road, or a glance at the stars from Mr. Goldingham's observatory, generally proved an overmatch for the most curious ceremonies of the Hindoo population. With the whole Black Town at command as a field for local inquiry, I never entered it but twice. The first time I was obliged to sound a hasty retreat, in consequence of the crowd, heat, and the most villainous compound of smells that ever offended nostrils. On the second occasion, I merely passed through it hastily, and not at all in quest of adventures, but in order to take tiffin or luncheon with a friend, who resided to the northward of the town.

After riding for some distance, I half repented of my purpose, for it was raging hot, and the first airs of the young sea-breeze had scarcely begun to fan the surface of the water along a narrow strip of the sea parallel to the beach. Only those native boats, called pattymars,[1] and one or two other small coasters, whose shallow draught of water enabled them to approach the shore could avail themselves of these fitful swirls, which swept from time to time towards the land, and then died away again, for a full hour before the regular sea-breeze blew in from the offing. As yet, however, not a leaf of any tree was put in motion, and not a bird could be seen; all nature, indeed, seemed to have fallen asleep—not a sound was to be heard except the ceaseless dash of the restless surf.

I rode slowly along, well-nigh suffocated for want of

[1] [A kind of latteen-rigged ship, common on the coast: the word is apparantly derived from *patta*, tidings.]

air, scarcely shaded from the direct rays of the sun by my old friends, the cocoanuts, and tormented by the dazzling reflection from the coral sand, almost as white as snow, which seemed to burn the horse's feet. So entire was the solitude, that I had not the least expectation of meeting a single soul, native or European; and I might reasonably enough have recorded the fact, that at such a season not only every kind of work was discontinued in India, but even their religious ceremonies were intermitted.

Just as I had made this reflection in the generalising spirit which is so very tempting, my ear caught the sound of a set of tom-toms, or native drums, sounding at a distance in the wood; and after advancing a few hundred yards farther, I came to an opening facing the sea, in which were assembled at least a thousand natives. In the centre of the area stood a pole or mast, some thirty or forty feet high, bearing across its top a long yard or beam, slung nearly in the middle, and stretching both ways to the distance of forty or fifty feet. One end of the yard was held down by several men, so low as nearly to touch the ground, while the other rose proportionately high into the air. Near the upper extremity of this yard, underneath a canopy gaudily ornamented with flowers and loose festoons of drapery, I was astonished to observe a human being suspended, as it seemed, by two slender cords. He was not hanging perpendicularly, like a criminal, by the neck, but floated, as it were, horizontally in the air, as a bird flies, with his arms and legs moving freely about. Round his waist there was slung a bag, or basket, filled with fruits and flowers, which he scattered from time to time amongst the delighted crowd beneath, who rent the forest with shouts of admiration.[1]

[1] [This is the ceremony of *Charak Puja* or hook-swinging, described by Abbé Dubois, Bishop Heber, and many other old travellers. It is now forbidden by law.]

On approaching nearer to the ring, I discovered, with no small astonishment and horror, that the native who was swinging about in the air, though apparently enjoying his elevation, was actually hung upon hooks passing through his flesh! There was nothing, however, in his appearance or manner indicating pain, though he must have been in no small suffering, I should suppose; for no rope or strap passed round him to take off the weight, and the only means of suspension consisted in two bright hooks, inserted in his back. At first I felt unwilling to advance, but the natives, who appeared to be enchanted with the ceremony, begged me to come on.

The man, who was sailing about in the air at the time of my arrival, having been lowered down and unhooked, another fanatic was summoned. He was not dragged along reluctantly and with fear, but advanced briskly and cheerfully from the pagoda, in front of which he had prostrated himself flat on his face. A native priest then came forward, and, with the tip of his finger, marked out the spot where the hooks were to be inserted. Another officiating priest now began to thump the victim's back with his hand, and to pinch it violently, while a third dexterously inserted the hooks under the skin and cellular membrane, just below the shoulder-blade. As soon as this was effected, the devotee leaped gaily on his feet, and, as he rose, a basin of water, which had previously been dedicated to Shiva, was dashed in his face. He was then marched in procession from the pagoda towards a little platform on one side of the area in which the mast and yard were placed. Numerous drums and shrill-sounding pipes, mixed with the sound of many voices, gave token of his approach.

On mounting the platform, he tore away a number of chaplets and coronals of flowers by which he had been ornamented, scattering the fragments amongst the eager crowd. His dress, if such it can be called, besides the usual langooti[1] or slight band round the waist, consisted of nothing but a very short jacket, covering the shoulders and half of the arm, and a pair of drawers, reaching nearly to the knee, both being made of an open network, the meshes of which were an inch wide.

As the natives, so far from objecting to my being present, encouraged me to come forward, I mounted the scaffold, and stood close by to make sure there was no deception practised. The hooks, which were formed of highly polished steel, might be about the size of a small shark-hook, but without any barb; the thickness being rather less than a man's little finger. The points of the hooks being extremely sharp, they were inserted without lacerating the parts, and so adroitly, that not a drop of blood flowed from the orifices; in fact, the native, who appeared to suffer no pain, conversed easily with those about him. I may add, as the contrary has often been reported, that there was not, on this occasion at least, the slightest appearance of intoxication. To each hook was attached a strong cotton line, which, after certain ceremonies, was tied to the extremity of the yard-arm, drawn to the scaffold by ropes. As soon as the lines had been made fast, the opposite end of the yard was again gradually pulled down by men on the other side of the ring, and thus the Sunnyass was raised fifty or sixty feet over the heads of the admiring multitude, who all shouted as he ascended.

To show his perfect self-possession, he took from the pouch tied round his waist handfuls of flowers, and, occasionally, a single lime, which, with a merry countenance and a cheerful voice, he jerked amidst the crowd. Nothing could exceed the eagerness of the natives to catch these holy rélics; and, in order to give all of them an equal chance, the men stationed at the lower end of the yard walked with it round the ring, so as to bring the swinger successively over the different parts of the

[1] [Hind. *langoti*, a loin-cloth.]

circle. To enable them to make this circuit, the centre of the yard was made to traverse on a double pivot, which allowed it not only to be lowered down at the ends, but to be carried round horizontally. In this way the suspended fanatic, who really appeared to enjoy it as a sport, was wheeled round three times, each circuit occupying about two minutes; after which he was lowered down to the platform, and, the lines being cast off, he walked back to the pagoda, accompanied, as before, by the tom-toms and squeaking pipes. The hooks were then removed from his back, and he joined the crowd who accompanied the next man from the pagoda to the platform—exactly as if he had not himself been exposed only the minute before to a trial which, let people say what they like of it, must have been very severe.

I remained near the spot for about an hour, during which four other men were hooked up in the same manner, and swung round, not one of them exhibiting the slightest symptom of uneasiness. During the whole time, I never detected anything even like impatience except once, when one of the men in the air appeared to fancy that the persons who were walking along with the lower end of the yard moved too slowly. He called out to them to quicken their pace, but with nothing angry in his tone, or any tremor in his voice, indicating suffering.

About four years after this time I had another opportunity of witnessing, near Calcutta, a number of these swingings, and a great variety of other tortures, to which these Sunnyasses exposed themselves, either in honour of their god, or in pursuance of some idle vow.

The effect of such exhibitions as that just described at Madras, when witnessed for the first time by a stranger from Europe, is that of unmixed wonder, and of curiosity highly gratified; but when he sees the same things repeated on an extensive scale, together with many hundreds of other examples of voluntary bodily exposure to sword, scourge, and even to fire, the degree of melancholy which it inspires in the traveller is very great. If it were possible to suppose that many thousands of persons of all ages could be subjected, by the agency of tyrannical force, to these severe sufferings, such a scene would be inconceivably horrible; but when the people themselves not only invite these torture, and press eagerly forward to claim the honour of being first cut to pieces, or pierced with irons, or burned with hot spikes, or swung round in the air by hooks, or, in the extremity of their zeal, leap from scaffolds upon the points of naked swords—the sentiment of indignation is changed into commiseration. For it is impossible not to feel grieved upon seeing a population so deplorably degraded; and surely there must mingle with this feeling a strong desire to ameliorate the condition of people sunk so low in the scale of human nature.

These reflections naturally give rise to the two important questions—What harm do such exhibitions really produce? And in what manner are they to be checked? For we must recollect, that it is not always by official mandates that the habits of a nation can be suddenly changed; and even the East India Company, though exercising infinitely greater authority, both military and moral, over those countries, than ever Zengis Khan or Tamerlane[1] possessed, cannot effectively interfere to change, on the instant, the manners and customs of their Hindoo subjects. They may upset one dynasty and reconstruct another—they may crush armies of hundreds of thousands of disciplined men,

[1] [Chingiz Khan (1162-1227) was the founder of the great Mongol Empire of Central Asia. Tamerlane (d. 1405) who claimed descent from him conquered half Asia, annihilated the Turks at Angora in 1402, ruled as far as Egypt, and was preparing to conquer China at his death. His great grandson Babur was the founder of the Moghul dynasty of India.]

and even climb the Himaleh mountains to dispossess other conquerors of lands which have been won by the sword of brave men. What is of far more importance, and far more difficult of execution—they may extend, and indeed have already extended the empire of law and justice far and wide over their vast possessions, and have given peace, security of person and property, and a wonderful degree of contentment, to the millions upon millions of their subjects. But with all this weight of influence, arising not merely from the possession of faithful armies and abundant wealth, but from the still higher source of authority—opinion, they dare not rashly interfere to stop many of those mischievous and superstitious proceedings of the natives, until all, or nearly all, the parties concerned are agreed in condemning them.

It becomes, therefore, the business of a statesman in India to watch his opportunity, and if he has reason to believe that the time has arrived when, with safety to the well-being of the state, he can interpose the high arm of authority to check abuses, he ought to act promptly and vigorously. The practice of Hindoo infanticide—thanks to the energy and sagacity of the late Colonel Walker[1]—has been long abolished in India. In this way, also, the extensive local experience of the present governor-general, Lord William Bentinck, showed him that in suppressing the abominable practice of Stuttees, or widow murder and suicide combined, he should carry with him the sympathies of the intelligent Hindoos themselves, and in no respect weaken our own political authority. He, therefore, boldly issued a Regulation [dated 4th December, 1829,] positively

[1] [General Sir Alexander Walker (1764-1831) was a brilliant Bombay political officer who was responsible for the settlement of Kathiawar in 1807. His greatest work was the suppression of female infanticide among the Rajputs. This was done to a great extent by raising a fund to provide dowries for Rajput girls at the time of their marriage.]

forbidding the practice—and declaring its abettors to be murderers. Thus, by a single stroke of the pen, at the right moment, one of the most shocking and deteriorating of all the Hindoo usages was totally and effectually abolished.

If future authorities shall act with equal discretion, and only take care to time their interference with equal skill, there can be no doubt that very great ameliorations may be safely effected among the natives of India. If, for example, the improvements in the judicial and revenue systems, already alluded to, be carried forward very gradually, and in that right spirit which seeks only to apply practical remedies to admitted evils, we may hope to see, even in our own day, no small moral change for the better in the vast population of our splendid Eastern empire.

CHAPTER IX

Palankeen Travelling—Irrigating Tanks in the Mysore Country

It was my rare good fortune, while actually serving in my proper calling as a naval officer in India, and without the loss of a single day's time, to make two land journeys across the peninsula of Hindustan, and thus to see the interior of the country, which is seldom visited by sailors.

"Fair friends make fair winds," says the sea proverb, and so it proved in my case; for my kind patron Sir Samuel Hood, who, in true Nelson style, was always endeavouring to discover what would be most agreeable and useful to those under him, bethought him of a method of serving me professionally, at the same time putting it in my power to make one of the most delightful trips possible.

About the middle of the year 1813, his Majesty's ship *Cornwallis*, a seventy-four gun ship, built of teak-wood from the coast of Malabar, was launched at Bombay, on the western side of India. The captain who was appointed to this new ship then commanded the *Theban*, at that time lying in Madras Roads, on the eastern side of the peninsula. But as this frigate required repairs which could be given her only at Bombay, she was ordered round to that port. Fortunately for me, the officer appointed to command the *Theban* happened at this juncture to be cruising in another ship far away to the eastward amongst the Moluccas of the Philippine Islands; and Sir Samuel Hood offered me the temporary appointment as acting commander until her proper captain should join.

"You will have to go to Bombay," he said, "to refit

the frigate and to bring her back to this side of India; but you may go either by sea, in the ship herself, or you may run over by land across the continent, only taking care that you reach Bombay in good time to relieve the officer in command of the *Theban*, that he may be free to go on board the *Cornwallis*."

I, of course, gladly availed myself of the alternative which enabled me to visit so interesting a part of India as the Mysore country, the scene of Hyder Ali's and Tippoo Sultan's wars, and so well-known in Europe by the splendid catastrophe of Seringapatam.

The preparations for the journey were very soon made, and I hurried away from Madras as fast as I could, being stimulated into extraordinary dispatch, not only by the wish to make the most of my opportunities, but by a latent apprehension that there must be some mistake in this piece of good fortune. I felt, indeed, as if it were all a dream, and could scarcely persuade myself that I was really and truly on the eve of making a journey through the interior of India, and that, in a week or ten days, I might actually be sleeping in the palace of Tippoo, or scrambling over the breach where that formidable enemy of the British name was found slain, under a vast pile of his devoted adherents.

I knew little or nothing of the mode of travelling in the East, and my stock of the language was as yet but small, albeit I had studied sedulously to acquire some knowledge of Hindustanee, which, although not the colloquial dialect of all parts of the country I was to pass through, I was told might be used for the purposes of travelling in every village. The cutwal[1], or head man, one of whose offices it is to assist travellers, can always speak this language, which, as I have been told, is a jargon, or lingua franca, consisting of Arabic, Persian, Sanscrit, a little sprinkling of Portuguese, and a still smaller dash of English, with here and there a stray

[1] [Kotwal.]

word of Malay origin. Unfortunately, all languages are nearly equally difficult to me; and, certainly, had I not travelled in the country, I should never have advanced beyond the elementary sentences, "Give me a glass of water;" "Bring the palankeen;" "Go faster;" and so on, together with a moderate stock of those truncated little oaths which everyone seems soonest to acquire, and without effort. But on a journey made quite alone, even the least apt mouth for languages is forced to model itself to the current speech of the high road. Hunger, thirst, and fatigue, are famous teachers of foreign dialects, and in all journeys there must occur many accidents which not only try the temper, but put the traveller on his mettle to explain his wants, or to extricate him from scrapes; and the emphatic lessons thus drilled into him, fix themselves on his memory, let it be ever so slippery.

The utility of languages to a naval officer is so great, not merely as a source of utility and enjoyment to himself, but of occasional advantage to the public service, that I would fain see it established as an Admiralty regulation, that no midshipman should be allowed to pass for lieutenant who, besides French, could not read and speak moderately well either Spanish, Italian, or Hindustanee, the four great dialects with which naval men are likely to be much concerned. Such a regulation would cause a famous hullabaloo amongst the rising generation of officers, and many a deep curse would be launched at the suggestor of such a measure; but, ere long, both these execrators and the public service would feel the advantages of the rule.

My first thought .was to cast about for letters of introduction; but an experienced Indian traveller told me not to mind such things, that they were scarcely ever required, and that my uniform alone would be an ample introduction.

"Take a passport with you," said my friend, "in

case of accidents, and your blue coat, merely to show who and what you are, but nothing more; you will find a welcome, and a hearty one too, at every station, civil and military, over the whole country. You cannot possibly go wrong," he added; "and if at any time you should be at a loss, you have only to apply to the nearest English station for assistance, and straightway all the resources of the spot will be at your command."

With this comfortable assurance, I set off; but I confess I felt queerish the first night when jogging along all alone on the high road, in a country totally unknown to me, and of whose language I knew so very little. After tumbling and tossing about, greatly to the annoyance of the bearers, for about an hour, I fell asleep, but only to dream of tigers and robbers, till at length the palankeen was suddenly and violently jerked on one side, and then thrown on the ground. I awoke, of course, in great alarm, and on thrusting out my head, I saw a snake twisting about amongst the feet of the foremost bearers, who had dashed down their load, and were leaping to the right and left into the jungle. As my sword lay on one side of the palankeen, I lost no time in drawing it forth, and, before the caitiff could effect his escape, cut him in twain, to the great admiration of the bearers, who dropped back again, one by one, to the road. It is singular enough, that this was the only snake, so far as I recollect, which I ever saw in a wild state in India, though I must have travelled many thousands of miles in that country.

Palankeen travelling may be compared in some respects to sea voyaging; inasmuch as the traveller carries his house, furniture, kitchen, and wardrobe with him. He is not dependent, indeed, upon the wind for his progress; but he is almost as much influenced in his comforts by the weather as if he were at sea; while the bearers, though docile enough to a certain extent, can no more be put out of their own particular way than the monsoons or trade winds. They must be allowed to travel at certain hours and at a certain rate, and they claim the privilege of making as much noise as they please during their progress, greatly to the discomposure of new-comers, but, it is said, greatly to their own relief. Every resident possesses a palankeen as a matter of course, just as we in Europe own a hat or an umbrella. A gig or a saddle-horse might seem better comparisons; but in England, alas! many people sport neither gig nor horse;—in India, no person moves without his palankeen. Those who can afford to do things in style, or who choose to be stylish whether they can afford it or not, keep a dozen bearers; but moderate men, except on a journey, content themselves with half-a-dozen.

The palankeen, which is generally kept in the verandah of the house, is taken up by the bearers in the morning, who brush it out, wash it if necessary, place it near the door in some shady spot, and, if their master be not ready to start immediately after breakfast they stretch themselves on the ground, in the shade, and either go to sleep, or continue chatting to one another in a low rumbling undertone, in which the words are scarcely articulated. On the appearance of their master, they instantly bestir themselves without bidding—for it is one of the delights of Indian service, that the attendants seem to possess an intuitive faculty of discovering what is wanted; and it very rarely happens that they require to be spoken to or lectured. In truth, no one, until he has visited India, can form any just notion of the immense comfort of being waited on by those truly angelic fellows, the white-robed serving men of the East, or estimate the positive addition it makes to the sum of human happiness, to be exempted from the wear and tear of looking after the habits, and studying the temper and humours of European domestics.

The palankeen-bearers, who form, I believe, a caste or class by themselves, are a faithful and diligent race of men; and, as it is their invariable custom to be honest, a traveller may leave anything loose in the palankeen with perfect safety. I have heard that it is not quite safe or fair to leave the brandy-bottle too much exposed, as poor human nature, under whatever colour of the skin it may be hid, is said never to be proof against the seductions of that wonderful tipple. For my part I do not believe I ever tasted it till I came to travel in India, and then I was as much taken in as the savage king, so cleverly described by Captain Cook, who mistook a bottle of this new-found beverage for an avatar of one of his gods. A worthy friend of mine at Madras, just as I was starting, thrust his head into my palankeen, and cried out:

"Why, man, you have got no brandy! You cannot possibly get on without some support, as we call it."

And running back to the house, he unlocked his private store, and deposited with me a small square, nicely cut crystal bottle of cognac, so delicious, that, he declared, it would bring a dead man alive again. I forgot all about this supply till some days afterwards, during a sultry, choky afternoon in the jungle, when there was hardly a breath of wind aloft of sufficient force to stir even the tremulous leaf of the bamboo-tree; while down below, where the ground was parched up and riven into a net-work of crevices by the heat, the still air had reached that suffocating pitch which makes one feel close to death's door. The bearers had stopped at a sparkling well, or rather a natural fountain, from which a small stream of cool water gurgled and splashed over the rocks, and spread its refreshing influence for many yards on either side. Being burnt up with thirst, I leaped out, and in the next minute would have plunged my face into the basin formed by the falling drops, and drank down the water to my own destruction had not one of the bearers gently interposed himself, and recommended me to put some brandy with the cold spring. I had no objection to this modification; but as I longed for a deep potation, I put only a couple of thimblefuls into a tumbler, and then filling it to the brim with water, swallowed the whole at one delectable gulp. The sensation produced by this experiment was so agreeable and new, that I could not well resist the temptation of repeating it; and, although the veteran bearer who dipped the water for me a second time, smiled as he filled the glass, I did not comprehend the meaning of his expression of countenance till some time afterwards. I also told him to fill one of the goglets, and to carry it in his hand, that it might enjoy the benefit of the breeze caused by our rapid advance. By and by I felt an irresistible desire to take another drop of the very weakest brandy and water; and, as it proved three times more delicious than the first, but left behind it a treble degree of thirst, I tried it again. I now became impatient, and called to the bearers to go faster.

"Go faster still!" I said, rather sharply.

Upon this they moved on so quickly that I was nearly jerked out. I then desired them to stop; an order more easily obeyed than the first. I took advantage of the pause to mix one more glass of what seemed very weak grog.

"Go faster!" I roared out—"go faster!" as I emptied the glass. But their utmost speed seemed to me a snail's pace; and, after a few more exclamations, reproaches, and threats, I leaped out of the palankeen, and rushing forward to enforce my orders, fell flat on my face in the dust! The terrified bearers dropped the palankeen on the road, and, scampering into the forest, left me all alone to crawl back to my nest as I best could.

I know not how long I slept, but on waking, I perceived that the bearers had again lifted the palankeen, and, having come to the termination of their night's journey, were just setting me down by the side of a tank, twenty or five-and-twenty miles from the spot where I had frightened them away the evening before.

The sun's rays were beginning to flicker through the lowest brushwood, dripping with dew; and the air felt so cool and elastic, that I begged to have a bath, to clear my noddle. I undressed myself accordingly; and, while I sat on the steps in front of the pagoda, allowed the bearers to pour in succession a dozen large jars of water over my head. After this, as soon as I was dressed, I called the men together, distributed the remainder of the brandy amongst them, and, in spite of my friend's assurance at starting, found I got on a great deal better ever afterwards.

When a journey of more than thirty or forty miles is to be made in India, it is usual to acquaint the palankeen-boys with this intention, that they may make the fitting preparations, in the shape of torches and oil, besides rice and curry stuff, and sundry other matters for themselves. Their cook, also, who makes the thirteenth man amongst them if it be a full set, sees his pots and pans in order for the march. A person—I think one of the bearers—is also got in readiness with a bamboo across his shoulder, to each end of which he attaches a light travelling trunk, made generally of basket-work covered with green wax-cloth. The night season, for obvious reasons, is generally chosen for travelling in India, both by bearers and travellers. The heat of the day interferes both with the length and speed of the journey; and although the person inside of the palankeen is shaded from the direct rays of the sun, he is sure to be well-nigh suffocated with the heat, or choked with the dust thrown up by the bearers' feet. At night, even in the hottest season, there is generally some dew to lay the dust, and the air is, of course, cooler.

People generally start after an early dinner; and as the night falls, the torch is lighted and held by one of the bearers, who runs along with it by the side of the palankeen. The torch, at first, may be about four feet long, and nearly as thick as a man's arm; it is made of rags and strips of cotton, well saturated with oil and grease, and then wound into a firm cylinder. The flame is supplied with oil from a tin vessel carried in the torch-bearer's other hand. Unfortunately for the traveller, it happens to be more convenient for the men that the torch should be held on the windward side of the palankeen than on the lee side, and consequently the smoke often blows right in upon him. During the early part of my journey, I endeavoured, by the wonted artillery of commands, scolds, entreaties, and bribes, to reform this matter, but all without effect. "Bap ke dustoor," was the only answer I got—"It is father's custom." The truth is, that if the torch be carried by a man to leeward, his shadow interferes with its light if he holds it in one hand, and the flame burns him if he holds it in the other. I have often made the musaljee change sides; but I could hear him chattering and growling sadly until he fancied me asleep, and then round he went again to windward. At length I discovered that it was much the best way to submit with what patience I possessed—which was not much—for I never found my stock of this virtue improved by attempting, in wretched Hindustanee, to explain to persons who did not wish to understand, the propriety of doing that which they believed improper, and felt to be exceedingly inconvenient. In some parts of the country, these torches are made of long slips of well-dried bamboo, occasionally of faggots bound up; and at other places they consist of long thick reeds. I could seldom prevail upon the bearers to use a lantern, unless when their stock of faggots had been burned out. The light, they said, was not sufficient for the safe guidance of their feet.

The palankeen is about six feet long by two and a half wide, and serves at night-time for a bed, in the day-time for a parlour. In the front part of the interior is fitted a broad shelf, underneath which a drawer pulls out, and over the shelf a net is stretched, such as we see in travelling carriages. In the after-part, as a sailor would call it, there is generally fixed a shelf for books, a net for fruit or any loose articles, and hooks for hats, caps, towels, and other things. There are two doors, or sliding partitions in each side, fitted with Venetian blinds in the upper panel; and in each end of the palankeen are placed two little windows. Many travellers choose to have a lamp fixed in one corner, with a glass face turned inwards, but trimmed from without, either for reading or for sleeping by—for your Indian must always have a light to see how to shut his eyes, as Pat said. The bottom, or seat is made of strips of rattan, like that of a chair, over which is laid a light elastic mattress, made either of horse-hair, or, which is still better, I believe, of the small shavings used in dressing the bamboo and rattan.

Across the palankeen, at a distance of a foot and a half from the end, is hung a flat square cushion, buttoned tightly from side to side, for the traveller's back to rest against; while his feet are prevented from slipping forwards by a cross-bar, similar in principle to the stretchers in a boat, against which the rowers plant their feet. This bar, which slides up and down in slits cut at the sides of the palankeen, is capable of being shifted nearer to or further from the end, according to the length of the voyager's legs, or to his choice of position. In the space behind the cushion or rest for the back, are stowed away, in the day-time, the sheets, blankets, pillow, and other night-things; and in the net above, two or three changes of clothes, in case of any accident separating the traveller from his heavy baggage. In the drawers may be kept shaving articles, and such knick-knacks as a compass, thermometer, sketch-book. On the shelf behind, a few books—among which, of course, will be found a road-book and a Hindustanee vocabulary—jostling with a tea-pot and sugar-canister. Under the mattress, an infinity of small things may be hid, provided they be flattish. In each corner of this moving house are placed little round sockets for bottles and glasses. Many other odds and ends of comforts and conveniences suggest themselves as the journey advances, or may be found cut and dry in expensive palankeens. I speak merely of what mine possessed, and it was a very ordinary affair—cheap, strong, and not too heavy. Along the top on the outside is laid a wax cloth cover, which, when not in use, is rolled up; but in rainy weather, or when the night air becomes chill, this cloth is let so loose as to envelope the whole palankeen.

At each end there is fixed a single strong, smooth bar, which rests on the bearers' shoulders. This pole, which is somewhat thicker than a man's arm, is possessed of none of the elasticity which gives such an unpleasant motion to a sedan chair, being secured tightly to the corners of the palankeen by iron rods. To one of these poles there is generally suspended a beautifully shaped rattan basket, holding a goglet or water-pitcher, which is still further defended from injury by an open tracery of split rattans, resembling not a little the work in relief on the buttresses and pinnacles of Henry VII's chapel in Westminster Abbey. This goglet is hung in front, that the dew which exudes from its pores may be evaporated by the current of air it encounters as the bearers move on; and thus, even in the hottest weather, a cool draught of water may always be obtained. Under the pole behind are hung a tea-kettle, coffee-pot, and a curious but useful kind of wash-hand-basin, imported from China, of cylindrical shape, made of wood highly varnished.

Some people add a brace of pistols to the equipment of their palankeen; but I preferred, if it came to the push, rather to be robbed in peace, than to fight a pitched battle with desperadoes about a trumpery watch, or a handful of pagodas. At the very best, one could only hope to repel the boarders, and perhaps put one or two of them to death; in return for which a broken pate, or a slice with a grass-cutter's knife, would remain as lasting evidences of the traveller's prowess in the jungle. As for tigers, I was assured that in ninety-nine cases in a hundred, they are quite as glad to make off from man as man is glad to get off from them; and, in truth, their instinct must be but small, or their hunger inordinately great, if they have not learned by this time, that Mr Homo is much more than a match for Mr Brute, with all his claws and teeth. Of this fact I saw ample proofs in the course of my journey, as I shall have occasion presently to relate in describing a great native festival near Seringapatam, where animals really wild, and not such tame creatures as are to be seen in our misnamed "wild beast" shows, were exhibited and baited for our edification, within twenty-four hours after being caught in the forest.

If the journey to be made in the palankeen be a short one, say thirty or forty miles, it may be run over in the night, with only one stop, during which the bearers light a fire and dress their supper. Including this delay, I have made, between eight in the evening and half-past six in the morning, a journey of full forty miles—that is, from Madras to the Seven Pagodas,[1] or

[1] [The famous group of temples, each exquisitely carved from a boulder of solid rock, at Mahabalipuram, between Sadras and Covelong, are the work of King Narasimha Varman (625-45 A.D.) of the Pallava dynasty of Kanchi.]

Mahabalipooram, the city of the great god Bali. On ordinary occasions, for short distances between house and house, when you are going out to dinner, only a couple of men run under each pole, and at such times the palankeen is carried at the rate of four or five miles an hour. But on journeys, there are generally three men to each pole, which employs six men out of the twelve, while the others run by their side, ready to relieve their companions at intervals. During the whole time they are in progress, they make a noise which it is not easy to describe. Sometimes it consists of a long, deep, but slightly varied groan, in which the whole party join in correct time. Mostly, however, the men in front use one kind of groan or grunt, which is answered by another from those behind. These sounds often approach to a scream, and frequently include words of warning against stones in the way, or pools of water; but these are articulated so indistinctly, that it is difficult to catch them. I remember one exclamation frequently used, "Kurab high!" [1] Occasionally, when it is wished to make a great exertion, the leader of the song suddenly calls out some such word as "Shabash!" [2] to which everyone answers, and away they spring at double speed, while the tone of the music, so to call it, is changed from a dull sort of grumbling bass, to an angry and sharp intonation, mixed with something almost insulting or reproachful in its tone.

A stranger, or griffin, [3] as he is called, on first getting into a palankeen at Madras, is naturally much alarmed, and often rather distressed, at these hideous sounds, as he naturally fancies the men must be suffering dreadfully under their load. There have even been instances of Johnny Newcomes so prodigiously sensitive

[1] [*Kharab hai*, Hind. "It is bad."]

[2] [*Shabash:* Hind. "Hurrah."]

[3] [*Vide supra*, p 110.]

or spoony, as actually to get out and walk in the sun to the particular amusement of the bearers, who, it is alleged, make their yells doubly horrible when they fancy they have caught a griffin. I do confess, that at first, it feels a little queer to be carried along on men's shoulders; but this is a great waste of sympathy, inasmuch as every man so carrying you is not only a servant at will, but a very well-paid, contented servant, and one of the caste whose greatest anxiety and pleasure is to be so employed—who makes money by it, and saves it, and buys land, and becomes, in time, a gentleman in his way. I never remember to have heard the brawny Highlanders, who carry people about in chairs in Edinburgh, Bath, and elsewhere, accused of any extra servility, because they lifted the box containing their employer, instead of driving the horses which dragged the carriage holding the same personages. In short, all these matters turn on usage, and the deuce is in it if the parties most concerned are not the best judges of what, upon the whole, is most to their mind. But the fashion nowadays is to cram compassion down contented people's throats, and, in the true spirit of the philosophers of Laputa, or the needy knife-grinder's friend in the the Antijacobin, to make happy men miserable, in order that they may be re-converted to happiness by some patent general principle—an invaluable process, always best known, it would appear, to those who are personally ignorant of all the practical details of the subject!

This song, or cry, or groan, or whatever it be, of the palankeen-bearers of India, is different in different parts of the country; while, at some places, as at Bombay they use none at all, but move along quite quietly. There seems to be as much art in carrying a palankeen as in driving a carriage or riding a horse. Some bearers shake you to pieces, while others glide along so gently, that you are scarcely conscious of any motion.

In every part of the country which I have visited, except Cananore and Mangalore, on the coast of Malabar, the palankeen is carried in a straight-forward direction, that is, parallel to the road, so that the hind-bearers follow exactly the footsteps of those in front. But at the places alluded to, on the western coast, they carry it nearly across the road, so that the hind-bearers are but little astern of the others, the poles making an angle with the direct line of about seventy-five degrees. This crab-kind of fashion of moving sideways, which resembles that of the abominable omnibuses of Europe, is anything but agreeable. I well remember the first time I encountered it feeling quite sick, and a little giddy. It was in the evening, about sunset, and I had shut to the doors to take a nap, when, after a little time, I thought there was something very odd in the motion, and I sat up to consider what it could be. On opening one of the doors, and looking out, I beheld all the objects passing by me at such a strange obliquity of angle, that I began to suspect I must have been again taking to the brandy bottle!

When a long journey is to be made, you must decide upon one of two ways, and either travel through with one set of bearers, which is the slowest method, or you must make arrangements for having relays of fresh men laid for you at different stations on the road. If one set go all the way, and be good of their kind, they will undertake to carry a moderate sized traveller about twenty-five miles a day for a continuance, which is surely great going. Travelling by dawk,[1] as it is called, or when the bearers are laid, is the most expeditious way of proceeding, but, of course, much the most expensive. Before starting, you must write letters to the different collectors of the various districts through which you mean to pass, stating the time you mean to set out, and the route you are to follow. It

[1] Hind *dak*, post.]

seems to signify little whether or not you are personally acquainted with these gentlemen, for it is the universal fashion in India to be obliging and hospitable. The bearers written for will, therefore, always be found waiting for you at their assigned stations. It sometimes answers equally well, and saves time and trouble, to send on as many sets of bearers as may be required to make the journey. Thus, when I left Madras on my second journey overland, I sent forward one set to the Mount, eight miles distant; another to Sri Parmatura, twenty miles further; a third to Baul Chitty's Choultry, twenty-four miles further, which was about twenty short of Arcot, my first halting-place. I have already mentioned, that each set of bearers consists of thirteen men, when a journey is to be made. The ordinary price of this description of labour, when I was in India, and I don't suppose it has changed materially since, was three fanams [or about sixpence and a farthing] to each bearer for every ten English miles, or six shillings and ninepence for the whole thirteen, which is about eightpence per mile. An additional sum is paid for those sets which are sent on past the first stage, and, of course, something extra is paid to them daily when they are kept waiting.

Fanams, rupees, and pagodas,[1] form the money current at Madras. There are twelve fanams in a rupee, and forty-five in a pagoda. The word rupee [or rupiya] means silver, and is applied to that metal generally. What we term fanam, I remember being told was called "fullum" by the natives; this, as etymologies go, is but a small shift. But where the

[1] *Pagoda:* [This word, probably derived from Pers. *but kadah*, "idol house," is applied to (1,) a Hindu temple; (2,) an idol; (3,) a coin (probably so called from the figure of the god which it bore). Accounts at Madras down to 1818 were kept in Pagodas, Fanams and Kas (cash); 8 kas = 1 fanam; 42 fanams = 1 Pagoda or Hun, equivalent to 3 rupees. In 1818, the rupee became the standard currency.]

word pagoda came from, I believe is not known; the coin so called by us is named "hoon," or "hoong", by the natives; but the temples which we style pagoda are called by them "dewul".[1] In China, the sacred edifices also receive at our hands the name of pagoda though, in the European slang of the spot, they are called Joss-houses—evidently from the Portuguese Dios. The word gentoo,[2] like that of pagoda, is also, I believe, entirely of European origin; but though much used by Orme[3] and other writers on India, I do not think it is anywhere a current word in that country, even amongst the English. I have indeed heard the name of Gentoos applied to the athletic race of palankeen-bearers who belong to a district north of Madras. They are naturally drawn to the presidency, which is the most wealthy spot in the country, just as the gallegoes of the north-west of Spain are drawn to Lisbon and other large cities of the European Peninsula; or like the hardy race of Pats and Donalds of our own country, to the rich foci of London and Edinburgh.

When travelling dawk or post, the same set of men will rattle you along for about twenty miles, without stopping, in five or six hours at most; and then, if all things have been well ordered, the palankeen will be transferred to the new set without its being allowed to touch the ground. You pay your bearers at the end of the stage—and it is amusing enough to trace a characteristic resemblance between these Asiatics and an animal apparently so dissimilar to them; I mean an English post-boy, or a French postilion. If you pay them their exact customary due, they make you a profound salam, and are perfectly contented; but if you

[1] [Hind. *Deval*, a temple.]

[2] [Port *Gentio*, gentile, Hindu, as opposed to *Moro*, a Moor or Mahommedan.]

[3] [Author of the standard *History of the Military Transactions of the British Nation in Indostan*, 1763.]

give them a single fanam over and above their allowance, they instantly smoke you to be a griffin, or an ignoramous, or both, and, therefore, fair game for plucking. So they either begin to beg for more money, or petition for a sheep for supper—their choicest feast—for they are not of the Banyan[1] race, who eat no animal food. They also exhibit such wretched looks of supplication, and make so many signals of starvation, that your purse opens even if your heart does not, and at last you yield to their much importunity. Here, however, the comparison with the post-boy ceases; for if you give him an expressly extra shilling, or a mug of ale to warm him, he drinks your honour's health, and looks pleased. But I never once contrived, by any stretch of over-payment, to extort or bribe a smile out of the palankeen-bearers of India. On the contrary, the more you give, the more discontented they look; alternately eyeing the cash and the road travelled over, and then, after glancing sulkily at one another in the most provoking style possible, they silently turn about and march off.

There is a current Joe Miller story in the East, of a gentleman who laid and lost a bet, that he would not only satisfy but astonish his bearers, whom he had taken only ten miles. In order to make sure, as he supposed, he gave them, besides their pay, a whole pagoda as a gratuity, being more than double their hire. They stood stock still, however—turned the piece of gold over in their hands, as if it had been a base coin;—and at length, with that dissatisfied tone and manner with which people so often shipwreck their prospects, by substituting the word claim for the word favour, they whined out, "Perhaps master will give us a sheep!"

I have mentioned that the travelling is generally at night; and, I believe, it is so stipulated, when you are moving with only one set of bearers, that they shall be

[1] [Hindu. *Vani*, the trading class of Gujarat.]

allowed the entire choice of the hours of motion and rest. When the bearers are posted on the road there is no necessity for this limitation; and the secret of agreeable travelling appears to lie chiefly in contriving to reach some military or civil station about the hour of breakfast, tiffin, or dinner. I have mentioned before, that I carried no letters of introduction with me, but trusted entirely to the habitual hospitality of the authorities scattered over the country, nor was I ever disappointed. I remember, one morning at sunrise, coming in sight of Nundydroog,[1] perhaps the most remarkable of those huge round-backed hill forts for which India is celebrated. It looks like a considerable mountain; for though only twelve hundred feet high, it rises so abruptly from the plain, that it appears double its real altitude. The morning air was cold and clear, and all things about us lay glistening with dew, which had settled on every leaf and every blade of grass, during one of those serene and starlight evenings, of which the month of October boasts, I think more than any other in the whole year. This applies to almost all parts of the northern hemisphere which I have visited, from the Missouri to the Yellow Sea.

Between the fort of Nundydroog and the rising ground on which we stopped to view the prospect, there extended a valley some six or eight miles across, the whole bottom of which was marked with a succession of artificial tanks, used for irrigating myriads of rice-fields lying below the level of these huge ponds. But as the best specimens of the picturesque and beautiful, or useful, always stand but a poor chance against the claims of a sharp-set appetite, I urged my fellows to jog on merrily, in hopes of reaching the military station in time for the commandant's breakfast; and,

[1] ["The fort of the Bull," once a stronghold of Tipu Sultan, from whom it was captured by General Meadows, October 19, 1791, and now a hill-station for the inhabitants of Bangalore.]

instead of admiring the landscape, I kept feasting my imagination all the way with visions of rich curries and hot rolls, and almost fancied I could snuff at a league's distance the aromatic perfumes of the delicious hookah.

"How shall I attack the commandant?" said I to myself; "for I have no letter to him, neither know I my future friend's name, nor even his rank."

As we entered the suburbs we fell in with a sepoy, of whom I asked whereabouts the commanding officer's house lay? "That is Captain Dowglas's house," he said, pointing to a bungalow near us. So in my bearers trotted without more ado, snorting and groaning with a double dose of yells, as if they had an inkling of my being an unbidden guest, and wished to give timely warning that a stranger was approaching. The owner of the mansion came forward in his white jacket to receive me.

"Sir," said I, to the commandant, "I am an officer of Sir Samuel Hood's ship, travelling towards Mysore, and I have done myself the honour of waiting upon you with my passport."

"Have you breakfasted?" was the characteristic reply, as he unfolded the paper and glanced slightly over it to learn my name. On my saying that I had not, he called out, "Boy! let us have breakfast instantly; put the palankeen into the verandah: we have a good deal to shew you here, and there are some pleasant people, whom I shall be glad to introduce to you."

My host, I found, had been seventeen years in India; and it was pleasant to be able to give him, in return for his hospitality, a budget of news from Antrim and Belfast. By and by several of his brother officers, and some of his friends in the civil service, came dropping in, all as anxious to be useful to the stranger in his researches, as if they had known him for years. I thus soon felt myself completely at home. A young officer accompanied me next day to the rock;

and as I had previously been "reading up", or cramming myself with the histories of Orme, Wilks,[1] and Dirom,[2] I surprised my friend by the minuteness of my knowledge of all the technicalities and the military events. What interested me, however, fully as much as the traces of Lord Conwallis's siege and unsuccessful storming of the fort of Nundydroog in 1792, was the view from the top of the rock, and particularly the sight of a vast number of those extraordinary tanks, or artificial ponds, for irrigating the rice-fields for which that part of the peninsula is so remarkable.

The table-land of Mysore, which stands several thousand feet above the level of the sea, is not strictly a flat plain, as the name would seem to imply; neither is it mountainous, or even very hilly; and yet the surface is extremely uneven, being moulded into gently sloping ridges, which form between them a succession of long valleys slightly inclined, broad and shallow, and winding about in all directions. Across almost every one of these valleys the natives have thrown embankments, some of them of very ancient date, though some are even so recent as the dynasty of Hyder. These walls, or bunds, as they are called, are made of considerable strength, and when of small extent, they generally curve upwards, so as to offer their convex side to the pressure of the water; but if they be a mile or several miles in length, the embankments assume a waving, snake-like shape, in what particular view I know not, but I suppose from some idea of strength. One valley was pointed out to me, which might be about a mile broad and forty miles long from end to end: this included between thirty and forty tanks, some large

[1] [Colonel Mark Wilks, Resident of Mysore, 1803-8, and author of *Historical Sketches of the South of India*, 3 vols., 1810-17, a classic of its kind.]

[2] [Author of *Narrative of the Campaign in India which Terminated the War with Tippoo Sultan in 1792*.]

and some small, every square yard of the intermediate space between the bunds being richly cultivated, while the surrounding country appeared to be condemned to nearly perennial sterility; indeed, I believe that almost the whole rice crop of Mysore is derived from artificial irrigation.

This vast supply of water is gained partly by the method of tanks just described, and partly by tapping the Cauvery and other rivers by means of subaqueous dams, called annicuts, built, during the dry season, diagonally across the bed of the stream. The effect of these dams is to direct a portion of the river into lateral trenches stretching far and wide over the country. From these it is again drawn off to water the rice-fields. I remember hearing a traveller describe the manner in which the greater river Indus is tapped, or drawn off in this manner to the right and left, for the purposes of agriculture, till the unhappy river is sometimes fairly exhausted, and its channel left dry! One is so much accustomed to consider the mighty mass of waters forming a river of any magnitude as something beyond the power of man to control, that it requires good evidence to satisfy our incredulity on this point. But if the Indus, in the districts alluded to, resemble the Mississippi and many other streams flowing over extensive alluvial countries, there need be no difficulty in conceiving such a transfer of the whole of its waters from the ordinary bed of the stream to the fields on either side; because rivers which traverse deltas almost invariably flow along the summits of ridges somewhat higher than the adjacent country. These ridges, it is true, are so wide and flat, that their elevation at most places can scarcely be detected by the eye; but still the inclination of their sides is abundantly sufficient to admit of water draining away from, instead of flowing towards the river.

The Chauvery, after traversing the Mysore country,

and forming, by one of its fantastic loops, the celebrated island of Seringapatam, is precipitated, over the edge of the table-land, into the Carnatic, in a series of magnificent falls, which I visited in the course of my journey. It then flows along quietly to the sea, past Trichinopoly and Tanjore, and joins the sea near Tranquebar. During the fierce struggles between the French and English in the south of India, the embankments of the river Cauvery were frequently cut, and the whole country, in consequence, laid under water. To explain this, it must be mentioned, that as rivers which run along deltas, or along ground nearly level, are liable to flow over their banks during the rainy season, it becomes necessary, in order to prevent the country being inundated, to raise walls or embankments to confine the stream. These [which are called in Louisiana, levées, in India, bunds,] being raised a little higher than the surface of the river at its highest, confine the stream within proper limits. But as the floods of each successive year bring down a prodigious mass of gravel and sand—the wear and tear of the mountains, fields, and forests, through which the tributary streams have passed—a certain portion of the largest and heaviest of these materials must subside, and remain at the bottom when the river reaches the low grounds, where its rate of motion is much diminished. This addition, though it be small in any one year, gradually raises the bed of the river. If this rise were not carefully met by a correspondent annual elevation of the artificial embankment, it is obvious that the water, in the course of time, would periodically flow over and submerge the country. The consequence of these alternate struggles between the waters trying to escape and man insisting upon confining them, has been to lift the whole body of the Cauvery in its passage across the Carnatic several feet above the highest level of the surrounding country. The power of deluging the adjacent district was, therefore, a very obvious though a dreadful weapon in the hands of whichever party held possession of the banks during those formidable wars in which the French and English contended for the sovereignty of Hindustan. In the long period of peaceful and secure repose which those regions have enjoyed since the contest has been terminated by the unquestioned supremacy of one party, the supply of water, so curiously raised into the air, has been appropriated exclusively to the irrigation of the country.

In the upper lands of Mysore, the peasants are dependent chiefly on their tanks for moisture, as the rains are uncertain in quantity, and transient in their effects. The stock of water collected in these numberless and extensive tanks or ponds, many of which well deserve the name of lakes, is capable of being distributed in the precise quantity and at the precise times required. I have often been amused at observing with what scrupulous care the persons appointed to distribute the water let it off from these magnificent reservoirs. The thirsty soil of Mysore, parched and riven by the heat, drinks up the fluid with a grateful kind of relish, a sort of animated enjoyment, at which I was never tired of looking.

In describing things which lie so much out of the ordinary course of observation, one becomes sensible of the poverty of language. Thus the word "Tank" suggests to most people the idea of a common cistern attached to a dwelling-house, and filled with rain-water from pipes along the roof. The word "Pond", again recalls images of muddy water, draggled post-horses, rank weeks, and a combined fleet of ducks and geese engaged in common warfare against frogs and worms. To call the tanks of Mysore by the name of lakes would be nearer the mark, for many of them well deserve that appellation. The Moota Talou[1] for example, or Rich

[1] [*Moti Talao,* Pearl Tank.]

Tank, near Seringapatam, I understand, is nearly thirty miles in circumference. I never saw that particular sheet of water ; but many of the artificial lakes which I did examine measured six, eight, and ten miles round; and so vast are their numbers, that I remember counting considerably more than a hundred at one view from the top of Nundydroog, nor do I believe that the least of these could have been less than two or three miles in circuit.

Dr. Buchanan,[1] in his journey through those countries, made by order of Lord Wellesley in 1800, shortly after the capture of Seringapatam, describes minutely the formation of these tanks, or Erays, as they are called in the Tamul language. The Symbrumbacum Tank, not far from Madras, he says, is eight miles in length by three in width, and its contents are sufficient to supply with water the lands of thirty-two villages for eighteen months, supposing the usual rains to fail.

I have mentioned the manner in which a traveller in India may get a breakfast or dinner, bed, board, lodging, and troops of friends, when he happens to be near any military or civil station of the East India Company. But it will sometimes fall out that he cannot exactly nick the hour of breakfast or dinner, and then he must trust to his own wits and those of his bearers. Such, however, is the style of doing things in that fertile and populous country, that he must be a sorry traveller indeed who need ever experience any real difficulty on this score. I remember enjoying many of these campaigning kind of meals, almost as much as I did the premeditated luxuries of the Residencies, and other head stations of the interior—those true palaces of enjoyment, wherein we find all that plenty, good taste, a fine climate, and hospitality grown into a habit, can produce.

[1] [Dr. Francis Buchanan, author of *A Journey through Mysore, Canara, and Malabar*, 3 vols., 1807.]

PALANKEEN TRAVELLING

After a night's run, in a part of the country remote from an English station, and just as the day is beginning to dawn, the weary bearers look out for some village on the road. Instead of entering it, they make for the little grove or tope, which marks the position of the pagoda and tank always to be found near a native village. The palankeen is then set down under the most shady tree which is to be found near these cherished nooks. The traveller, if not awake before, is, of course, roused by the grating sound of the palankeen on the ground. He steps out in his slippers and sleeping trousers, and speedily plunging into the clear pool, proceeds, after a good swim, to make his toilet, with his shaving apparatus, glass, and basin, ranged on the top of his movable house.

While he is thus engaged, one of the bearers on the opposite side of the palankeen takes out the blankets, sheets, and pillows, to give them a good shaking, and after the interior has been well swept out, to arrange all things for day travelling, by stowing away the night furniture, hanging up the back cushion, and placing the footrest across. A couple of the men are likewise dispatched to the village for milk and eggs; and if, by good fortune, there be a running-stream near, they may bring a newly-caught fish. By the time these foragers have returned, a fire has been kindled, the little kettle set a-boiling, and the tea made. The eggs are then put on, the fish split and grilled on the embers, and the milk heated. Countless slices of toast are now prepared in rapid succession; and the nipping morning air having quickened the hungry edge of the traveller's appetite, he casts himself on the corner of his cloak, spread out for a table-cloth, and feasts away right joyously.

CHAPTER X

The Dessera Festival at Mysore[1]

I THINK I have already mentioned, that little or no intercourse of a domestic nature takes place between the natives of India and the Europeans resident among them. The habits, in fact, of the two races of men are so dissimilar in all respects, that it is scarcely possible to conceive much agreeable or useful association. Some missionaries, indeed, by adopting the dress and language of the people, and by conforming to all their customs, have succeeded in domesticating themselves with the Hindoos; but the great points they aimed at were little, if at all, accomplished by such unwonted degradation—for it is a degradation—and, what is more to the purpose, has always been so considered by the natives. Curiosity may be gratified by such an experiment, but nothing more. The taste, even of a very coarse-minded European, must revolt at usages so foreign to his ideas of delicacy; and the influence which he might readily acquire by other means, more consistent with his own station, must vanish under this sort of condescension. The Abbé du Bois,[2] and others, furnish us with enough, and more than enough, of the details of the private life of this singular people; and I can safely refer the curious in such matters to the

[1] [The *Dasara* is a great Hindu festival, lasting for ten days, held in the month Asvin [October] at the end of the rains. Under the old Hindu Raj, great military reviews and parades were held on this day, as the troops were then moved out of winter-quarters, the campaigning season having now commenced.]

[2] [The celebrated French missionary, who, having passed his life among the Hindus of Southern India, wrote *Hindu Manners, Customs and Ceremonies* (Moeurs, Institutions et Cérémonies du peuple de 'Inde) 1817, which has now become a classic.]

THE RAJAH OF MYSORE IN HIS STATE CARRIAGE

[face p. 193

Rev. W. Ward's[1] book on the history, literature, mythology, manners, and customs of the Hindoos.

The usages of savage life in the cold regions of the world, for example of the Esquimaux or the Cherokees, are essentially revolting in every shape, whether in reality or in description. Pretty nearly the same thing may be said of the domestic manners of the Asiatics, which are only less disagreeable to us, I suspect, from their being unaccompanied by the misery and filth which belong peculiarly to cold climates. The Hindoo, who is eternally bathing his person, cleaning his house, and scouring his brass kettles, casts over his shoulders his light and graceful wrapper, as white as snow; while your western savage would consider it a disgrace to wash his hands. The Esquimaux, after gorging himself with the raw flesh of a seal, draws the monster's skin round him, and goes to sleep in the mud. In this case, as there occurs nothing but what is disgusting, we dismiss the subject as speedily as we can without a wish to see or hear more of it. In truth though these savages be human in form and speech they seem so close to the brute creation, that any sympathy with them is out of the question.

It is so far different with the Orientals, whose civilisation, in some respects, is considerable. Our wonder, indeed, is often excited by the most anomalous mixture of pure barbarisms with refinements of a high order. The institution of castes, and the rigorous ceremonial discipline which it imposes, appear fatal to any improvement in manners, by rigidly defining the course of every action. The utter extravagance, also, and measureless absurdity of their superstitions, which pervade every thought, word, and deed of their lives,

[1] [*A View of the History, Literature and Religion of the Hindoos.* Serampore, 1811. Carey, Ward and Marshman were the famous trio who established the fame of the celebrated Baptist Mission of Serampore in the early part of the last century.]

seem effectually to place a bar against amelioration in that quarter. What time and change of political circumstances may bring about, it is difficult, if not impossible, to say.

The public festivals, and other out-of-door habits of the Hindoos, however, do certainly include some points of transient interest. But they are so entirely without taste or fancy, that the attention of a European becomes fatigued, as soon as his mere curiosity is satisfied. I remember experiencing this process in the interior of the South of India on two different occasions, between which an interval of more than a year elapsed. My headquarters, in both cases, was the British resident's house, or residency, at Mysore, a town about ten miles from Seringapatam. The country of Mysore, after we had conquered it from Tippoo, was restored by us, as I have already mentioned, to the original native dynasty of the Hindoos. As a measure of precaution, however, we retained the island of Seringapatam,[1] in the river Cauvery, garrisoned it, and kept the British flag flying on the forts. It was stipulated, also, that a subsidiary force, consisting of several thousand men, partly European and partly native, but all officered by English, and under the command of a general officer, should be maintained by the Company, in the heart of the country. The object of this subsidiary force [so called from a subsidy being

[1] [This famous fortress, the capital of Haidar Ali and Tipu Sultan, lies on an island in the Cauvery, about 77 miles from Bangalore. It was twice taken by the British, in 1792, and again by storm in 1799, when Tipu fell in the breach. The old Hindu *raj* was then restored in the person of Sri Krishna Raja Wodeyar, a boy of five years of age, who was supervised by the celebrated Diwan or Prime Minister Ramrao Purnia. Ten years later, the young raja dismissed his minister and, as we may well expect from reading Basil Hall's account, entered upon a life of extravagant misrule, which led to his deposition by Lord Bentinck in 1832. Lord Ripon restored the kingdom in 1881.]

paid by the native power to maintain it,] was to prevent invasions from abroad, and also to render it unnecessary for the Hindoo government to keep an army in the field. The civil administration, however, of the country, the collection of the revenue, the execution of the laws, the appointment to office—in short, every detail of government, was left in the hands of the native rulers. In order to secure compliance with the various stipulations of the treaty, re-establishing the Hindoo dynasty on the throne of Mysore, a British resident was appointed to live at or near the court, to watch what was going on, and, in case of need, to interfere by remonstrance, or, in extreme cases, by force.

This was certainly not independence, nor was it intended to be so. It was essential to our political existence in India, that we should retain a preponderating influence in Mysore, and other countries similarly circumstanced; but the same course of measures which secured our authority, afforded peace, security, and, it was hoped, contentment to the great mass of the nation. That some of the chiefs should sigh for more uncontrolled authority, according to the despotic customs of the East, is not to be wondered at, nor ought it to be disregarded; on the contrary, it requires the greatest delicacy of treatment on our part to keep them in tolerable good humour. Sir John Malcolm[1] well remarks on this subject, that "while we are supported by the good opinion of the lower and middling classes, to whom our government is indulgent, our power has received the rudest shocks, from an impression that our system of rule is at variance with the

[1] [*Sir John Malcolm*, 1769-1833, was a famous Persian scholar, diplomatist, and soldier. He went on three diplomatic missions to Persia, was secretary to Lord Wellesley, served with distinction in the Maratha wars in the Deccan and subsequent settlement, and wrote a *History of Persia*, now a classic, a *Memoir on Central India*, a Life of Clive, and other works.]

permanence of rank, authority, and distinction in any native of India. This belief," he adds, "which is not without foundation, is general to every class, and its action leaves but a feverish existence to all who enjoy station and high name. The feeling which their condition excites, exposes those who have left to them any portion of power and independence, to the arts of the discontented, the turbulent, and the ambitious. This is a danger to our power which must increase in the ratio of its extent, unless we counteract its operation by a commensurate improvement of our administration."—*Central India*, Appendix, No. XVIII. p. 434.

As the British resident, of course, wished to keep on the best terms, personally, with the native ruler near whose court he was stationed, he introduced, on all occasions of ceremony, such private friends as might chance to be living with him; and the Rajah, on his part, was no less careful to mark, by his reception of such guests, the high consideration in which he held the officer appointed to watch him. Both parties might, at heart, be hating one another like cat and dog; but none of this came to the surface, for your Asiatic, like a Spaniard, knows well how to be courteous under almost every trial of temper.

I had the good fortune to arrive at Mysore during the Dessera feast, a celebrated Hindoo festival in honour of Shiva, and known to the natives by the name of "Nuwwee Rátree," or nine nights—though the word Dessera means "tenth." I lost the first four days, but I saw more than enough in the last five to satisfy me. The Rajah's palace, in the fort of Mysore, lay at the distance of half a mile from the British residency, from which the resident and his suite set out generally about four o'clock in the afternoon. It was not considered etiquette to move till we had been summoned by a message from the Rajah, stating that he was ready to receive us. As soon as the order to march was given, off we scampered to the door; and, while some of us flung ourselves into the palankeens, others mounted their horses, and the whole moved along as fast as the crowd would permit. The bearers set off at a full run, shouting and screaming as usual, and preceded by about fifty men carrying spears in their hands fourteen feet along. At the head of the procession, a fellow, blessed with powerful lungs, sounded a long slightly curved sort of trumpet, called a colleroy horn,[1] to announce the resident's approach. The blast sent forth by this wild instrument rang far over the plain with a note such as I never heard before, rising towards its close into a pitch of shrillness which pierced the head from ear to ear. As we rushed along towards the gate of the fort, the palankeens, to the number of a dozen or twenty, frequently came into smart collision with one another. As the road contracted, there remained only room for three abreast; but, as all seemed equally anxious to get in first, the mêlée became trying enough for those who possessed weak nerves. Besides our own party and immediate attendants, there pranced along the resident's body-guard of troops, and many hundreds of native horsemen —all struggling for admission, and casting up clouds of dust as high as the topmost pinnacle of the adjacent pagoda—every man shouting, screaming, and jostling, apparently trying who should make most noise, and occasion most disorder.

Within the gate, a little more room was found; and the apprehension of being upset and trodden under foot diminished for a time; but the row and risk proved even worse as we entered the quadrangular court of the palace, in the centre of which the ring for wild

[1] [A long brass horn with a hideous note, used at Hindu funerals and festivals. The name was corrupted, by an amusing "Hobson Jobson," into *Cholera Horn*. It may be derived from Tamil *kallar*, thief, being used to scare thieves or give warning of their approach.]

beast baiting was fixed. On the outside of the ropes such a dense mass of the multitude were jammed, that the poor Sepoy guards stationed there to keep a lane clear for us to pass, could with great difficulty obtain an opening barely large enough for two of the party. Into this narrow strait, however, four or five palankeens used to make a determined rush together; and, on one occasion, such was the momentum of their charge, that both the protecting lines of soldiers were toppled down exactly in the fashion of the child's play at cards, known by the title of Jack sent for Mustard. The palankeens were instantly closed upon by the crowd, like the hosts of Pharaoh when the Red Sea collapsed upon them; but, in spite of the chance of being squeezed to death, it was impossible for us not to laugh. I can remember to this minute the shout which a merry countryman of mine set up—o'ertopping all but the skirl, as he called it, of the colleroy horn.

On reaching the inner side of the palace square, we rolled out of our palankeens dusted over like millers, at the bottom of the stairs, where the resident was received by the prime minister or dewan, Ram Row by name and another high officer of state, whose name and station I forget. It appeared to be the practice first to make salam to these functionaries, and then to shake hands with them—ceremonies, doubtless, typical of the mixed nature of a subsidiary government—half native, half English. As soon as we had all been received, the resident and the dewan—unquestionably the two most important men of the country, and the real managers of all public affairs—moved on, while we followed upstairs according to our rank and consequence, such as it was. At the top, we entered a long gallery, or verandah, open towards the court. A row of pillars in front sustained a low roof, richly gilt, and gaudily painted with flowers; to match which a brilliant set of cotton carpets had been spread under foot—so gay, indeed, that one felt it almost a shame to tread upon them.

In the middle of the front row sat his highness the Maha Rajah, Kistna Rajee Oudaveer, on a throne formed exclusively of gold, silver, and ivory. This gorgeous seat was shaded by a canopy of similar materials, supported by four polished steel pillars, and festooned round its edge with such strings of such pearls as might have drawn sighs from a dozen grand duchesses. On the top of all sat a bird, composed, as it seemed to our dazzled view, entirely of precious stones, the eyes sparkling to the life, being two diamonds of a brilliancy far surpassing all the rest.

It was more satisfactory than I can well describe, to behold the Rajah thus rigged out in the very garb which youthful imaginations bestow upon all monarchs, but in which, to the mortification of many a youth and many a maid, few monarchs actually exhibit themselves. Except, indeed, in the shop of Messrs. Rundell and Bridge, so many jewels are rarely to be seen collected in one space; at least, I never but once beheld such a load of riches on the person of any individual. In the front part of his Hindoo highness's turban blazed a battery of diamonds, twice as large as the splendid ornament which most of the present generation may remember to have seen on the forehead of that great Ranee, or queen of song, Catalani, valued at ten thousand guineas. From the right side of the Rajah's turban rose a curved pedestal of gold, from the projecting part of which hung down a cluster of enormous pearls, on different strings, forming a bunch larger than one hand could grasp. This weight of wealth gave his majesty a slight "list to starboard," but, as one of our party remarked, a man might be content to go with a crick in his neck for the remainder of his life, in consideration of the honour and glory of such ballast. Our royal host, however, was also pretty well weighted below, for over his neck and shoulders he had cast about a dozen chaplets of precious stones, some of them reaching to his middle, and others clasping his throat. From each ear was suspended a thick ring of virgin gold fully three inches in diameter, carrying a huge ruby, sparkling above all the other jewels which loaded his person. To his left arm, from the wrist to the elbow, there appeared to be fitted a broad gold plate, like a piece of armour; but what its purpose might be we knew not. On each day of the festival, the Rajah's turban and his robes were different: one day his tunic consisted of a white ground, with small red spots; another day it was entirely red; and on a third, the whole consisted of gold cloth. But the jewels seemed to be the same on each day, and thence our inference was, that the whole stock of "barbaric pearl and gold" belonging to the crown of Mysore, was produced on these occasions.

On entering the gallery, we marched up in a row to the foot of the musnud or throne, salaming all the way; and, after shaking hands with his highness and salaming again, we backed away stern foremost, exactly as in European courts, to the seats assigned for us in the first row. The space behind us, between our chairs and the wall, was occupied by the sovereign's family and officers. Close to the Rajah on the right hand, sat the Dewan, the British resident on his left, and then various near relatives and official folks—not to mention two attendants of high rank, whose sole business appeared to consist in popping into his highness's mouth, from time to time, the proper portion of betel-nut!

I forget exactly at what stage of the interview an officer of the household, dispatched by the Rajah, came along the line and cast over our necks a chaplet of white flowers, each person, of course, rising and salaming towards the throne as this high honour was conferred upon him. Next followed an attendant bearing a silver dish, on which were laid some bits of betel-nut, with a few leaves, and the proper proportion of lime to chew with them. Some of the party did actually go through this ceremony—on the principle, I suppose, of Captain Cook, who ate and drank everything. I have sometimes, by the way, thought, in reading the accounts of our great voyager, that he must have been blessed with the stomach of an ostrich, to whom spike-nails are no harder of digestion than asparagus, as is said and believed on board ship! Close behind the betel-nut bearer, came an attendant with a tray of small nosegays, followed by a boy with a bottle of highly perfumed oil, one drop of which he bestowed on each bunch of flowers, thus literally "adding a perfume to the violet."

Last of all came a most important personage, whose office everyone could appreciate. The business of this welcome messenger consisted in throwing a pair of the finest cashmere shawls over each of our shoulders! Never shall I forget the effect which this present produced on my mind and feelings. Up to that moment I had been in the habit of thinking as ill as possible of the Rajah of Mysore; and, with the ready indiscretion of youth, and all the confidence of recently acquired and partial knowledge, had never failed to state in company, without any measure in the terms, that the government of his highness Sree Kistna was most oppressive. But ever since feeling the delicate pressure of these beautiful shawls, I have been unable to bring myself to say one word against the giver.

The East India Company very judiciously take care that none of their servants shall be exposed to such temptations; for every present whatsoever, given to any officer, civil or military, in their employ, must immediately afterwards be handed over to a person appointed to receive it. An exact equivalent being, as a matter of course, presently returned, in some shape or other, to the treasury of the Rajah, Sultan, or other native authority who gave the present. As I was not within reach of this provoking ordinance, I was allowed to keep my pair of shawls, and though rather the worse for twenty years' wear, they still figure on the necks of some fair friends of mine at home.

Many a time have I witnessed the intense mortification of the wives of the East India Company's servants, on their being obliged to relinquish the beautiful presents which they and their husbands brought home from the Durbar. I remember once seeing, or thinking that I saw, a tear or two drop and mingle with a handful of pearls which a lady was in the act of returning, according to regulation.

"Why!" said I to her, "what does it matter? What could you do with the jewels here? You have no society amongst whom you could desire to wear such valuable ornaments?"

"No," she replied, "that is very true; but my two poor girls at home, whom I have not seen for these three long, long years, would look so becoming in them!" And then the mother's tears flowed fast and in earnest, as she thought of her children, between whom and her rolled ten thousand miles of sea!

The Rajah having ordered the sports to commence, we turned our eyes to the area below with much curiosity, to see what should first happen. In the middle of the great square, an enclosure or ring, about thirty or forty yards across, had been formed by means of a double line of posts, ten feet apart, and ten feet high, over which was cast a strong netting, forming a secure wall of ropes, but so loose that it hung in folds to the ground. The populace filled the rest of the square, along with the guards, some mounted, some on foot, and I am afraid to say how many elephants there might be—twenty or thirty, at the least, together with numerous bodies of policemen bearing long poles with flags at the end. These, I presume, were intended for show; but another set carried immense long whips, with which the sovereign people were kept from pressing in too great numbers upon the ropes. A dozen native bands of music, consisting of sharp sounding drums, and a number of shrill pipes, resembling in squeak that of our penny trumpets, only most painfully louder, and all playing at once, grievously disturbed us during the whole exhibition.

One one side of the space within the ring two beautiful leopards stood chained to separate posts. As these animals had been caught in the jungle the day before, nothing could be more sleek and glossy than their coats. Near these noble beasts, as if in contrast, were turned in, quite loose, two jackasses, each of which drew behind him, tied to his tail, a globular empty leathern bottle, called, I think, a dubbah, about as large as a man could grasp in his arms. Into these machines a handful of gravel or dried peas had been inserted, to make a noise as the poor donkeys moved about. On the other side of the arena two painted wooden figures of men were placed in a leaning posture against stakes fastened in the ground.

Exactly opposite to the Rajah, at the further side of the ring, a huge cage, composed of strong wooden bars, had been wheeled close to the ropes. A door on that side of the cage which faced us being now drawn up, we discovered a large royal tiger sitting in the attitude of the sphinx, apparently all ready for a spring. He looked exceedingly fierce, and no wonder, for the poor wretch had been kept with little or no food ever since his capture in a pitfall in one of the great teak forests of the Malabar Ghauts upwards of two days before. The royal animal seemed very ill disposed to afford sport to folks who had treated him so uncourteously, for not an inch would he budge even when the netting was drawn up, and a clear course opened for him into the ring.

Perhaps he felt alarmed at the dreadful hullabaloo of so many thousands of people bawling out, drums beating, and horns sounding, rows of elephants tossing up their trunks, and horses snorting and prancing all round. Possibly, too, he might not have felt much tempted by the dainty company of the jackasses with their bottles of peas. At all events, no poking of sticks or thumping on the cage could make him start tack or sheet, till his hind-quarters were blown up by a handful of squibs and crackers cast into his den.

The instant the explosion took place the tiger gave a tremendous roar, and sprung forwards with great violence into the circle, where he stopped suddenly, and then glared his eyes round and round with a most suspicious scowl. After surveying the ground for a few seconds, he turned tail, and, in a most cowardly fashion, ran back; but observing the door of his den closed, he swerved on one side, and leaped with prodigious violence against the ropes. Had the cords not been left so loose that his force became expended before they were drawn tight, I verily believe he might have broken through the meshes, or pulled down some of the posts. Instead of this he merely got entangled with the lines, and losing all his patience, if he ever possessed any, he raged and roared, lashing his tail about in the most furious style till he got free. Then turning round, he shot across the area like a congreve rocket, and after making an immense cat-like spring, pounced upon one of the mock figures of men, the head of which he twisted off in an instant. During this proceeding he gave utterance to a fierce growl, or murmur of satisfaction, enough to make one's blood run cold. As soon as he detected the trick, he first flung the head violently from him, and tore the figure all to pieces with his claws, then made another attempt to break through the enclosure, but with no better success than at first.

I really thought at one time he would have effected

his escape, by climbing over at the place where his cage stood. Both his fore paws were actually on the roof, and, with no great struggle, he might have gained the top, from whence his leap into the midst of the crowd must have produced a pretty tolerable sensation, I guess! Fortunately, a courageous little boy, about twelve years old, who had perched himself on the cage to see the fun, stood quite firm when all his older companions scattered to the right and left, in terror of the tiger's open jaws close to them. This bold young fellow held in his hand a short, stout club, and the instant the tiger showed himself above the ropes, he lent him such a sound rap on the nose, that the animal fell back again into the enclosure, heels over head, with a sort of inverted somerset. While a shout of applause rung over the whole space, an old Mahometan soldier, an officer of the extinct dynasty, remarked to us in a whisper, that this exploit was just the sort of thing which his former master, Hyder Ali, might have been expected to do in his youth.

The baffled tiger now attacked the other figure of a man, and wrenched off his head as he had done that of the other; but instead of getting into a passion, as he had done on the first occasion, when he discovered the cheat, he stood perfectly still, with his tail on the ground his head drooped and turned away from the figure, as if he felt ashamed of having been twice deceived. In this attitude he remained several minutes, with his eyes half closed, slightly moving his head from side to side; after which he deliberately laid himself down. A dozen yelping dogs were now turned in, some of which prudently contented themselves with taking a distant look at the royal beast. Not one of them approached him except an English greyhound, and even he was not such a fool as to press matters too far, but merely barked and snarled; once or twice he came so close to the tiger's nose that we wondered the monster had not laid his paw upon him, and crushed him at a blow. Meanwhile, the rest of the dogs, in a body, attacked one of the chained-up leopards—a most unfair contest; but as he had the good fortune to catch one of them on the hip, he gave such evidence of his capacity, that the barkers, leaving the nobler game, one and all scampered off in chase of the donkeys. These poor beasts, terrified by the sound of the bottles at their tails, and worried by the dogs, were soon dragged to the ground, after which a distant action was recommenced against the leopards, with no results, as military men express it.

By this time, probably the Rajah, and certainly his company, were pretty well tired of so much nonsense; and his highness, turning to one of his courtiers, desired him to go down to the court with a bow and arrow which was handed to him. The officer descended accordingly, and having passed round to that side of the ring where the tiger lay, very deliberately shot an arrow at the unoffending animal. He immediately sprang at the ropes; but upon receiving another arrow in his breast, the poor creature fell back, and stood looking reproachfully at his opponent. This gave the unconcerned courtier time to draw a third arrow from his quiver, and so on, till the wretched beast was literally bristled all over like a porcupine; yet, to our great surprise, he still kept his feet. As the arrows pierced his side, he merely turned round his head, and broke them off with his mouth, leaving the barb far within. We observed one arrow pass clean through his body from side to side, and could not but remember the old song of Chevy Chase, where the grey goose-quill, a cloth yard long, is wet with the heart's blood of a warrior. As nothing could be more disagreeable than this method of putting so noble an animal to death, some of us sent up a petition to the Rajah, that one of the party might be allowed to go down for the purpose of despatching him *à l'Anglaise*. This favour was readily granted ; and it was curious to observe how instantaneous death followed the passage of a single musket-ball, though eight or ten arrows had already gone through and through him without producing any visible effect.

Persons who have only seen those beasts which are called [ironically, I suppose,] wild, though the tamest and most docile of God's creatures, can form but an imperfect idea of the beauty of the skin and the nobleness of the air of those truly wild inhabitants of the tropical forests, thus inhumanly "butchered to make an Indian holiday." We had a good opportunity of studying the habits of the tiger at the British residency hard by, where one of the most remarkable specimens of his tribe was kept in the open air. He had been brought as a cub from the jungle a year or two before, and being placed in a cage as large as an ordinary English parlour, in the centre of the stable-yard, had plenty of room to leap about and enjoy the high feeding in which he was indulged. He devoured regularly one sheep per day, with any other extra bits of meat that happened to be disposable. A sheep in India is rather smaller—say ten per cent—less than our Welsh mutton ; so this was no great meat for a tiger four feet high. The young hands at the residency used to plague him occasionally, till he became infuriated, and dashed with all his force against the bars, roaring so loud that the horses in the surrounding stables trembled and neighed in great alarm. Indeed, it was very difficult even for persons who were fully satisfied of the strength of the cage, to stand near it with unmoved nerves. He would soon have made famous mincemeat of half-a-dozen of us could he but have caught the door open for a moment.

But what annoyed him far more than our poking him up with a stick, or tantalising him with shins of beef or legs of mutton, was introducing a mouse into his cage.

No fine lady ever exhibited more terror at the sight of a spider than this magnificent royal tiger betrayed on seeing a mouse. Our mischievous plan was to tie the little animal by a string to the end of a long pole, and thrust it close to the tiger's nose. The moment he saw it he leaped to the opposite side, and when the mouse was made to run near him, he jammed himself into a corner, and stood trembling and roaring in such an ecstasy of fear that we were always obliged to desist from sheer pity to the poor brute. Sometimes we insisted on his passing over the spot where the unconscious little mouse ran backwards and forwards. For a long time, however, we could not get him to move, till at length, I believe by the help of a squib, we obliged him to start ; but instead of pacing leisurely across his den, or making a detour to avoid the object of his alarm, he generally took a kind of flying leap, so high as nearly to bring his back in contact with the roof of his cage !

I heard afterwards, with much regret, that his noblest of tigers had been put to death. One day, a drunken, useless fellow of the soodra caste,[1] the lowest rank amongst the Hindoos, happened to be passing through the court-yard, and not being able to steer very straight, he ran foul of the cage. In the stupidity of his intoxication, he allowed one of his arms to pass between the bars, upon which the tiger, naturally supposing this was an invitation to help himself, snapped off the man's arm in a moment, and before assistance could arrive the man bled to death. The British resident, very properly considering that the feelings of the natives would be outraged if, after such an accident, the animal were permitted to live, ordered him to be shot.

We were promised a grand day's sport one afternoon, when a buffalo and a tiger were to be pitted against each other. The buffalo entered the ring composedly

[1] *Soodra :* [The lowest of the four Hindu castes.]

enough; but after looking about him, turned to one side, and rather pettishly, as if he had felt a little bilious, overturned a vessel of water, placed there expressly for his use. The tiger refused for a long time to make his appearance, and it was not till his den was filled with smoke and fire that he sprang out. The buffalo charged his enemy in a moment, and by one furious push capsized him right over. To our great disappointment, the tiger pocketed this insult in the shabbiest manner imaginable, and passing on, leaped furiously at the ropes, with which his feet became entangled, so that the buffalo was enabled to punish his antagonist about the rump most ingloriously. When at length the tiger got loose, he slunk off to a distant part of the arena, lay down, and pretended to be dead. The boys, however, soon put him up again, and tried to bring him to the scratch with squibs and crackers; and a couple of dozen dogs being introduced at the same moment, they all set at him, but only one ventured to take any liberty with the enraged animal. This bold dog actually caught the tiger by the tail, but a slight pat of the mighty monster's paw crushed the yelping cur as flat as a board. The buffalo, who really appeared anxious to have a fair stand-up fight, now drove the dogs off, and repeatedly poked the tiger with his nose, and even turned him half over several times with his horns.

As the gentleman showed no pluck, the Rajah requested one of us to step down to give him the *coup de grâce*. I accordingly loaded a musket which was placed in my hands, but on reaching the arena I felt rather unwilling to fire, as I just heard a story of a gentleman who, the year before, in firing at one of the animals in the ring by the Rajah's directions, not only shot the animal, but also killed an old woman who stood on the other side of the ring, the ball having continued its course after piercing the tiger's head. On my expressing a wish to try, in the first place, the effect of cold iron upon his tough hide, a very sharp-pointed spear was given me, and I tried with my utmost force to pass it through his hide, but in vain. He rose, however, on being pricked by the steel, and by making a violent effort to clutch my hand, thrust his head fairly through one of the meshes of the net, to my no small dismay. Either the ropes were not very strong, or the seizings weak, for they began to break, and in the next minute, as it appeared to me, the infuriated monster might have forced his whole body through. In this emergency I quite forgot all about humanity and old women, and catching up the musket, placed the muzzle by the piece at the tiger's head, and blew his brains out in a moment.

A more manly, though not a pleasing kind of sport succeeded, in which the Jetties, or native Athletæ, exhibited before us. Mysore is the only part of India, as far as I know, in which these Oriental prize-fighters are still kept up. The Jetties, whose institution is said to be of very ancient origin, constitute in Mysore a distinct caste of persons, trained from their infancy daily in the most laborious exercises, or what we should call gymnastics, but far more varied and extraordinary than any I ever saw in Europe. Whether they spring from a peculiarly handsome stock, or whether it be that the nature of their unremitted exercises develops the beautiful points of the human form, I know not; but certainly nothing except the statues of antiquity go beyond them in symmetry. The beau idéal, if I understand the term correctly, consists in the appropriation and just disposition of the most characteristic forms of each department, selected, not from one or two individual specimens, but from the whole class. Judged by such a severe test, every one of these Jetties would, of course, be found wanting in many respects. But I cannot doubt, on the other hand, that a sculptor or painter in search of materials to fill up, by observation of actual nature, his own conceptions of ideal excellence, would consider the exercising room of these singular people a capital studio. At all events, their attitudes, and even some parts of their limbs, recalled to me so strongly the surpassing wonders of the Elgin marbles, that I went very often to their quarters to see them rehearse.

The Jetties intended for the real combat are brought forward, two at a time, wearing no other dress than a pair of light orange-coloured drawers, extending half-way down the thigh. The right hand of each is furnished with a weapon which may be called a cæstus; for though it is somewhat different, I believe, from the Roman instrument of that name, its object appears pretty nearly similar. Colonel Wilks, in his *History of Mysore*, says it is composed of buffalo horn fitted to the hand, and pointed with four knobs resembling very sharp knuckles, and corresponding to their situation, with a fifth of greater prominence at the end nearest the little finger, and at right angles with the other four. This instrument, if properly placed, would, he conceives, enable a man of ordinary strength to cleave open the head of his adversary at a blow; but the fingers being introduced through the weapon, it is fastened across them at an equal distance between the first and second lower joints, in a situation which does not admit of attempting a severe blow without the risk of dislocating the first joints of all the fingers.

The set-to or battle consists of a mixture of wrestling and boxing, but the head is the only object allowed by the rules of the ring in India to be aimed at. The Jetties are led into the arena and placed in front of the Rajah, by the two masters of the fight, always old-stagers, who have fought in their day. The right hands of the two combatants being then held up by the masters, to shew that all is fair, the Rajah nods his approbation, and this is considered a signal to commence. The Jetties may either strike at arm's length, or close and grapple, or, if they can, they may throw each other down—everything, in short, is considered fair, except striking with the cæstus lower than the head. The guards for defence, I have heard persons skilled in boxing say, are all of them extremely good and scientific. These refinements, like the niceties of English boxing and French fencing, are, I need scarcely confess, quite unintelligible to ignorant eyes. However, this be, there is no mistaking the nature of a successful blow, though it often baffles the quickest observation to discover how it was given. Every such cut lays the skin open, rattles smartly on the skull, and sends down a stream of blood from top to toe of the wounded man. This is all very disagreeable, but we were assured never dangerous. The wrestling part of these contests was really admirable, and being unmixed with anything painful, interested us much more than the savage cutting and maiming alluded to. Sometimes the combatants continued for several minutes prancing round a common centre, in attitudes very like those of our boxers, facing one another, each eyeing his antagonist with the utmost intentness, and watching for a favourable opportunity to close with him. During these movements, which frequently recalled to my mind the figures in the Spanish bolero, the fingers of the left hand are kept in perpetual motion, and that arm constantly waved about in the most graceful way possible, the purpose of each fighter being to catch the eye of the other, and so to draw away his attention from the meditated point of attack. The whole muscles of their bodies, at this period of the fight, appeared to be made of highly elastic springs ; for as their feet touched the ground, their bodies rose again into the air, as if they had become actually buoyant.

Suddenly one of the parties, seizing his moment,

rushes in, makes his blow, and having cut a gash into the other's head so deep as to shew for an instant, by a bright white line, that the skull is laid bare, he grapples his antagonist by the shoulders, or clasps him round the body, or even seizes him by the leg, and tries to throw him over. This is by far the most interesting part of the battle. The elasticity of the muscles already alluded to, seems now quite gone, for every fibre appears to have become rigid as a bar of steel. The violent exertion of the limbs swells out the muscles between the joints into firm knobs almost as hard as the buffaloes horn of the cæstus. For a long time the centre of gravity of the two bodies keeps within the well-marked base carved deeply in the sand by their feet during the struggle ; but at length, down they go together with a most formidable crash. It is not always, I took notice, that the wrestler who is undermost comes worst off ; for it frequently happens, that the upper one is obliged to weaken his guard in order to keep the other down, and thus, although he has the superiority in position, he gets many a severe pegging from the armed knuckles of his prostrate antagonist. In this manner they lie rolling about in the sand for a long while, struggling to regain their feet, and occasionally giving each other such blows on the head that they become dreadfully disfigured.

After battling in this way for some time, without any decided advantage on either side, they cast up many petitioning looks to the Rajah, who at length makes a signal for them to desist. The victor if there happens to be an obvious superiority, generally goes off the ground in half-a-dozen somersets, to show his undiminished vigour, as our champions in the prize-ring cast up their hats when they have won and say they are ready for a fresh fight. Meanwhile, the loser puts on a pathetic or wistful look ; and first bending towards the Rajah, makes a low salam towards the lattices, behind which the ladies of the court are seated, so as to view the sport, while they themselves keep out of sight of the profane world. Presents, consisting of gilt or silver armlets, turbans, webs of cloth, and so on, are then thrown down from the throne to the Jetties, upon which the bleeding combatants again prostrate themselves in the dust before the Rajah, and make similar obeisances on both sides of the court to the invisible ladies above.

Immediately after these rather painful exhibitions, were were entertained with stilt dancing by a set of men the soles of whose feet were raised, on slender poles, more than seven feet from the ground. They stalked about amongst the crowd, and in this elevated position went through the whole series of what are called the Persian exercises. One strong fellow, thus elevated, presented himself before the Rajah with a couple of full-sized ploughs on his shoulders, a feat which called forth much admiration. We had then a fight between two buffaloes, which ran their heads against each other with a crash that one could fancy shook the palace to its very foundation ; indeed, the only wonder was how both animals did not fall down dead with their skulls fractured. But there appears to be a wonderful degree of thickness or hardness in this part of the animal structure both in beast and in man, for just after these buffaloes had given evidence of the hardness of their heads, a dozen persons came forward and placed themselves before a large pile of cocoanuts stripped of their outer husks. These being cast successively high into the air, were caught in their descent by these hard-pated fellows, who stood erect, and received the cocoanuts, I presume, on their " bumps of resistiveness". In every case the shell was literally dashed to pieces, and the milk scattered in showers over the crowd. Such a cracking of heads I never heard, except once at a fair in Ireland. Thus, our careful mother, Dame Nature, it should seem, has taken good care to defend the brain, though it may perhaps be surmised, that folks who furnish such hazardous evidence of the thickness of their skulls, have no great stock of brains to protect.

The prettiest game, to our taste, during the whole of this long and rather wearisome festival, was one which might be imitated with some effect by the figurantes of our own Opera. From a ring in the middle of a pole stretched horizontally over the centre of the area, were suspended eight differently coloured silk strings, the ends of which were held in the hands of as many little boys. Upon a signal being given, and music striking up, these eight young persons commenced a dance, the purpose of which was to plait up the separate cords into one rope. After working about a couple of feet of this line, the music changed, and the little weavers, inverting the order of their dance, undid the silken strands of their party-coloured rope, and stood ready to lay them up again, according to the same or any other pattern which might be ordered by his highness the Maha Rajah of Mysore.

CHAPTER XI

Granite Mountain Cut into a Statue—Bamboo Forest—Rajah of Coorg

During my stay in Mysore, I made an excursion thirty miles north of Seringapatam, to examine a huge statue of solid granite, nearly seventy feet in height, at a place with a name almost as long as the statue itself—Shrivanabalagol. It is wonderful how indifferent most people, living on any given spot of the earth's surface, become to the sights in their immediate neighbourhood; for when I asked at the Mysore residency for information about this extraordinary colossal statue, which lies within one night's journey, I found the greater number of the party had never seen it ; nor could I prevail on any person to accompany me on the expedition. I set out, accordingly, alone, about sunset, went to bed in my palankeen, and never awoke till the bearers set me down, next morning, on the pavement of a choultry near the spot. As I could see nothing of the statue, however, for an intervening grove of trees, I ran to the corner of the wood, where I suddenly obtained a view of this astonishing work of art, standing up boldly against the sky, and shewing itself above a low range of intermediate hills.

I certainly never saw any work of man before or since, which gave me so complete an idea of a giant, as this extraordinary statue. It has sometimes been described as an image of Boodh ; but I understand that it represents Gomuta Raya, a celebrated saint of the Jains — a sect of Hindoos, differing in some important respects from the Brahminical, and also from the Boodhist varieties of Oriental superstition.[1]

I possessed no exact means of measuring its height; but the authorities I have consulted on this point vary between sixty-seven feet and seventy feet three inches, which is the height stated by Dr. Buchanan; and, from such estimates as I could make, I am sure it cannot be much less. It is admirably placed for effect, as it stands on the summit of a conical granite hill about two hundred feet high, which serves for a pedestal. The statue still constitutes a part of the solid rock, which originally may have been three hundred feet high, the stone which formed the upper part of the mountain having been carved away, until nothing but the figure remained. The original shape of the hill cannot, indeed, be correctly inferred from anything we now see, but it probably formed a steep cone, or peak, of which the bold sculptor has taken such magnificent advantage.

I have often, when travelling since in foreign countries, been struck with natural forms and positions, which, by the hands of a man of genius, might easily be turned to account for the construction of similar colossal figures, calculated, under certain circumstances, to produce a much greater effect, at incalculably less cost, than the ordinary methods of casting and carving can accomplish. I was therefore much rejoiced to hear a great modern sculptor declare, that he had long entertained a project of constructing such a statue in this country. On my shewing him the sketches I had made of the gigantic figure in Mysore, and

[1] [The famous Sravana Belgola colossus, standing in solitary grandeur on a small rocky eminence, represents the legendary saint Gommata or Bahu-balin of the Digambara or naked Jain sect. It was erected, as an inscription informs us, by the minister Chamunda Raya, 983 A.D. Similar Jain Colossi are to be seen at Venur and Karkala in Southern Kanara. It is cut out of solid gneiss rock. The height is 59½ feet, and width at hips 13 feet.]

describing it as minutely as I could, he remarked to himself, " I'll beat this big Indian man yet ! "

In looking at Buchanan's account of Mysore for a description of the statue at Shrivanabalagol, I found the following remark : " Sir Arthur Wellesley visited the place lately ; " and on inquiring amongst the officers who had belonged to the army which marched from Seringapatam to the Mahratta country, some time after the fall of Tippoo, I learned that the general had actually gone upwards of thirty miles out of his way to see the statue, and then galloped back to rejoin the troops, whose march was never interrupted.

I had also the curiosity lately to ask the Duke of Wellington himself, whether this account was correct, and what he thought of the statue ? He said it was quite true, and added, that he had never seen anything so magnificent in its way. It will therefore be interesting enough if Mr. Chantrey, with such an example before him as the Indian statue, and such a subject at hand, shall make good his boast of beating the Oriental sculptor.

During my stay at the residency of Mysore, I took many trips to Seringapatam, for I never felt tired of wandering amongst the fortifications and other spots so celebrated in our Eastern history. I got hold of an intelligent old corporal, a pensioner, who had actually entered the breach as one of the storming party when the place was taken in 1799. I easily induced him to go regularly through the whole siege, Uncle Toby fashion, from thc beginning to the end—from the first hour the ground was broken, to the capture of the city and the discovery of Tippoo's body. The trenches and breaching batteries, of which scarcely any traces now exist, had been formed on the right bank of the river, not far below the spot where the river divides itself into two streams, which, after running apart for about three miles, again unite, and thus form a loop,

A VIEW OF SERINGAPATAM

[face p. 221

within which stands the island of Seringapatam. On the upper end of this island, which is sharp like a spear-head, is erected the fortress, by no means in a good situation, as I understand from military men, nor well constructed in itself. That, however, signifies little, as it is now dismantled. The breach had been built up ; but although fourteen years had elapsed since the siege, the difference in colour of the modern masonry rendered the spot quite distinct. We could even count numerous shot-marks and shot-holes on the different faces of the bastion adjacent to the breach, which was made in the curtain of the work. The river happened to be so low, that Corporal Trim and I managed, at the expense of a pretty good wetting, to follow the exact line of the storming party across the bed of the stream, and over the Fausse Braye wall. We were obliged to make a little circumbendibus to enter the works, for we carried no scaling ladders with us.

The readers of the history of the campaign, which terminated so gloriously, will remember that a huge ditch was found within the ramparts by the astonished storming party, and, had it not been for a few planks inadvertently left by the troops of Tippoo, they might never have been able to cross, and the beseigers have been repulsed. As the waters rose in the river to seventeen feet in depth, within a day or two afterwards, the fort might then have long withstood its assailants, had the moment of attack been deferred.

On these visits to Seringapatam, I slept in one of Tippoo Sultan's palaces, called the Dowlut Baug, or garden of riches ; but I paid dearly for my temerity. Indeed, I believe that island is nearly the most unhealthy spot in the East Indies. What is curious, however, I felt none of the evil effects of the malaria poison as long as I remained on the high level of the Mysore country ; but within a few days after reaching the sea-coast of Malabar, was seized with what is called the jungle fever, of which I feel the consequences to this hour. The Duke of Wellington [then Colonel Wellesley] when governor of Seringapatam, lived in the same palace, which he rendered more commodious than it had ever been in the days of Tippoo Sultan, or even of his father Hyder Ali. He filled it with European furniture, and made it less unhealthy by placing glass sashes in all the windows, by which some portion of the noxious air of the night could be kept out.

A characteristic touch of the same hand was pointed out to me in the Dowlut Baug. On the walls of the verandah, on that side of the palace which is most conspicuous, there had been represented, with much minuteness of detail, but with a total absence of perspective, the native version of Colonel Baillie's defeat—a disaster which, as I have already mentioned, occurred some twenty years before [1780] under the reign of Hyder. As the success, upon that occasion, was undoubtedly on the side of the Mahometans, there could be nothing fairer, in the way of nationality, than blazoning the victory on the walls of the palace. By the same right of conquest, the new governor of the island might undoubtedly have ordered a brush to be passed over the original painting, and have substituted in its stead the storming party in the breach where Tippoo fell. The English warrior's taste, however, was of a different description. He sent for the best native artists in Seringapatam, and made them carefully restore the original work, which had been much destroyed, desiring them to omit no item which the fallen dynasty had sanctioned. In consequence of this fresh painting, I saw, so late as 1813, the whole disastrous story displayed to public view, in the glaring colours in which Hyder had originally delighted to exhibit the prowess of his arms.

In the same manly taste, though possibly with

higher political motives, the custom which, antecedent to our conquest of Mysore, had been religiously observed, of reading the Koran several times a day beside the tomb of Hyder, was continued by the Duke of Wellington ; and, in fact, it is continued to this hour. During the few days I lived in the palace, I went repeatedly to hear these moolahs offer up their prayers. All the Mussulman priests of the subverted dynasty were pensioned by the British government, and also most of the principal officers and civilians of Tippoo's court. This wise policy included the celebrated old Purneah, the late sultan's prime minister—the Talleyrand of India—who, though he served at different times many different masters, behaved to each and to all with rigid fidelity, and stood by them heartily as long as they kept their respective heads above water.

After remaining about a fortnight, wandering over the Mysore country, I turned my steps to the westward, with the intention of passing the Ghauts and reaching the coast, where I considered it would not be difficult to procure a sea conveyance to Bombay. The resident of Mysore advised me to call at the Rajah of Coorg's capital on my way, and furnished me with a letter of introduction to that native prince.

Early in the morning, therefore, of a beautiful day in the latter end of September, I set out from the bare table-land of Mysore, and proceeded towards the hilly and thickly-wooded regions overhanging the Malabar country. When I awoke in my palankeen, I knew not very distinctly where I had got to, for I had been dreaming all night about the monstrous statue at Shrivanabalagol, I sat up, drew the door gently back, and, looking out, found myself in the midst of one of the most curious and magnificent scenes which my eyes had ever beheld. It seemed as if I were travelling among the clustered columns of some enormous and enchanted Gothic cathedral compared to which the minster at York, or the cathedral at Winchester, would have seemed mere baby-houses. The ground extended on all sides as smooth, and flat, and clear of underwood, as if the whole had been paved with grave-stones. From this level surface rose on every hand, and as far as the eye could penetrate into the forest, immense symmetrical clusters of bamboo, varying in diameter at their base from six feet to twenty or thirty, and even to twice that width, as I ascertained by actual measurement. For about eight or ten feet from the ground, each of these clusters or columns preserved a form nearly cylindrical, after which they began gradually to swell outwards, each bamboo assuming for itself a graceful curve, and rising to the height, some of sixty, some of eighty, and some even of one hundred feet in the air, the extreme end being at times horizontal, or even drooping gently over, like the tips of the feathers in the Prince of Wales' plume. These gorgeous clusters stood at the distance of fifteen or twenty yards from one another, and being totally free from the interruption of brushwood, could be distinguished at a great distance—more than a mile certainly, in every direction, forming, under the influence of an active imagination, naves and transepts, aisles and choirs, such as none but a Gothic architect ever dared to conceive. Overhead the interlacing curves of the bamboos constituted as complete a groined roof as that of Winchester or Westminster, on a scale of grandeur far beyond the bold conception even of those wonderful artists who devised that glorious school of architecture, which, in the opinion of many people, has raised the dark centuries immediately subsequent to the era of the crusades almost to the level of the days of Pericles.

On counting the separate bamboos in some of the smallest, and also in some of the largest clusters, I found the numbers to vary from twenty or thirty to upwards of two hundred, and the height generally from sixty to a hundred feet from the ground to the point of intersection of the curves overhead. Most of the bamboos were somewhat thicker than a man's thigh at the ground, where, as I have before said, they are clustered so close as to be almost in contact. They then taper off very gradually to the extreme end, where the point is not thicker than a quill. There occurs a joint at about every foot and a half, distinguished not only by a slight flat ring or fillet, but by a set of small branches, eight or ten feet long, striking out at right angles to the main bamboo. These minor sheets are again divided into joints, from which minor series of shoots, still more minute, are thrown out ; and so on for many successions, the last always terminating in a sharp-pointed narrow leaf, two or three inches long, and half an inch wide in the middle, not unlike a large tea-leaf when spread out.

As each bamboo of the hundred or more forming the clusters sends out shoots from every joint, and as all the joints of these subordinate branches do the same, a compact mass is formed by these innumerable little branches, which cross one another at every possible angle. If a person were to fill a hat full of pins or needles, and shake it about for some minutes, it might give a notion of the inextricable confusion which is presented to the eye on looking into one of these clustered columns of bamboos. It is only at the top where the bend takes place, that the foliage has full room to play or where the tapering arms of this magnificent plant form, by their meetings and crossings, a complete system of pointed arches.

What surprised me very much, and greatly puzzled me at first, was to observe that, notwithstanding the multitude of lateral shoots from each of the main bamboos, and from all the subordinate branches, not a single trace of displacement, or the slightest obstruction to the growth of any branch, could be detected. Every person must have heard of the astonishing rapidity of the growth of the bamboo. It is said, indeed, that in one season it starts up to its whole length. I do not know if this be true, but am quite certain that if one of the main bamboos were to spring from the ground in the centre, or even near the sides of the cluster, and that from its joints there were at the same time to sprout out the lateral branches I have described, it would be impossible for the main stem to force its way through the obstructions presented by the net-work, formed by the little branches growing from the joints of the other bamboos in the cluster.

After examining a considerable number of the clusters, however, we can, I think, discover how Nature manages this difficult affair. When the bamboo first springs out of the ground, it is about as thick as a man's wrist, but it is armed with a very sharp point, not unlike that of a wooden instrument called a fid, which sailors make use of in splicing ropes. As this point is extremely hard, and the bamboo always highly polished, it readily makes its way through the very thickest masses of the little branches, as one might thrust a sword through a quickset hedge. Thus, the bamboo, whose growth is prodigiously rapid, starts upwards, and, by reason of its smooth sharp end, and perfectly smooth sides, easily makes its way to its extreme length and thickness, without, as I conceive, sending out a single lateral shoot from any of its joints till the utmost extent has been gained. The subordinate branches from the joints then, but not till then, begin to start out horizontally, all these being, after the manner of the principal stem, exempted from lateral shoots at their joints till their utmost length has been reached. In consequence of this beautiful arrangement, none of these successive branches, however numerous or delicate, find any difficulty in piercing the confusion.

I saw bamboos in every different stage of this process, and, in particular, I noticed several of the main stems rising to the height of seventy feet and upwards, of a clear yellow colour, and evidently of recent growth; but without a single lateral branch growing from their joints from top to bottom; and this led me to infer that their extreme height had not yet been attained, or was just attained.

On reaching a pretty little town, with the long name of Eerajunderpet, I was received by an officer of the Rajah of Coorg, whose dominions I had entered. A guard of sepoys, with several elephants, and a most inconvenient allowance of ear-splitting music, were placed at my disposal by the Soubadar,[1] as he styled himself. I begged him, as delicately as I could, to stop the tom-toms, and then insinuated something about breakfast. I suspect this functionary had often before been sent to meet my countrymen similarly circumstanced, for I could see the ends of his huge whiskers gradually curling upwards by the muscular action of that kind of smile called a broad grin, as he listened to my demand, and pointed to the choultry, or caravansary, close at hand. In truth, in spite of the picturesque beauties of the bamboo forest, and the witchery of the still more magnificent scenery which embellishes the summit ridge, or crest of the Ghauts, I had not been able to exclude from my thoughts the chances, pro and con, of a good meal at the end of the stage. Accordingly, I felt my heart leap as I caught sight of a table-cloth, flapping in the breeze in the verandah, above which rose a goodly range of dishes, a huge tea-pot, and a bowl brim-full of eggs. The attendant lifted up the covers, and displayed a pyramid of rice shining like a snow wreath in the sun, supported by a curry, the savoury smell of which spread so far as to reach the senses of the tired bearers of my palankeen, who

[1] [A native officer of the rank of Captain.]

seemed as hungry as myself. In the joy of the moment, I presented them with a whole sheep, of the small mountain breed, for their dinner.

During the rest of this day I travelled, sometimes in the palankeen, and sometimes on the back of one of the elephants sent me by the Rajah of Coorg,[1] for whose capital, Markara, I was now bound. The road wound about amongst the hills, or along the valleys of the Ghauts, and across numberless small streams, besides the great Cauvery, now shrunk to a rivulet, which we forded repeatedly during this journey. When the sun became disagreeably hot, at those places where the woods opened, I had only to dismount and pop into the palankeen; but, when we plunged into the forests, and enjoyed the shade of the teak tree, iron wood, banyan, and tamarind, I again got on the back of my elephant. She was an exceedingly fine animal, in the prime of her life, as I was told, being only fifty years old, called Bhigelee,[2] or lightning. Your grand folks in India, upon state occasions, place a howdah, or castle, on their elephants, and ride about in triumph, like Darius in Le Brun's pictures of Alexander's battles. But, for ordinary travelling, a good thick matting, or rather a pad, answers the purpose; in fact, this method is the more agreeable of the two on a journey, for there is less motion felt when one is seated close to the elephant's back, than when perched three or four feet higher, and wagged about like the head of a Chinese mandarin over a chimney-piece. Even with the pad, it is not very easy to keep on when the road is steep; and this would be impossible, were not a piece of cloth, twisted up like

[1] [*Coorg*, a little hill-state in Mysore, about 3,000 feet above the sea, now a great centre of the coffee estates, is celebrated for its mountain scenery, and the excellent shooting to be obtained in its primeval forests. It was ceded to the British by Tipu Sultan in 1792. The Raja whom Hall visited was deposed for misgovernment in 1834. Merkara, the capital, is about 75 miles from Mysore.]

[2] [Hind. *bijli*, lightning.]

a rope, placed before and behind, which may be grasped by the hand, according as the inclination of the road is upwards or downwards.

An elephant is proverbially one of the surest-footed animals in the world; but we came, during this journey, to some passes so very steep, and so much covered with loose stones, empty water courses, broken trunks of trees, and all the other débris left by mountain torrents, that I quaked not a little at times, as we passed along the edges of precipices. But our trusty Bhigelee appeared perfectly self-possessed on these occasions; and, as the mahout, or driver, made me remark, she never took her foot off one stone till she had made sure of a solid foundation for the next step. Sometimes she made this inspection with her trunk, sometimes with her foot; but she never once made a false move, though occasionally she slid down for a yard or two on all fours.

At one place, the bough of a tree happened to cross our path, upon which the elephant raised her trunk and wrenched it from the stem in a moment, in order to use it as a fly flap, and so brisk were her movements, that she had very nearly whisked both the mahout and myself into the valley. At another turn of the road, where we crossed a running stream, her thirsty ladyship sucked in a hogshead or two, and then, having filled her trunk, and wishing to cool herself, she squirted the contents so dexterously over her sides and back, that we were both completely drenched. For this trick, Miss Bhigelee received a suitable correction at the hands of her guide, albeit his age, as he said, was less than that of the elephant by about a dozen years. He told us, that he had scarcely been absent from her a whole day since he was born; and that, even when a mere crawling infant, he used to be left by his mother under the elephant's care.

It was at the close of twilight when I reached

Markara, the Rajah's capital; and not a little astonished was I to be shown into a large house, built in the taste of the English bungalows at Madras, furnished, also, in the European style. In one of the rooms, which was brilliantly lighted up, I found a table laid with twenty covers; and, before I had been there three minutes, a sumptuous dinner was placed on the table, as if it had been brought by magic. A couple of dozen mutes, in white robes, stood round like the ivory attendants of the Black Prince in the fairy tale. I lamented that I had not twenty mouths, to do more justice to my host's ultra hospitality. As it was, however, I did pretty well; for the keen air of the Coorg mountains, and the rough riding of the elephant, had set my appetite so sharply, that I felt rather provoked to receive a summons to attend the Maha Rajah of Coorg, Lingra Jender Wadeer, just as I had smoked out my first chillum, and was considering whether or not to break in upon a second bottle of claret, for the Rajah sported some of "Maxwell and Key's best long cork." Not a moment was to be lost, however; so I jumped up, and being shown to another suite of apartments, found a bedroom and dressing-room, for all the world like those of any hotel in Jermyn Street. I rigged myself in my best coat, tucked in my sword, screwed on my cocked hat, and rattled away to the Durbar.

This worthy Rajah's whim, as I soon discovered, was to have everything in one department of his palace, as much as possible, in the English style. In this view, the floor of the room in which he received his European guests was laid with Brussels carpets, and round the walls stood pianofortes and organs, music books, sofas, card-tables, writing-desks, clocks of a dozen shapes and sizes, mirrors, and pictures—all English. He seemed enchanted with my amaze at this strange jumble of upholstery; nothing, however, was ordered aright, and it looked more like one of Mr.

Dowbiggin's warehouses in Mount Street, than an English drawing-room, which it was intended to represent. As I entered the Durbar, the Rajah claimed my admiration of the disposition of his goods in such a way, that it was impossible to contradict him. In one instance, indeed, the sagacity of the native outran his taste; and, in the midst of much that was trashy, and even childish, betokened a degree of knowledge of character for which, indeed, the Hindoos are peculiarly distinguished. He led me up to a picture of Sir Arthur Wellesley, sent to him by the general, at the Rajah's request, after the great campaign against Tippoo.

"There," said he, "look at that picture; there is the portrait of the greatest man we have ever known in India."

Just as these words were interpreted, I was surprised to hear a band of music strike up the tune called, I think, "The Hunting of the Stag," of which song the burthen is "Hey ho, chevy!" To this most incongruous tune, a set of Indian figurantes, or notch girls, were made to dance before us, and very strange work they made of it! After a short audience, the Rajah observed that I must be tired with the day's journey, and allowed me to retire.

Next morning I got up betimes, and took a survey of the grounds, which satisfied me, that although nothing could be more picturesque in the way of mountain scenery, a more absurd spot for a stronghold could not have been selected in Asia. It would indeed be a famous place to keep a state prisoner in, for the fort stands in the centre of an amphitheatre of hills, each overlooking, and either commanding it, or the approaches to it, within half cannon shot. I returned to the fort, after standing on the top of one of these knolls for about half an hour, watching the mist as it gradually stole out of the valleys, and became invisible in the higher air, whenever it mixed with sunbeams as they peeped over the eastern ridges of the Ghauts. Meanwhile, the light wind, which generally flits about at that hour, shook down the dew drops from the branches of the well-steeped forest; and I had almost forgotten, in the coolness of the air, and more than Alpine beauty of the Indian landscape, how far I had wandered from the scenes which it recalled. At the door of the bungalow, I was met by half a dozen attendants, who salamed to the ground, and led the way to the parlour, where a feast sufficient to have satisfied twenty half-pay officers, was laid on the table. I counted eighteen dishes, and I forget how many silver tea-pots, cream-jugs, besides crockery enough to have equipped an Indiaman—such was the magnificent pleasure of the Rajah of Coorg.

In due season, a message came to me from his highness, to say he wished me to go over the new palace, which he was fitting up like an English house, and upon some of the details of which he desired to have my opinion. As things were in actual progress, I took the liberty of suggesting a few changes, with which he was greatly pleased. He had already made some very erroneous arrangements, probably from acting upon imperfect information; and, as even his queer taste revolted as these incongruities, he felt delighted to have a European's authority for making further alterations.

On returning to the great square in the centre of the building, we found three chairs placed for us on a Turkey carpet, spread on the ground in the open air. The Rajah took a seat and made me come beside him, after placing his son, a nice little boy, nine or ten years of age, on my right hand. This young fellow was gaily dressed, with a huge overspreading turban. A dark circle, about the tenth of an inch broad, was painted round each of his eyes, which gave him a strange staring look; and on his cheeks, brow, and chin, were placed small black marks, or beauty spots, about twice as large as the head or dot of a note in music.

The whole area of the court was now begirt with soldiers, each holding, as high as his face, an immense bill-hook or knife, the blade of which near the extremity, could not be less than three inches wide, and diminishing gradually towards the hilt. This formidable instrument, well known in Indian warfare under the name of the Coorg-knife, is often used as a sword, and when handled by men who are not afraid to close with their antagonists, is said to be a most efficient weapon.

On a signal given by the Rajah, a folding door was thrown open on one side of the court, and in stalked two immense royal tigers, held by several men on each side by long but slight ropes attached to collars round the animals' necks. These beasts appeared very tractable, for they allowed themselves to be led close to us. I confess I did not much like this degree of propinquity, and eyed the slender cordage with some professional anxiety. Meanwhile the Rajah and his son, and the officers of the household, appeared quite unconcerned, though the tigers passed within a few yards of them, and, as it seemed to me, might easily have broken loose. What degree of training these animals had undergone, I know not; but, after a little while, the Rajah, probably to increase the surprise of his guest, directed the men to let go the ropes and to fall back. There we sat, in the midst of the open court, with a couple of full-sized tigers in our company, and nothing on earth to prevent their munching us all up! The well-fed and well-bred beasts, however, merely lounged about, rubbed their noses together, and then tumbling on the ground, rolled about like a couple of kittens at play. I could, however, detect the Rajah spying at me out of the corner of his eye, and half-smiling at the success of his trick. After a time the men were recalled and the tigers dragged off.

A pair of lionesses and two furious-looking buffaloes were then introduced, but nothing could be more innocent or more respectful to the Rajah and his son. Like Falstaff, indeed, they seemed to have an instinctive knowledge of the true prince. Yet, for all this, I caught myself several times edging my chair back a little bit, and looking out for a clear place to escape, as the monsters stalked up and down the court, and once or twice actually touched the edge of our carpet with their feet. On these occasions, that part of the circle of guards which stood behind us, advanced just so far as to bring our chairs on the outside of their ring, and to place themselves between the beasts and us. On clapping their hands and flourishing their knives, the lionesses and other beasts moved a little farther off after which the guards again dropped to the rear. Still, this seemed rather a poor protection; at least, I had my recollection so full of the rapid motions of the same class of animals which I had seen baited at Mysore, that I could discover nothing which need have prevented the tiger from whipping off the heads of the Rajah and the heir-apparent, or, at all events, that of their guest, who, having no particular claims to the throne of Coorg, could reckon on none of the benefits of instinctive respect.

A troublesome story, too, respecting a touch of insanity in the Rajah's family, recurred to my thought occasionally. I had heard somewhere of his predecessor calling for a fowling-piece one day in open Durbar, and having ordered forth his cabinet-ministers, he deliberately popped them off, one by one, like sparrows —an honour to which, it is said, they submitted with edifying patience and propriety. I confess I felt rather queerish when he sent one of his family for a double-barrelled gun, a beautiful piece of workmanship, bearing the name of Joe Manton on the lock. I admired it, of course.

"That piece," said the Rajah, "was made here by one of my people."

I ventured respectfully to point to the name of the London maker.

"Pooh!" cried his highness, "what's in a name? The man who could make such a piece as this could surely copy a name. Bring the London gun."

And, strange to say, when the model from which one of his native gunsmiths had made the piece was placed in my hands, so exact was the imitation, I could scarcely tell which was the original, which the copy. On pulling the trigger of each, however, the difference in the vivacity of the spring made the distinction apparent. I had often heard of their powers of imitation, but had no idea before of its extent.

When we had satisfied ourselves with an inspection of these pieces, the Rajah gave orders for half a dozen tiger's cubs, about eight months old, and as many puppy-dogs, to be set to play before us on the carpet, while a full-grown royal tiger was at the same time dragged forward and pitted against a bear for a real battle in the open court. Anything more disproportionate or absurd cannot be conceived than this match; and so, perhaps, the poor brutes thought, for fight they would not, although both of them were well thumped and forced against each other by the attendants. At length a brilliant thought struck the Rajah.

"Tie them together!" exclaimed his majesty; and accordingly the rope which was fastened to the tiger's collar was hitched to the belly-band of the bear.

Neither party liked this. The tiger roared, and the bear growled, while the Rajah and his son laughed and clapped their hands in ecstasy at their own good joke. Of course, the guards and courtiers joined in the mirth, and the whole quadrangle rung with mixed shouts of the soldiers, the growl of the bear, and the roar of the tiger. Of all the parties in this singular concert, the tiger appeared to be the most discomposed. His eye flashed fire, his tail waved from flank to flank in the most ominous style. I thought at one time this was to turn out no laughing matter; for, if the angry animal, when at length he lost all patience, had taken a direction towards us, he might have demolished the dynasty of Wadeer, or at least made a vacancy for an officer in his Britannic Majesty's Navy. Fortunately, he chose exactly the opposite course, and running furiously across the court, made a flying leap right into one of the low windows of what the Rajah called his English drawing-room. The glass and frame-work of the window were, of course, dashed to pieces in a moment, and the pianos, pictures, and bookcases, must soon have shared the same fate, had not the tiger's progress been checked by the weight of the wretched bear, which hung outside, halfway between the window-sill and the ground, somewhat after the fashion of the golden fleece over a mercer's door. The tiger we could no longer see, but we could hear him smashing the furniture at a great rate.

The Rajah, who naturally thought this was a little too much of a good thing, desired his people to enter the room, in order to catch hold of the ropes fastened to the tiger's collar, by which he had been brought forward in the first instance. This being accomplished, and the tiger secured, the rope connecting him and the bear was cut, upon which poor Master Bruin tumbled to the ground, no great height, indeed, and off he moved very sulkily to his den. Meanwhile, the tiger was dragged out of the house by main force, and sent to the rear.

As soon as order was restored, five elephants made their appearance, none of them standing less than thirteen feet high. At the bidding of the Rajah, these grand fellows knelt down, prostrated themselves, rolled over, on their sides, lifted their keepers in their trunk, and whirled them high in the air. In short, they went through all manner of gambols.

"Now," said the Rajah, "let us have an elephant dance!"

I forgot to mention before, that on one side of the court a group of pretty dancing girls had been exhibiting all the time of the show, without attracting much notice. These ladies being ordered forward, one of them was stationed before each of the elephants as a partner, and the keepers, slipping down from the animals' necks, seated themselves cross-legged on the ground, in front, and within reach of the animals' fore-feet. The music now struck up, the girls began to dance and sing, while the keepers, by touching the elephants' feet gently with little sticks, made them hobble likewise. As the unwieldy monsters jogged from side to side, they beat time with the ends of their trunks on the bare heads of their keepers, shook their monstrous ears, and stared at the girls. Never was anything more grotesque! The effect, indeed, was so ludicrous, that even the poor Indian girls themselves appeared at a loss whether to laugh or to cry at being set to dance a jig with elephants to the tune of "Drops of Brandy", or some such exotic air—villainously played by Hindoo pipers—a glorious concourse of absurdities! The day was pretty well advanced before these sports were over, for we had still to witness sundry sheep-fights, and ram-fights, and an endless variety of antics by human tumblers.

At last the Rajah broke up this queer Durbar, or levee, ordered out the palankeens, wished me a safe descent of the Ghauts, and, as I thought, was about to dismiss me rather unceremoniously; but, on the contrary, he did me the high honour to accompany me as far as the outer gate of the fort, on the hill, a distance of at least a mile from the palace. A double row of soldiers lined the road the whole way; and these being joined by many hundreds of labourers from the adjacent fields, the crowd became quite dense towards the end of the line. The most profound silence was observed, however, and as each person stood with his broad-bladed knife in his hands, raised nearly to his mouth, in what we should call an attitude of prayer, the palms being pressed together, the effect was very lively and striking. On reaching the gate the Rajah presented me with one of the Coorg knives already described, and a handsome sandalwood walking-stick.

The dress of these bold mountaineers is simple, and not inelegant. On their heads they wind a long white cloth into a broad flat turban, and round their bodies wrap a loose, white frock, reaching two inches below the knee. This robe or tunic is tied round the waist with a shawl of more or less richness, according to the wealth of the parties.

In the evening I found my way back to Eerajunderpet, and strolled into the woods in quest of adventures. What should I meet but a Roman Catholic priest, "all shaven and shorn," speaking a strange mixture of Portuguese, Spanish and Hindustanee! As I possessed a slight smattering of each of these languages, we got on pretty well. Although this good padre had passed much more than half his life away from Portugal, he still took a lively interest in those distant scenes, which, as he said, he never hoped to visit again. He had heard, he told me, of the peninsular war, but he knew none of the details. The worthy missionary's thoughts, indeed, were much more earnestly engaged in works of peace and charity than in those of war and conquest. He shewed me his native school, where a number of boys were taught to read, and, with an air of exultation, assured me he could reckon upon there being at least nine or ten hundred Christians in the Coorg country, of which the population is said to be fifty thousand.

Next morning I descended the celebrated Poodicherum Pass in the great Malabar Ghauts—a gorgeous specimen of rugged but well-wooded mountain scenery. At the bottom of the pass I found bearers who carried me to Erricore, and so onwards to Cananore, a very interesting trip along the coast.

After various commonplace adventures and worrying delays, I reached Tellicherry, and lastly Mangalore, where I considered myself most fortunate in catching an English ship just sailing for Bombay, loaded with teak timber for the dockyard. By taking advantage of the land-winds at night, and the sea-breezes in the day, we reached our port within a few hours of the time to which Sir Samuel Hood had limited my excursion.

CHAPTER XII

Visit to the Sultan of Pontiana, in Borneo—Sir Samuel Hood

In the summer of 1814, Sir Samuel Hood made a voyage, in his majesty's ship *Minden*, to the eastern parts of his station. We called first at Acheen, on the north end of the island of Sumatra, where we held some very amusing intercourse with the king of that district, whose capital the Admiral visited. From thence we steered over to Pulo Penang, or Prince of Wales' Island, and thence down the Straits of Malacca, entering the China Sea by the beautiful Straits of Singapore. The Admiral's chief object was to visit Java; but as there lay three routes before him to choose between, viz., the Straits of Gaspar, the Straits of Banca, and the Caramata passage, he preferred taking the last and widest, which also led him near the western shore of the immense island of Borneo. On reaching the equator, he steered in for the mouth of the great river Lava, which passes the town of Pontiana. The weather being very favourable, the ship was anchored, and the barge got ready for an expedition.

At four in the morning, on receiving the joyful intimation that I was to be officer of the boat, I lost no time in getting together everything likely to be useful—sextant, artificial horizon, spy-glass, chart, compass, and Nautical Almanac, besides a Malay dictionary; for Sir Samuel, with his wonted ardour, had already commenced the study of that language, saying, and saying truly, that before our cruise amongst the eastern islands was over, he should cut us all out in speaking Malay. This boast he afterwards made good; for before he completed his travels in Java, he could maintain a conversation with the natives with very little assistance from the interpreter, merely by the help of a vocabulary, which he made for himself and carried in his pocket. He actually travelled over more than twelve hundred miles of ground on that island, during the last quarter of which, at the eastern end, I had the good fortune to accompany him. I had previously visited alone about seven hundred miles of the interior of that noblest of all our insular possessions in the East.

It is truly grievous to think how unwittingly we allowed that magnificent possession to slip through our fingers, in 1814, at the grand settlement of affairs. But after the downfall of Bonaparte, such a game of chuck-farthing was played with kingdoms, that even a gigantic country like Java failed to excite its due share of notice, or was totally lost sight of in the haze which obscured everything at a distance from the scene of excitement.

We had some little difficulty in finding our way in the barge, for the mouth of the river of Pontiana lay so completely hid amongst low cane brakes, mangroves and other aquatic trees and shrubs, which grow thickly along the western shores of Borneo, that until we came quite close, no inlet was perceptible. The first hit we made proved wrong, and lost us three or four miles; and it was not till nearly noon that we reached the rush of fresh and troubled water, which indicated the true entrance. The Admiral desired greatly to observe the sun's meridian altitude, saying, he had a childish sort of anxiety to take an observation exactly on the Equatorial line. His excellency, however, though he could command many things, could not command this; for although our fellows gave way lustily, so as to stem the current running out, and we had a full half hour to spare, we could not effect a landing in good time. On reaching what had seemed the shore, no footing could be found anywhere. Even the little boat which we carried with us in tow of the barge, though she threaded the mangrove stems and roots, and went in much further than the barge, could not reach anything like dry land. As the main bank refused to afford us a resting place, we put off, and rowed as briskly as we could to a small island about half a mile from this treacherous shore; but this, too, proved a cheat, for what we took to be solid ground consisted merely of a mass of green shrubs, growing on the ridge of a soft slippery mass of mud just peeping above the water.

As the sailors, by this time, were pretty well exhausted with rowing so long in the hot sun, they hailed with great joy the sea-breeze which just then set in. They soon stepped the masts, hoisted the sails, and laid the oars in.

"Now go to dinner, men," said the considerate chief, "this rattling breeze will not carry us up far; and you will pull all the better for a good bellyful."

Just as this judicious order was given, and while we were still laughing at the recent adventure, which reminded us of Sinbad's mistaking a whale for a solid rock, our eyes were attracted by the sight of another island, much smaller than the first. It seemed, indeed like a little grove or tuft of palm-like foliage rising out of the water somewhat in the fashion of our Prince of Wales' feather. None of the party had ever seen such a tree before, and everyone tried to guess what it might be; but all were puzzled. At length, a diminutive moving black speck shewed itself at the root, or centre, from which these fairy-like branches radiated.

"It is a rock with a tree on it," cried one.

"Pooh!" said Sir Samuel, "there are no rocks hereabouts; the soil for many a league is alluvial."

"It skims along like a witch," exclaimed a third; "it is surely alive!"

"Let us sail to it whatever it be," said the Admiral, waving his hand to the coxwain to sheer the barge further from the side of the river.

As we drew near, we discovered our phenomenon to consist of a fishing canoe, gliding along merrily before the sea-breeze, with no other sails than half a dozen branches of the cocoa-nut tree placed in the bow, and spread out like the feathers of a peacock's tail. These were held together by a slender bar of bamboo, and supported by small strips of bark to the stern, in which sat a naked Malay.

The Admiral proved a true prophet, for the deceitful sea-breeze presently lulled, and it cost us a very hard row to accomplish our purpose against the stream. The town of Pontiana stands on a low point of land formed by the confluence of two mighty rivers, names to us unknown. This particular spot is always held sacred in India, and is known under the Hindoo name of Sungum. I suspect, however, that the Malays and other Mahometans, who inhabit the coasts of most of the Indian Islands, acknowledge no superstitious predilections for one spot more than another, and consider such things as mere prejudices unworthy of the followers of Mahomet, their great military prophet. Probably the Sungum point has some local advantages belonging to it, as I observe it is generally appropriated by the strongest party in every country. At all events, it has the advantage of communicating directly with both the rivers, by whose junction the Sungum, or solid angle, is formed. In the instance of Pontiana, the Mussulmen had taken possession of it, though it was formerly a Dutch settlement, while the Chinese were left to occupy the corners opposite to the Sungum, on the right and left banks, respectively, of the river formed by the junction of the two streams. Thus three considerable cities had been built facing one another, and each displaying on the river a multitude of boats and barges, canoes and proas, in crowds which would not have disgraced the show at London Bridge, and, of course, indicating considerable wealth and activity.

We came upon this grand view quite abruptly, and having no expectation of encountering anything so magnificent, were taken rather by surprise. Two enormous Chinese junks occupied the centre of the stream, each of them rising out of the water nearly as high as the poop of a line-of-battle ship. Along the shore, on both sides, lay a fleet of eight or ten sailor junks, some of them very large, and all bearing enormous white flags, in the centre of which sprawled huge dragons and other monsters familiar to the eyes of all fanciers of old China jars.

This was the first time that many of us had seen genuine or unmixed specimens of Chinese or Malay towns on a great scale, and our admiration was great accordingly. In strict language, it cannot be said that these Chinese are at home in Borneo; but in point of fact, they certainly are so. The truth is, that China Proper is so much over-crowded, that its surplus population must find vent somewhere and somehow; and, in spite of the severest laws forbidding people to leave the Celestial realm, they emigrate in vast numbers. In this respect the enactments of England against the export of guineas bear a close resemblance in their efficiency to those of China against the exportation of human beings. Be this as it may, it has so happened, that all the islands which lie to the eastward and southward of the China seas—the Philippines, the Moluccas, and the Isles of Sunda—possess large colonies of Chinese on their coasts.

I remember hearing, when I was in Batavia, that the Chinese population of that city alone amounted to thirty-five thousand. Indeed, persons who have attended much to the subject on the spot, assure me there is good reason to believe, that in process of time the Chinese will occupy exclusively the whole of the eastern islands. They are the most industrious of human beings, and are physically strong and energetic; they also possess a cheerfulness and patience of disposition which makes them careless about danger and difficulty. Nor are the Chinese entangled with any of the ritual superstitions of their Hindoo neighbours, and in that respect are even more free-souled than the Malays, their only rivals on the coasts of the Oriental archipelago—although I suspect that they are not very straight-laced Mussulmans. The Malays form at present a fringe of population round most of the islands in those seas, whatever may be the description of the inhabitants in the interior. This we certainly find to be the case along four or five hundred miles of the north coast of Java, but the moment we strike inland, a different and indigenous race appears. The Malays are the masters by sea, and, like a certain nation "throned in the West," are said to lord it in tolerably imperious style. On the other hand, the Chinese, who are the worst possible sailors, but who are agriculturists by nature and by necessity, as well as taste, are gradually outmastering the Malays along shore; and in time, I have little doubt, they will become the chief proprietors of the soil. They may then build forts at the mouths of the rivers, and bully the good folks of the interior. Thus, ages hence, Pontiana may become a second Antwerp; and protocols in Chinese, Malays, and Bornese, occupy all Eastern men's thoughts from Timor to Formosa!

In the meantime, as there existed no dispute about the navigation of the River Lava, we rowed up very peaceably towards the great city of Pontiana. On our meeting a canoe with a Malay in it, the Admiral, who had been studying Marsden's dictionary all the way, stood up in the barge, made the men lie on their oars, and to their great astonishment, and probably to that of the native, called out in the Malay tongue:

"Which is the way to the Sultan's house?"

To Sir Samuel's unspeakable delight the man whom he addressed understood him, and after offering to shew us the landing-place, paddled off ahead of us. Our fellows gave way as hard as they could, but the Malay kept the lead; and as we shot past the Chinese towns, one on each bank, the natives crowded to the beach, as much astonished, no doubt, with our strange cocked hats, swords, and oddly shaped boat, as we could be with their long tails and wild-looking junks, or with the creases which every Malay carries by his side. This fierce-looking weapon is not, in form, unlike the waving sword one sees in the pictures of the angel Michael, though it is not above a foot and a half in length.

The Sultan's cousin received the Admiral and his party at the gate of the palace, and led him by the hand along a causeway of flag stones to the residence of the monarch. Directly in the middle of the gateway, which was only ten feet wide and about as many in height, there stood a twenty-four pounder gun. On the top of the arch there was built a small square room, from holes in which peeped out the muzzles of five or six field-pieces, the whole affair resembling very much that part of a child's box of toys which represents the stronghold or castle. Within the high wall surrounding the palace, we counted innumerable large guns scattered about, apparently with no other object than to be seen—as if the mere look of a cannon were expected to do the work of a fight! The same number of mock barrels of gun-powder, similarly disposed, would have answered the purpose equally well, or perhaps better, for there appeared no way in which the guns could be fired, without doing much more injury to the besieged than to the besiegers.

On we went, till we were met by the Sultan himself, at the inner side of the quadrangle. He courteously conducted the Admiral to a large room or hall of audience, and having begged his guest to sit down at a small table, took a chair by his side, and began a conversation as if they had been long acquainted. Of course, in spite of the Admiral's proficiency, this could not be accomplished without an interpreter; and the services of a very clever Malay boy, whom we had brought with us from the ship, were brought into requisition. The hall, in which we were first received, might have been about fifty feet square, bleak, unfurnished, and comfortless, with an uncovered mud floor. It was so feebly lighted by a few windows almost hid by Venetian blinds, that we could only discover that the roof had been left bare and unfinished. After sitting for about ten minutes, the sultan rose and led the way to another apartment apparently of still larger dimensions, but literally so dark, that, had it not been for the light entering by the door we had left, and the one ahead of us, we could not have moved along without breaking our shins over the stones, sticks, and other rubbish lying in the way. We had next to make rather a difficult transit along a precarious kind of bridge, formed of a single plank laid across an ominous-looking pool or puddle of mud, which divided these two branches of the palace from each other.

All at once we were ushered into a splendid room, seventy or eighty feet square, brilliantly lighted, and not ill furnished, but strongly contrasted with the darkness and dirtiness of the suite we had passed through. This total want of keeping, it may be mentioned, is quite in Oriental taste. They know tolerably well how to be magnificent on occasions; but they never learn how to be uniformly decent. The Asiatics, and even some other nations which might be named nearer home, can seldom afford to be taken by surprise. Indeed, I am not sure if more than one country can be alluded to, in which the people are at all hours ready to receive strangers, and have no occasion to make a fuss, or to change anything when a rap comes to the door.

In the centre of this gorgeous room, on a part of the floor raised to about a foot and a half above the level of the rest, and laid with a rich Turkey carpet, stood a long table, at the top of which the Sultan placed the Admiral, and then made the signal for tea. First entered an attendant, bearing a large tray, on which were ranged several dozens of exceedingly small cups. This he placed on the carpet, and then squatted himself down, cross-legged, beside it. Another attendant soon followed bearing the tea-pot, and he likewise popped himself down. After a conjuration of some minutes the cups were brought round, containing weak black tea, exquisite in flavour, but marvellously small in quantity. There appeared no milk, but plenty of sugar candy. Some sweet sherbet was next handed round, very slightly acid, but so deliciously cool, that we appealed frequently to the vase or huge jar from which it was poured, to the great delight of the Sultan, who assured us that this was the genuine sherbet described by the Persian poets. It was mixed, he told us, by a true believer, who had made more than one pilgrimage to Mecca.

At the upper end of the apartment, in a deep recess, partly hid from our view by a rich festoon of shawl drapery, we could just discover the sultan's bed, flanked by large mirrors, beyond which, in an adjacent chamber, was probably stowed away the Sultan's most favoured wife. But all this department of the establishment was thrown into such deep shade, that we could see none of the ladies, nor any of his highness's progeny, except one little boy, whom he introduced to us at supper. He appeared to be about five or six years old, very like his papa in miniature, rigged with turban and robes of cloth of gold. At first the little fellow looked somewhat startled, but he soon recovered his dignity, and sat on our knees, without much apprehension of being swallowed up.

Both the upper corners of the room were screened off by white curtains, eight or ten feet high, so as to form smaller chambers. One of these served the purpose of a pantry, or subsidiary kitchen, at least we observed the dishes issuing from it, and thought we could distinguish the well-known sound of the cook's angry reproaches—a note which, like that of muttering thunder, is nearly the same in every climate. The other corner we soon made out to be a sort of temporary nook, from which the ladies of the palace and the young sultans and sultanas might spy the strangers. This we ascertained from seeing sundry very pretty faces thrust out occasionally between the folds of the curtain, and by the sound of many an ill-suppressed giggle amongst the peeping damsels.

A half-choked squall from some rebellious baby, or a sound thwack on the pate of an over curious urchin, betrayed the nursery in terms not to be mistaken. Indeed, I do not wonder at their eagerness to look at the Admiral, whose very appearance, in any company in the world, or under any circumstances, must have claimed no small share of admiration. The characteristic prominence of the Hood nose, so well-known for a glorious half-century in the navy, with the tall and gallant bearing of our lamented chief, to say nothing of the Nelson-like circumstance of his right arm having been shorn away in battle, and, I may add, the peculiar sweetness of his voice, and the benignant expression of his countenance, which, while they won all hearts to him, showed a mind entirely at peace with itself. Everything, in short, that was great and amiable, conspired to render Sir Samuel Hood one of the most interesting officers of his time.

The Sultan appeared to enter into his guest's character at once, and neither overloaded him with attentions, nor failed to treat him as a person to whom much respect was due. I heard Sir Samuel say afterwards, that he was particularly struck with the Sultan's good breeding, in not offering to assist him in cutting his meat. The Sultan merely remarked that few people were so expert as his guest even with both hands; adding, neatly enough, that on this account the distinction which his wound had gained for him was more cheaply purchased than people supposed. While the Admiral was hunting for some reply to this novel compliment, his host remarked, that in Borneo it was considered fashionable to eat with the left hand.

The supper, which soon followed the tea, consisted of about a dozen dishes of curry, all different from one another, and a whole poultry yard of grilled and boiled chickens, many different sorts of salt fish, with great basins of rice at intervals, jars of pickles, piles of sliced pine-apple, sweetmeats, and cakes. Four male attendants stood by with goglets of cool sherbet, from which ever and anon, they replenished our glasses; besides whom, a number of young Malay girls waited at a distance from the table, and ran about nimbly with the plates and dishes.

All persons who approached the Sultan fell on their knees, and having joined their hands in the act of supplication, lowered their foreheads till they actually touched the ground. The Sultan held out his hand, which the people eagerly embraced in theirs, and pressed to their lips. What they had to say was then spoken, and after again bending their foreheads to the ground, they retired. This ceremonial took place only in the outer room or hall of audience, for no one, except the strangers and one or two of the principal officers of state, was permitted to approach nearer than twenty or thirty feet of the raised part of the floor where we sat.

At that distance, a group of about twenty persons, probably the nobles of the court, sat cross-legged on the ground in a semicircle facing the Sultan, and in profound silence during the whole supper, no part of which appeared to fall to their share.

Soon afterwards the cloth was removed, and a beautiful scarlet covering, of the texture of a shawl, substituted in its place. This might, perhaps, give us a hint for after dinner. Instead of dull mahogany, or dazzling white, why might not we spread over the table a cloth *couleur de rose* for the benefit of the complexions of the company?

The Sultan now produced a letter which he had received from Lord Minto when governor-general, thanking his highness for the friendly disposition he had always manifested towards the English people trading to the great city of Pontiana, and in a particular manner expressing his obligations for the manner in which Mr. Palmer, a wealthy merchant of Calcutta, had been received by the Sultan, when his ship was wrecked on the west coast of Borneo.

"Mr. Palmer," said the Sultan, "lived for some weeks with me, and on returning to Calcutta, sent me these beautiful mirrors and chandeliers. But," added he, pointing again to the governor-general's letter, "much as I value embellishments so splendid, I esteem far more this little signature, and these few words from Lord Minto. Still," continued his highness, "my wishes in this respect have never been fully satisfied. I have long desired to possess a specimen of Sir Samuel Hood's writing; and though I never ventured to hope that I should have had an opportunity of seeing his signature written with his own hand, I have always felt how essentially that circumstance would add to its value in my estimation."

It was wonderful how well the shrewd little Malay interpreter expressed all this rigmarole to the Admiral, who cheerfully agreed to the proposal, and desired me to send for his writing-case. As I rose, the Admiral whispered to me, "I wish you would contrive, at the same time, to see what the boat's crew are about. Try, also, if you can get them something to eat; the fellows must be hungry enough by this time—but mind they don't get too much toddy."

I found the crew seated on the mud floor of a large room close to the beach, and open on all sides, like a tent without walls. The Johnnies were in such high glee, that I feared they had already trespassed too deeply on the toddy pot; but I was glad to find that their satisfaction arose from a safer source, in the shape of a glorious hot supper, which Jack was tucking in to the delight and astonishment of the natives, who had been ordered by the Sultan to supply them with as much curry and rice as they chose to eat. The cook had no sinecure of it that evening!

I soon returned to the palace, and the Admiral, having written several lines for his host's album, expressed his wish to retire to rest. The Sultan instantly rose, and having conducted his honoured guest to the outer door, he left him in charge of half-a-score of the principal officers of the palace, amongst whom were several of the Sultan's own near relatives. This guard of honour accompanied Sir Samuel to his bed-room, and it cost him a good deal of trouble and some address to free himself from his company—their intention evidently being to bestow their tediousness upon his excellency all night.

Scarcely were this party dismissed, when, to our great surprise, the Sultan himself came to the door of the house in which the Admiral and his suite were lodged. Sir Samuel feared that he might possibly have given offence to some of the worthy connections of the Sultan, by dismissing them too abruptly, and that the Sultan had called for "an explanation." The honest Asiatic had no such gunpowder fancies in his head. On the contrary, the object of his visit was to press upon the Admiral's acceptance two large and beautiful diamonds. The poor Admiral was now reduced to a great dilemma. He could not, he thought, with any official propriety, accept the present; and yet he felt very unwilling to hurt the generous Sultan's feelings, especially as his highness had paddled at midnight through the mud of his own approach to make the offer. The Sultan saw at a glance what a mistake he had made, and instantly withdrew, laughing however, and saying that such was the custom of his nation. I think the Admiral was sorry afterwards that he had not carried in the boat some trinkets of correspondent value, or that he had not accepted the diamonds and afterwards sent something still more precious to the Sultan.

Very early in the morning, long before there was the least peep of dawn, the Admiral roused us all out of bed, ordered the boat to be manned, and declared his intention of dropping down the river while it was yet cool, so as to reach the ship before the fierce heat of the sun had set in. I suspect, also, that he wished to escape the salutes and other fussifications, of which he had seen some preparations over night. But in this he partly reckoned without his host, for scarcely had we gained the distance of two or three hundred yards from the shore when the heavy guns of the batteries began to fire a royal salute. The night was uncommonly dark and still, and the successive flashes and reports of the cannons were followed by a long series of echoes from the edges of the damp forests lining the banks of the three different branches or forks of the river. The Admiral, who had the finest perception possible for all that was picturesque or beautiful, was exceedingly struck with the grandeur of his nocturnal salute, and having made the men lay their oars across the boat, while she drifted quickly down the river, he stood up in the stern-sheets in order to enjoy the scene more completely. At each of the first dozen discharges we were near enough to be illuminated by the flash, and a smile of delight could be seen on the veteran's countenance as sounds so dear to him once more caught his ear. It is not improbable that they recalled to his memory the glorious night action of the Nile; in which it is not too much to say, that amongst all the distinguished warriors whom Nelson had gathered round him, there was not one on whom his great chief more firmly relied in battle, or to whom, personally, he was more attached in private life.

A trifling incident occurred shortly afterwards, which suggested to our thoughts another important service of Sir Samuel Hood's, which, although it be familiarly known in the navy, may not be so fresh in the recollection of persons on shore. A question arose in the boat as to whether or not the land-wind was blowing. Some said there was a breeze up the river, while others maintained that the wind blew down, towards the sea. The Admiral let us go on speculating and arguing for some time, and then said, "You are both wrong; there is not a breath of air either up or down the river. At all events we shall soon see, if you will strike me a light." This was done accordingly; and the Admiral, standing on the after-thwart, held the naked candle high over his head, while the men ceased rowing.

"There, you see," exclaimed he, "the flame stands quite upright, which proves, that if there be any breeze at all, it blows no faster than the stream runs down."

As he yet spoke, the flame bent from the land, and in the next instant was puffed out by a slight gust from the forest.

"Ay! that's something like!" exclaimed the commander-in-chief; adding, in an undertone, as he resumed his seat, "I have known the time when a flaw of wind not greater than has just blown out this candle has rendered good service to his majesty."

We knew what was meant, and so will every naval man; but others may be interested by being told, that early in the year 1794, when Captain Hood commanded his majesty's ship *Juno*, he had very nearly lost his ship in a most extraordinary manner. The port of Toulon, though in possession of the English at the time of his departure on a short trip to Malta, had been evacuated while the *Juno* was absent; and as the land was made in the night, no suspicion of that important change of affairs arose in the mind of anyone. With his wonted decision, therefore, into the port he dashed; for, although the *Juno* carried no pilot, Captain Hood's knowledge of every port he had once visited rendered him comparatively indifferent on that score. A couple of the sharpest-sighted midshipmen were stationed with glasses to look out for the fleet; but no ships were seen —for the best of all reasons—none were there!

One vessel only, a small brig, could be detected, and the captain, supposing the fleet had run into the inner harbour during the recent easterly gale, resolved to push up likewise. The batteries all kept quiet, and though the brig hailed the frigate as she passed in a language so indistinct that no one could make it out, not the least suspicion was excited.

Captain Hood, in his official letter to Lord Hood [see *Naval Chronicle* for 1807, vol. xvii. p. 11,] says, "I supposed they wanted to know what ship it was, and I told them it was an English frigate called the *Juno*." The brig, however, was not quite so courteous in return; for they merely replied by the word "*Viva*," but made no answer to the captain's repeated inquiry, both in English and French, as to the brig's name, and the position of the British Admiral's fleet. As the *Juno* passed under the stern of this treacherous little craft, a voice called out "Luff! luff!" which naturally induced Captain Hood to put his helm down, from an idea that shoal water lay close to leeward of him. Nothing could have been more adroitly managed by the Frenchmen, for before the frigate came head to wind, she struck fast upon the shoal, to which the words "Luff! luff!" had no doubt been intended to direct her.

A boat was now observed to proceed from the brig to the town. As there was but little wind, and the water perfectly smooth, the *Juno's* sails were clewed up and handed; but before the men were all off the yards, a gust of wind came sweeping down the harbour, and drove her off the shoal so suddenly as to give her brisk stern-way. The anchor was speedily let go, but when she tended, the after part of her keel took the ground, and the rudder could not be moved. The launch and cutter being instantly hoisted out, the usual preparations were made to lay out a kedge, to heave the ship off.

At this critical moment a boat came alongside. The people appeared anxious to get out of her, and two of them, apparently officers, came up the side. They said it was the regulation of the port, as well as the commanding-officer's orders, that ships should go further in to the harbour, there to perform ten days' quarantine. In the despatch relating this transaction, Captain Hood says, "I kept asking them where Lord Hood's ship lay;" and those who remember Sir Samuel's impatient manner when anyone to whom he addressed himself trifled with his questions, will easily imagine how he must have perplexed and overawed the two Frenchmen, who really knew not what to do or say next. In the meantime, one of the mids, who happened to be thrusting his head forward after the investigating manner of this enterprising class of officers, said apart to the captain,—"Why, sir, they wear national cockades!"

"I looked at one of their hats more steadfastly,"

says Captain Hood in his narrative, " and by the moonlight clearly distinguished the three colours."

" Perceiving they were suspected," continues Sir Samuel in his narrative, " and on my questioning them again about Lord Hood, one of them replied, ' *Soyez tranquille, les Anglais sont de brave gens—nous les tratons bien ; l'amiral Anglais est sortie il y a quelque tems.*' "

Sir Samuel well says, that it may be more easily conceived that words can express what he felt at that moment. In one instant, the situation of the poor *Juno*, which was almost desperate, became known throughout the ship. The officers naturally crowded round their captain to learn the worst, while the Frenchmen, bowing to the right and left, grinned and apologised for the disagreeable necessity of making them all prisoners ! The rest of this singular story, unique in the history of the Navy, and altogether wonderful, considering the formidable nature of the trap into which the frigate had fallen, will be best told in the words of the accomplished officer himself, to whose presence of mind, courage, and professional dexterity, the escape of the ship was entirely due. The personal regard in which the captain was held by every officer, man, and boy on board, and the thorough confidence which they possessed in his talents, enabled him to undertake a service which an officer held in less esteem might have found it very difficult to carry through. It used, indeed, to be said of Hood's ship, that, fore and aft, there was but one heart and one mind.

After describing the deportment of the French officers, he goes on to say, in his despatch, that " a flaw of wind coming down the harbour, Lieutenant Webley[1] said to me, ' I believe, sir, we shall be able to

[1] Now Captain Webley Parry, C.B., long afterwards the friend and follower of Sir Samuel Hood, who, as may well be supposed, never forgot any of the men who stood by him at that most trying hour of his professional existence.

fetch out if we can get her under sail.' I immediately perceived we should have a chance of saving the ship ; at least if we did not, we ought not to lose her without some contention. I therefore ordered every person to their respective stations, and the Frenchmen to be sent below. The latter perceiving some bustle, began to draw their sabres ; on which I directed some of the marines to take the half pikes and force them below, which was soon done. I believe in an instant such a change in people was never seen—every officer and man was at his duty ; and I do believe, within three minutes every sail in the ship was set, and the yards braced ready for casting. The steady and active assistance of Lieutenant Turner and all the officers prevented any confusion from arising in our critical situation ; and, as soon as the cable was taut, I ordered it to be cut, and had the good fortune to see the ship start from the shore. The head sails were filled ; a favourable flaw of wind coming at the same time gave her good way, and we had every prospect of getting out if the forts did not disable us. To prevent our being retarded by the boats, I ordered them to be cut adrift, as also the French boat. The moment the brig saw us begin to loose sails, we could plainly perceive she was getting her guns ready, and we also saw lights in all the batteries. When we had shot far enough for the brig's guns to bear on us, which was not more than three ships' lengths, she began to fire ; also a fort a little on the starboard bow, and soon after all of them, on both sides, so they could bring their guns to bear. As soon as the sails were well trimmed, I beat to quarters to get our guns ready, but not with an intention of firing till we were sure of getting out. When abreast of the centre of Cape Sepet, I was afraid we should have been obliged to make a tack ; but, as we drew near the shore, and were ready to go about, she came up two points, and just weathered the cape. As we passed very close along that shore, the batteries kept up as brisk a fire as the wetness of the weather would admit. When I could afford to keep the ship a little off the wind, I ordered some guns to be fired at a battery that had just opened abreast of us, which quieted them a little. We then stopped firing till we could keep her away, with the wind abaft the beam, when, for a few minutes, we kept up a very lively fire on the last battery we had to pass, which I believe must otherwise have done us great damage. At half-past twelve, being out of reach of their shot, the firing ceased."

The whole of this admirable piece of service was performed so quickly, and at the same time with so much coolness, that there occurred little or no opportunity for any remarkable individual exertion. Everything, as I have heard it described by Sir Samuel Hood himself and by the officers, went on as if the ship had been working out of Plymouth Sound at noonday. One little incident, however, which caused much amusement in the ship, will help to show the degree of regard in which Sir Samuel was held by those immediately about him ; and to disprove the proverb of no man being a hero to his *valet de chambre*.

Dennis M'Carty, an old and faithful servant of Captain Hood's, who was quartered at one of the main-deck guns in the cabin, stood firm enough till the batteries opened on the *Juno*. No sooner had the firing commenced, and the shot came whizzing over and through all parts of the ship, than Dennis, to the great amaze and scandal of his companions, dropped the side tackle-fall, and fairly ran off from his gun. Nothing in the world, however, could be further from poor Pat's mind than fear—except fear for his master, behind whom he soon stationed himself on the quarter-deck ; and wherever Captain Hood moved, there Dennis followed, like his shadow. The poor fellow appeared totally unconscious of any personal danger to himself, though the captain was necessarily in the hottest of the fire. At length Sir Samuel, turning suddenly round, encountered the Irishman full butt.

"Ho! Master Dennis," exclaimed the captain, "what brings you here? and why do you keep running about after me? Go down to your gun, man!"

"Oh, by the powers! your honour," replied Dennis, "sure I thought it likely you might be hurt so I wished to be near you to give you some help."

There was no resisting this; the captain laughed in the midst of the battle; and poor Dennis was allowed to take his own way, having no care for himself.

It would be quite impossible within any moderate compass, even to enumerate the important services which Sir Samuel Hood rendered to his country, both before and after the time alluded to; nor can it be necessary to do so, for they are still so fresh in the recollection of the Navy, that they are often quoted as examples in every walk of duty. His forte appears to have been that invaluable quality of all great commanders, promptitude in seeing what was best to be done, and decision of purpose in carrying it into execution. At the moments of greatest doubt and difficulty, and when scarcely anyone else could see through the confusion, he appears invariably to have taken those useful practical views, which the calmest subsequent reflection proved to have been the most expedient.

One of the most important, and also the most amusing instance of the effect of his resolute and characteristic presence of mind and boldness of manner, occurred in the summer of 1797, when Nelson attacked the town and fortifications of Santa Cruz, in Teneriffe. The enterprise failed; Nelson was wounded and carried on board in the only boat not captured or destroyed, while the remaining officers and men were necessarily left without any means of defence or escape. Sir Thomas Troubridge and Captain Hood now found themselves in the very heart of the town, at the head of only a handful of seamen and marines carrying merely a few pikes, but surrounded by several thousands of well-armed Spaniards. As the boats had been all demolished in the surf, or knocked to pieces by the fire of the batteries, retreat became impossible, and capture or destruction would inevitably have awaited them the moment daybreak showed their small numbers and wretched plight. In this dilemma, Captain Hood went forward alone to the Spanish governor, and said he was sent by the commanding officer of the British troops and seamen within the walls to state, that as they had been disappointed in their expectation of finding treasure in the town, they were disposed to return peaceably to their ships, if boats were provided them for that purpose, but that should any means be taken to molest or retard them, they would then set fire to the town in different places, and force their way out of it at the point of the bayonet. With the utmost deliberation, and without betraying the smallest haste or anxiety, he then pulled out his watch, and said, " I am directed to give you ten minutes to consider of this offer."—See the *Naval Chronicle*, vol. xvii. p. 19.

Don Antonio, the governor, looked amazed at the coolness of this proposal from persons whom he conceived—and with good reason—to be his prisoners. He proposed to hold a council of war immediately, and let the British commander know their determination in the course of an hour ; but Captain Hood saw the impression which his argument had produced, and again holding up his watch, declared he could not spare his excellency a single second ; and, as the fatal minute approached, he turned round and prepared to rejoin his shipmates. The governor, alarmed at the possible consequences of driving men so commanded into extremities, acceded to the proposals made by Captain Hood, and agreed to provide the defeated party with boats.

Next morning, accordingly, the Spaniard, having once pledged himself to certain terms, kept good faith, and not only allowed them all to return to their ships, but, previously to the embarkation of the invaders, he considerately furnished each of the sailors with a bowl of wine and a biscuit, filled their boats with fruit and other refreshments, and gave orders that such of the British as had been wounded, should be received into the Spanish hospital !

It is by such deeds of true nobleness that the asperity of actual war is softened, and that kindly feelings take the place of that bitterness which only excites to angry retaliation, without at all advancing the great objects for which opposing nations are contending.

I have often thought that much of this kindness on the part of the generous Don, as well as the more important part of the service, may have been due chiefly to the mere personal address of Sir Samuel Hood, whose appearance and manner were at all times unspeakably winning, and especially pleasing to the well-bred Spaniards. As these outward qualities were backed by solid judgment, professional knowledge, and the most thorough disinterestedness, he became almost irresistible, even on occasions when most other men might have seen little hope of success. It is not, then, surprising, that a mind like Nelson's should attach itself cordially to that of Sir Samuel Hood, or that every successive incident of their joint services, should rivet more closely and firmly the alliance of such kindred spirits.

There entered into the character of Sir Samuel Hood some peculiarities, which, although I have never seen them stated, appear well to deserve the attention of professional men. When it is said that he was thoroughly disinterested, it must not be thought that he was indifferent to his own share of credit which belonged to meritorious service : for he conceived his own reputation, and that of the profession, as identical with that of the country, and, in proportion as he rose in fame and rank, so this obligation to preserve his renown unsullied appears to have pressed upon his mind. But, whenever the accession of credit became merely individual or personal to himself, and did not seem in his eyes calculated likewise to augment the honour of the service as well as his own, he not only felt careless about it, but actually staved off the honour and glory, which other men might have eagerly courted.

Of this a remarkable instance was afforded at the battle of the Nile. Previous to entering into that great action, Nelson, as everyone recollects, hailed Captain Hood's ship, and consulted him as to the best method of attack.

"What think you," said the Admiral, "of engaging the enemy to-night?"

"I don't know the soundings," was the answer, "but with your permission, I will lead in and try."

The result is well-known; but I believe it is not so generally known that, in the first draft of the despatch, which Nelson wrote, he gave to Captain Hood the merit of confirming him in his determination of attacking the French fleet that night. On showing this letter, however, to Hood himself, he entreated that it might be altered, saying, "that they were all brothers, engaged in the cause, and that the Admiral would have received exactly the same advice from any other captain in the fleet whom he might have consulted." The paragraph was therefore omitted in the despatch. But, on many accounts, this omission is certainly to be regretted; for it essentially adds to the true credit of Nelson himself, instead of diminishing it, that he not only knew how to estimate such concurrence in opinion, but how to acknowledge and reward the services of men of Sir Samuel Hood's stamp.

I have this anecdote of the change in the despatch

from one of his nearest connections, and one of the dearest friends to his memory. He himself particularly wished the alteration in the despatch not to be told at the time; but, as the story crept out somehow, it seems very material that the facts should be well authenticated. When the circumstance was mentioned to Sir Samuel Hood many years afterwards, by the friend from whom I have received authority to state it, and he was asked if it were true, he confessed that it was so; but exclaimed:

"How the devil could all this have got wind?—I never mentioned it before to a living soul."

As there is hardly any professional anecdote which retains its freshness of interest more entire than the memorable parley above described between Nelson and Hood, on the eve of the battle of the Nile, I venture to give another version of it, which is substantially the same, and is calculated to confirm, in a pleasing manner, all that is essential. The following particulars I have been favoured with by Captain Webley Parry, then first lieutenant of the *Zealous*.

When steering for the enemy's fleet, Sir Horatio Nelson hailed the *Zealous*, and asked Captain Hood if he thought he might venture to bear up round the shoals. The answer was—

"I cannot say, sir; but if you will allow me the honour of leading into action. I will keep the lead going."

"You have my permission, and I wish you good luck," was the reply; and, as Nelson said this, he took off his hat. Captain Hood, in his hurry to return the courtesy of his Admiral, dropped his hat overboard. He looked after it, laughed, and exclaimed:

"Never mind, Webley, there it goes for luck! Put the helm up, and make all sail."

Captain Foley of the *Goliath*, being close to the *Zealous*, perceiving this manœuvre, guessed what the orders were, and bore up likewise, so that when the two ships had shaped their course, they were nearly abreast of each other. The *Goliath*, being a little in advance, which of course was rather annoying, Capt. Hood stood on for some time, in hopes of being able to take the lead in the *Zealous*, but finding this could not be without jostling and confusion, he turned round and said——

"This will never do! Well—never mind; Foley is a fine, gallant, worthy fellow. Shorten sail, and give him time to take up his berth. We must risk nothing that will tend to the enemy's advantage; and we shall all soon have enough to do."

This was instantly done; the *Goliath* shot ahead, and Captain Foley had the glory of leading the British fleet into action. By some accident, however, he failed to place the *Goliath* in opposition to the headmost ship of the enemy's line. The experienced eye of Hood instantly saw the inevitable consequence, and while the *Goliath* passed on to the second in the line, Sir Samuel placed his own ship, the *Zealous*, alongside the first, exclaiming in the joy of his heart, "Thank God! my friend Foley has left me the van ship!"

The following private letter, written some time afterwards, from Lord Nelson, is so characteristic of the writer, and so flattering to Sir Samuel, that I venture to insert it.

"St. George, March 13, 1801.

"MY DEAR HOOD—Many thanks for your kind letter; and believe me, there is not a man breathing that loves you more than myself. I am glad you have quitted the *Courageux*; she would have drowned you in chase of an enemy's squadron. I have directed four crosses to be made, and they are this day sent to Mr. Davidson's, I expect. I send you an order [of St. Ferdinand and Merit.] No; I have written to Davidson to deliver it to Troubridge, who will send it you; it is to be worn round your neck like the order of St.

Anne. I send you a piece of riband to suspend it by. We sail to-morrow for Yarmouth. I only hope Cornwallis will meet the French fleet, and that you will be in company. Ever, my dear Hood, your obliged and

"NELSON AND BRONTE.

"CAPT. HOOD."

The mixture of affection, business, playfulness, and professional allusions, in this short letter, is strikingly indicative of the intimacy and full understanding which existed between these distinguished officers. It is always delightful when one gets a peep behind the scenes, to find such men on terms of true friendship.

The whole life of Sir Samuel Hood proves, that he never took into his calculations what effect any particular measure might or might not have upon his individual reputation or fortunes, but that he looked exclusively to its probable effect upon the interests and honour of his country and the service. He possessed, it is true, the keenest possible relish for well-earned fame ; but he enjoyed no applause which came unconnected with the general good ; and his anxiety about his own reputation, which was very great, and to which I have already alluded, rested upon what he conceived the true view of professional principle and public spirit, in its most genuine acceptation. Every action of his life showed that he was not only far beyond the reach of any envious feeling, but that his chief pleasure was to bring forward merit wherever it was to be found, and he was always more ready to bestow distinction than to claim it for himself. Whenever it became his good fortune to act with the army, he brought these principles into the most useful play, to the advancement of the public service, and greatly to the satisfaction of his sister service.

It is also highly delightful, as well as instructive, to

know that these generous sentiments were speedily participated by all those who enjoyed his confidence, and worked along with him. I am indeed persuaded that he very often converted selfish and sulky officers into useful and cheerful public servants, in no great length of time, and not unfrequently to their own great surprise. What, then, must have been the extent of his influence over the minds of men similarly disposed with himself?

When, unfortunately for the profession and for his country, he fell sick at Madras, and knew that his last moments were fast approaching, he called his faithful friend and old follower in many ships and many actions, Lieutenant [now Captain] Walcott, to his bedside, and said to him——

"It will be too hard, Walcott, to die in this cursed place; but should I go off, let nothing deter you from going home and accounting to the Admiralty for my command of the East India station."

These were nearly the last intelligible words he uttered; and they serve to shew how strong, even in the hour of death, was his sense of professional duty. As Lieutenant Walcott had served during the whole of Sir Samuel's India command in the double capacity of flag-lieutenant and secretary, and had enjoyed the Admiral's entire confidence, he, and he alone, possessed the means of "accounting to the Admiralty" for the measures completed, or in progress, for the good of the service, and therefore the Admiral suggested to him the propriety of his going home to report matters in person.

The senior officer, who succeeded to the command in the India seas, felt so desirous of following up the friendly intentions of his lamented predecessor, that knowing the late Admiral's attachment to Lieut. Walcott, he offered to promote him into a death vacancy, which had either actually taken place, or was certain to fall within a week or two. Moreover, he assured him, that after the necessary time had been served, he should have the first vacancy for post promotion.

These were indeed tempting offers to a young officer devotedly attached to his profession ; but they had no influence over a man bred in the " Sam Hood school". The Admiral's dying injunction appeared to this right-minded officer fully as binding, or, if possible, more so, than a written command must have been in his lifetime.

To England Walcott went accordingly ; and the difference in professional standing which it made to him was this :—had he remained in India, as Sir Samuel Hood's successor proposed, he would undoubtedly have become a post-captain of 1816, instead of which, his name now stands in 1822, six years later on the list ! Had it been sixty times six, however, it would have made no difference in his conduct.

Along with all this professional merit, which won for Sir Samuel Hood the devoted respect of everyone who served with him, there were mingled qualities of a nature more domestic and endearing, but not less decided. The unaffected suavity of his disposition, the absence of all affectation from his manners, and the kindly alacrity with which he entered into the wishes and feelings of others, won all hearts to him, from the depths of the cockpit even to the "throne's height". Of this some pleasing examples occurred when we returned to England, immediately after the loss of his arm.

When it was decided that he should be taken ashore at Ryde in the Isle of Wight, his cot was laid on a grating, and the cabin bulk-heads being knocked down, the wounded chief was hoisted out and lowered into the boat. " The whole ship's company, man and boy, came on deck, and I never shall forget this most affecting scene," writes an eye-witness, " for you would really have thought every man in the ship was his brother ! "

In the course of the same evening, a lady and gentleman called at Sir Samuel's lodgings at Ryde, not for the idle curiosity of asking how the wounded commodore was, but with the considerate purpose of mentioning what they imagined would give him pleasure. They had that day received a letter from a gentleman holding a high situation in the household of George III., stating that the good old monarch, who was much attached to Sir Samuel, had actually shed tears when he heard of his loss, and exclaimed :

" Would to God the French had their frigates again, and poor Hood his arm ! "

The affectionate respect of his ship's company in the morning had touched him closely ; but this extension of sympathy quite unmanned the veteran warrior.

Of his friendly disposition to all persons whom he had it in his power to oblige, I could give many anecdotes. The following little circumstance, however, is so characteristic that it may suffice.

When the army returned from Spain, after the battle of Corunna, in 1809, there were between twenty and thirty officers accommodated in Sir Samuel's cabin. Notwithstanding the almost constant pain in his leg from an old wound, he gave up his cot to one of these gentlemen who was wounded, and slept himself either on the deck, or on a corronade slide during the whole passage. It happened that amongst these officers there was a distant connection of Lady Hood's, and so remarkable did the Admiral's attention to him appear, that the young man very naturally ascribed the notice he received to this circumstance. But when the father and mother of the young man afterwards called upon the Admiral to thank him for the uncommon kindness he had shewn to their son, they learnt that Sir Samuel had not only been totally ignorant of the connection alluded to, but did not even know that a person of that name had been on board his ship during the passage !

" Indeed," said he, " I hardly knew the names of half my guests. But who," he continued, " would make any distinctions amongst such war-worn and brave fellows ? "

The curious fact is, such was his general kindness, that each of these military officers, his passengers, fancied the Admiral was more civil to him than to any one else. He suspended on this occasion all the usual strait-laced etiquettes of the quarter-deck discipline, and permitted the harassed soldiers to lie down and read between the guns, or wherever they pleased. His great delight was to coddle them up, and recompense them, as far as he could, for the severe privations they had undergone during Sir John Moore's retreat, and nothing entertained him so much as seeing the relish with which these hungry campaigners partook of his hospitality. On the day after the battle of Corunna, when these gentlemen came on board, he ordered a cock to be driven into a hogshead of prime old sherry ; and his satisfaction was perfect, when his steward, with a rueful countenance, communicated to him, on arriving at Spithead, that " his very best cask of wine had been drunk dry on the passage by the soldier officers ! "

INDEX

INDEX